THE AXEMAN OF NEW ORLEANS

the true story

MIRIAM C. DAVIS

First hardcover edition published 2017
First paperback edition published 2018
Published by Chicago Review Press Incorporated
814 North Franklin Street
Chicago, Illinois 60610

ISBN 978-1-61374-868-8 (hardcover)
ISBN 978-0-912777-71-9 (paperback)

The Library of Congress has cataloged the hardcover edition as follows:
Names: Davis, Miriam C., author.
Title: The axeman of New Orleans : the true story / Miriam C. Davis.
Description: Chicago, Illinois : Chicago Review Press Incorporated, [2017] | Includes bibliographical references and index.
Identifiers: LCCN 2016047629 (print) | LCCN 2017017263 (ebook) | ISBN 9781613748695 (PDF edition) | ISBN 9781613748718 (EPUB edition) | ISBN 9781613748701 (Kindle edition) | ISBN 9781613748688
Subjects: LCSH: Serial murders—Louisiana—New Orleans.
Classification: LCC HV6534.N45 (ebook) | LCC HV6534.N45 D38 2017 (print) |
DDC 364.152/320976335—dc23
LC record available at https://lccn.loc.gov/2016047629

Cover design: Natalya Balnova
Cover image: John J. Miller Photography/Getty Images
Typesetting: Nord Compo

Printed in the United States of America
5 4 3 2 1

For my brother Tim, who gave me the idea

Contents

Preface

ONE HOT SUMMER AFTERNOON about thirteen or so years ago, my brother Tim and I were sitting on my front porch drinking bracingly cold English cider. The conversation turned, as it always does on these occasions, to the subject of serial murder. . . .

Tim told me about a case he had read about as a boy, about a killer who went around New Orleans whacking Jewish bakers with an axe. Ever since I read Ann Rule's account of her erstwhile friend Ted Bundy, I have been fascinated, in a scared sort of way, with serial killers. I don't know what moved me to look into this further; I was deep into another topic at the time. Probably it was nothing more than the urge to procrastinate. But look into it I did, and found that the New Orleans case involved not Jewish bakers but Italian grocers. Eventually, I got hold of Robert Tallant's *Ready to Hang*, which formed the basis of most other accounts of the Axeman. Robert Tallant was a New Orleans writer of the mid-twentieth century who, according to one reference librarian in the New Orleans public library, may well have gotten much of his information by hanging out in New Orleans bars.

In a chapter titled "The Axman Wore Wings," Tallant tells the story: On the morning of May 24, 1918, Joseph and Catherine Maggio, Italian immigrants who ran a small grocery, were discovered dead and bloody in their bedroom. They'd been assaulted with their own axe and had had their throats cut. Nothing appeared to have been stolen. The assailant had gotten in by cutting out a panel in the back door.

In the course of their investigation, police found a peculiar message written on the banquette (an old New Orleans term for sidewalk) near the Maggios' home and grocery: "Mrs. Maggio is going to sit up tonight just like Mrs. Toney." The police remembered that seven years earlier, in 1911, three other Italian grocers had been murdered with an axe; in two cases their wives had also been slain. Tallant gave the grocers' names as Cruti, Rosetti, and Tony Schiambra. Was Tony Schiambra's wife the "Mrs. Toney" of the sidewalk message? Tallant asked. Was this a message from the Italian Mafia? Had the couple been slaughtered by gangsters for some unknown misdemeanor? No one was ever charged with the murders, so these questions were never satisfactorily answered.

The next month Louis Besumer, a Polish grocer, and Harriet Lowe, the woman who lived with him, were also attacked with an axe and seriously injured. Again, the weapon had been the grocer's own. Again, a door panel had been removed. And again, nothing was reported stolen. This time both victims survived, at least temporarily, and Lowe, who changed her story several times, accused Besumer first of being a German spy and later of having tried to kill her. When she died of her wounds two months later, Besumer was charged with murder.

Over the next fourteen months, the killer, nicknamed "the Axeman" by the press, racked up a litany of victims: Mrs. Edward Schneider, August, 5, 1918 (survived); Joseph Romano, August 10, 1918 (died); Charles, Rosie, and Mary Cortimiglia, March 10, 1919 (Mary died); Steve Boca, August 10, 1919 (survived); Sarah Laumann, September 3, 1919 (survived); and Mike Pepitone, October 27, 1919 (died). In almost all cases the modus operandi was the same: back door panel cut out, the victim's own axe used, weapon abandoned at the scene, and nothing stolen. Most but not all of the victims were Italian grocers. Fear of the Axeman paralyzed the immigrant community. Some terrified Italians couldn't sleep at night without posting guards to stand watch. Phantom Axemen were seen everywhere. Stories circulated about grocers waking in the morning to find a door panel chiseled off and an axe outside their door.

Louis Besumer was acquitted of Harriet Lowe's murder, but his was not the only trial. Rosie Cortimiglia accused two neighbors, elderly grocer Iorlando Jordano and his son Frank, of having attacked them and having killed their two-year-old daughter out of business rivalry. Even though her husband, Charles, testified that the killer had not been either man, father and son were convicted of murder and eighteen-year-old Frank was sentenced to death. Later, Rosie admitted that she had lied because she hated the Jordanos.

Shortly after the Cortimiglia attack, the *New Orleans Times-Picayune* received a letter purporting to be from the murderer. He was "a fell demon from the hottest hell," the letter claimed, and would descend on New Orleans the coming Tuesday night looking for a victim, sparing anyone listening to jazz. Tallant reported that the designated evening, March 19, was Saint Joseph's Night, and it was "the loudest and most hilarious of any on record" as jazz blared all over the city.

After the death of grocer Mike Pepitone in August 1919, the attacks finally stopped. And in Tallant's account, the story seems to have had a dramatic—and satisfactory—sequel out in California: On December 7, 1920, Esther Pepitone, the widow of Mike Pepitone, shot and killed a New Orleans man named Joseph Mumfre in Los Angeles. She told the police that Mumfre was the Axeman, that she had seen him as he fled after murdering her husband. Convicted of his murder, Tallant wrote, she served only three years before being freed.

According to *Ready to Hang*, Joseph Mumfre was a career criminal who was well known to the New Orleans police. And the dates he'd been in and out of prison matched the dates when the Axeman attacked and when he seemed to have disappeared.

So, was Mumfre the Axeman? Tallant said that the evidence was only circumstantial, and most New Orleanians believed that more than one killer was responsible. The two main theories were that the Mafia was responsible, or the killer was a "homicidal maniac," a "Doctor

Jekyll and Mr. Hyde" type as suggested by one of the investigating detectives.

This was the story that I found on the web and in crime anthologies when I first began researching the Axeman case. Most of the available sources basically repeated Tallant's version of events.

While Tallant left the question of the Axeman's identity open, I found that some writers seem to have swallowed whole the theory that Joseph Mumfre was the killer. In a list of male serial killers, for instance, forensic psychologist Eric Hickey listed "Joseph Mumfre" as the Axeman of New Orleans. In *Bloodletters and Badmen*, crime writer Jay Robert Nash argued that Mumfre was a professional killer who used an axe to kill Pepitone and other victims as part of a Mafia vendetta.

Others, however, questioned aspects of Tallant's account. In an early edition of his *Hunting Humans: The Encyclopedia of Serial Killers*, vol. 1, crime writer Michael Newton reported that city records showed that no Italian grocers named Cruti, Rosetti, or Schiambra had been killed—by an axe or anything else—in 1911.

I had an opportunity to check out some of these questions in the early 2000s soon after I became interested in the Axeman case. At the time, my husband and I visited New Orleans once or twice a year. On one of our visits, I popped out of the French Quarter to visit the city archives, located in the public library conveniently across Canal Street in the Central Business District. Examining homicide and coroners' records for 1911, I discovered that while no Cruti, Rosetti, or Schiambra had been murdered that year, a sleeping Italian grocer named Joseph Davi had been—his skull fractured and his wife cut up in the middle of the night. That such a basic fact about the case and one so easily discoverable had been missed suggested that the story had never really been properly investigated. Maybe, I thought, there's a book here.

Since I began working on *The Axeman of New Orleans*, two well-done works on the subject have appeared (both times nearly giving me a heart attack): Keven McQueen's chapter on the Axeman in *The Axman Came from Hell*, and the account given by Gary Krist in *Empire of Sin*. If either narrative had been available when I first read about the Axeman,

I might have never written this book. Both are useful, well-researched explorations of the Axeman's crimes. But both, I will argue, are incomplete. They don't answer questions that can, in fact, be answered.

In the course of examining the tale of the Axeman, moreover, I became fascinated by the experience of the Italian—usually Sicilian—grocers he preyed on, particularly in the case of the Jordanos, the father and son accused by Rosie Cortimiglia. The teenaged Frank and his elderly father, Iorlando, were as much casualties of the Axeman as any of his other victims. The story of Frank and his family merits telling because it illustrates the experience of Italian immigrants and the niche they carved out for themselves in the social hierarchy of early twentieth-century Louisiana as well as the social prejudice against them.

Mafia aficionados shouldn't worry. The story also involves the gangsters of the Sicilian underworld.

What follows is the result of my own investigation into the Axeman of New Orleans murders based on an examination of all available sources. This has been a different kind of history than I was trained to write in graduate school. I wanted to write something analytical that would be fully grounded in the sources but would also appeal to a wide audience by telling a story rather than merely being an analysis of a list of murders.

A college friend of mine who was studying English once remarked that the great thing about being a lit major was that unless someone could prove you absolutely wrong, you could say anything you wanted. I assure the reader that this is *not* the approach I have taken here. While I've tried to tell the story as what is sometimes called creative or narrative nonfiction, I've stayed true to my obligations as a historian. Everything I write can be justified on the basis of what is found in the historical record, although I've sometimes had to use my judgment when choosing between conflicting accounts in, for example, rival newspapers. On occasion, I've relied on deduction and common sense to connect dots and piece together what must have happened and what must have been experienced by the individuals in my story.

Anything in quotation marks is from a written document, usually a newspaper, police report, or court record. Sometimes these quotations have been condensed or edited for clarity, especially when they're based on varying accounts found in different newspapers. I have sometimes modernized spelling. *Italicized* dialogue has been imaginatively reconstructed when I felt that something like it must have been expressed but didn't have direct evidence of exactly what was said. I've been careful to remain faithful to the historical evidence and context. In some cases I've inserted personal thoughts or feelings—but, again, always based on deductions from the historical evidence.

Full passages of italicized text indicate a re-creation of scenes that no one but the killer himself was witness to. For insight into the elusive killer, I've relied on modern forensic psychology.

Endnotes have been consolidated as much as possible, while still providing full documentation. Anyone wishing to retrace my footsteps should be able to do so.

Among the questions that I began my research hoping to answer were:

- Were all the killings named by Tallant actually Axeman crimes?
- Did the Axeman murders begin with the murder of Joseph and Catherine Maggio?
- Was the Mafia involved?
- Were all the Axeman's victims Italian, and if they were, why did he target them?
- Why did Rosie Cortimiglia accuse Frank Jordano and his father of murdering her daughter? Did she later change her story, and if so, why?
- Did Esther Pepitone murder Joseph Mumfre?
- Most important, was Joseph Mumfre the Axeman? And if he wasn't, who was?
- How do the answers to these questions help one understand what it was like to live in New Orleans during the Axeman's reign of terror?

In the course of my investigation, I discovered that Tallant was wrong in many details, some unimportant, some not. At the end of "The Axman Wore Wings," he wrote, "It is extremely doubtful that anyone will ever know more" about whether Mumfre was the Axeman. He was wrong about that.

1

Evil Descends

3 AM, Sunday, March 9, 1919

THE KILLER BALANCED ON *the chair as he looked through the window, straining to see the figures in the bed. It was a moonless night; he couldn't see much by the light of the one electric bulb dimly illuminating the room. It didn't matter. He knew they were there. He went around to the back and broke in in the way for which he was famous, carefully chiseling out a panel of the heavy kitchen door. He worked steadily, taking his time, pausing when he needed to; no reason to hurry. When the panel finally came off, he slipped his gloved hand through the door and eased back the bolt. Once in, he moved surely through the tiny kitchen, in stocking feet so his heavy boots wouldn't clatter on the wood floors, straight through the dining room, past the door leading to the small grocery, and stopped at the bedroom door. He paused, listening to the breathing of the sleeping figures. Then, getting a tighter grip on the heavy axe, he entered the bedroom.*

Minutes later, his work done, he walked unhurriedly through the dining room and the kitchen, out the door, and down the steps. He tossed the axe carelessly under the house, human hair still clinging to the quickly drying blood. Sitting down on the stoop, he pulled his boots back on, tugging at them firmly before lacing them up. Then he vanished into the night. The Axeman of New Orleans had claimed another victim.

Carnival had just ended. Only four days before, the murderer and his victim had both jostled with the crowds flooding the streets of New Orleans. Mardi Gras was meant to be a sedate affair this year, very unlike the one two years before in 1917. That year it was celebrated with all its magical grandeur, perhaps with a little more intensity than usual given that anyone could see that the United States was about to go to war. The Carnival season, between Epiphany and Lent, was a season of balls, pageants, parades, and general exuberance. It culminated in two hedonistic days before Ash Wednesday. New Orleanians were not reticent about enjoying themselves in anticipation of Lent; maybe they thought they needed the pagan holiday to get through the penitential season.

Each year on the eve of Mardi Gras, Rex—King of Carnival, Monarch of Mirth—arrived at noon, steaming up to the landing at the foot of Canal Street in his royal yacht, where he was met by thousands of his frolicsome subjects. Dressed in white satin and silver cloth, he led his parade through the heart of the city, accompanied by mounted police, artillery battalions, sailors, marines, National Guardsmen, and Boy Scouts. At city hall, the mayor presented Rex with the keys of the city, inaugurating his merry thirty-six-hour rule. On Fat Tuesday, Rex again processed through the streets, leading a parade of floats so elaborate they took their krewes a full year to create. In 1917, framed in a great golden crown, Rex had led a dazzling pageant of twenty floats whose theme, "The Gift of the Gods to Louisiana," used glittering images from ancient mythology to illustrate the wonders of the state. The crowds loved it.

Mardi Gras wasn't just about parades and pageants. On Fat Tuesday the population itself took to the streets in costumes and masks. Clowns, gypsies, elves, and pirates packed into Canal Street and danced to jazz bands playing on street corners; red devils and black-faced minstrels added a touch of the grotesque, children dressed as bumblebees a touch of the comical. The city center became a playground for high-spirited antics. Identities safely hidden, people dared what they'd never do unmasked. Maskers danced with complete strangers; respectable women invaded bars; masked matrons peeked into houses of ill repute on Basin Street.

But in 1919, Rex announced that this year he would not leave his palace in Araby the Blest to descend upon New Orleans. Celebrations had been canceled in 1918 because of the war. Such frivolity didn't seem quite right with American boys dying in French mud. The thousands who enjoyed the pageants and parades and costumes swallowed their disappointment and looked forward to the resumption of festivities at the end of the war. March 1919, however, just four months after the end of a conflict that left over 116,000 Americans dead, still seemed too soon. The celebration of Carnival was scaled back. A few modest parades were planned, private masked balls were permitted, but the *Times-Picayune* tried to lower expectations: "There will be no gorgeous pageants to fill the streets with a blaze of color and light."

Apparently, no one checked with the people of New Orleans.

By ten on the morning of Mardi Gras, the spirit of Carnival had overwhelmed the city fathers' reluctance and spontaneously impelled thousands of masked merrymakers into the streets. Costumed in bright silks, satins, and velvets, revelers swaggered up and down the banquettes, hung out of slick new automobiles, and hitched rides on horse-drawn wagons. The twang of banjos and the reedy hum of clarinets floated through the air. A truck carrying a calliope pushed its way through the crowds, adding its steam-driven whistles to the general din. Elves, gnomes, hula dancers, Spanish dons, Cherokee warriors, and harem beauties made their way down Saint Charles Avenue. Cross-dressing was surprisingly popular, with young women uniformed as soldiers competing for attention with grown men made up as Japanese geishas. No "modest, even . . . somber Carnival" was this. By midday any pretense that the day was in any way normal had vanished; the city was one big party. Businesses closed. Housewives found themselves abandoned by household help who had joined the masked throngs. Even the weather cooperated, an approving sun driving out threatening clouds.

Frank Jordano and his girlfriend Josie Spera joined the flood of humanity that darkened the Central Business District, floating along with the crowd down Canal Street, laughing at the masked sprites, the satin-clad cavaliers, the women dressed as redbirds. They tried to listen to the primitive jazz band at the corner of Saint Charles and Canal, heroically attempting to make its ragtime heard over the cacophony of the crowd. They gaped at the red devils and harlequins driving delivery wagons. They ate hot dogs on Canal Street from a vendor hawking them from the back of his wagon. All day and into the night, they shared the streets with the happy crush of surging humanity.

They also shared the streets with a more sinister companion. He, too, enjoyed the crowds and the masks and the music. But his was a malevolent spirit that threatened Frank and Josie and their future happiness.

That night, that memorable Mardi Gras, Frank was a happy young man, ambitious and optimistic. An exemplary son of Sicilian immigrants, he worked hard and made big plans. At seventeen he was already an insurance agent and engaged to Josie, a sweet local girl; he anticipated a flourishing American life, a happy family, a prosperous business. But three nights after Mardi Gras, Josie had a dream. She dreamed that evil was about to descend on the neighborhood. She was prescient. Frank's life was about to become a nightmare.

Screams tore through the quiet Gretna neighborhood on an otherwise tranquil Sunday morning. Hazel Johnson, a young black woman, bolted out of the Cortimiglias' combination residence and grocery, yelling for someone, anyone to help—the Cortimiglias had been murdered!

Frank Jordano was upstairs in bed when his twenty-year-old sister Lena's hysterical cries—"Oh, Jesus! Oh, Jesus! Oh, Jesus!"—punctured his sleep. Panic-stricken, thinking something had happened to their mother, he tumbled down the stairs, dressing on the way. Facing his sister, shirt unbuttoned, shoes on without socks, he demanded, "Lena, what's the trouble? Is it Mama?"

"They're dead," she wept. "Mr. Cortimiglia, Mrs. Cortimiglia, and the baby are dead." Dazed, he stared at her: "Do you mean that?"

"Yes," she insisted. "Hazel Johnson came running out hollering that they were dead."

At that moment, he looked up to see Ella Kennedy, Hazel's aunt who had accompanied her on her errand to the store, coming out of the alley that led to the back of the Cortimiglias' place, screaming that the baby was dead.

Still buckling his belt and buttoning his shirt, Frank raced into the alley that separated his home from that of the Cortimiglias, ran down it and around to the kitchen entrance to the Cortimiglia home. Despite the recent dispute between the families over rental property, he liked the Cortimiglias. And he adored their little girl. Sprinting up the steps to the little house, he joined the growing crowd that crammed into the single, small bedroom. Peering over the heads of the others who'd already arrived, what he saw there changed his life.

Charles Cortimiglia and his young wife Rosie lay draped across their bed from opposite sides; the body of their dead toddler lay still between them. The room was soaked in crimson. Blood drenched the bed; it speckled the wall and stained the curtains; it pooled on the floor. You could have wrung buckets of it out of the mosquito bar, the gauzelike netting that had covered the sleepers. From one wall, a picture of the Virgin Mary gazed serenely down on the pain and blood.

Frank's parents had beaten their son to the scene. Even old Mr. Jordano, achy with rheumatism, had moved faster than he'd done for months and had followed his wife from their house to their neighbors', curious and frightened at the same time. Mrs. Jordano took in the situation at a glance: Rosie lay still. Charlie was barely conscious, awash in his own blood, half on and half off the bed, kneeling with his upper body slumped across it. Going over to him, Mrs. Jordano asked, "Mr. Charlie, Mr. Charlie, what can I do for you?" A voice from the back of the crowd advised, "Don't do anything until the doctor comes." Charlie Cortimiglia could barely shake his head. Feeling helpless but desperate to do something, Mrs. Jordano went to get a bucket of water and a cloth to bathe his bloodied face. Frank took her place by the side of the bed, asking, "Charlie, for Christ's sake, who done this?" Charlie couldn't

THREE GRETNA VICTIMS OF AX MURDERER

These photographs show the Cortimiglia family, victims of the latest axman mystery, and their Gretna home. The child, Mary, aged 2 years, was slain outright. Charles Cortimiglia and wife are shown in the lower lefthand corner. Cortimiglia is dying in the Charity Hospital. His wife's condition is serious. In the upper righthand corner is a diagram of the interior of the Cortimiglia home. The arrow designated "A" points to the rear door where the murderer entered by cutting out the panel of the lower lefthand portion. It also shows the steps under which the ax was concealed. The arrows indicated by "B" point to a trunk and dresser found rifled. The broken dotted line ending in an arrow pointing to the bed where figures of the Cortimiglias and their child are indicated as they were found, show the path traversed by the ax murderer from the rear door to their sleeping chamber.

Pictures that appeared in the Times-Picayune *after the attack on the Cortimiglias.*

speak before he passed out. Frank cradled his neighbor in his arms as he kept him from falling over. As he did so, he glanced at the body of the toddler lying beside him. The little girl had been playing at his house only days before. Frank—big, husky, 275-pound Frank—began to cry.

Charlie came to and moved his lips as if trying to speak. Frank leaned down to make out what he was saying. Charlie was only able to get out "Frank, I'm dying. Get my brother-in-law" before lapsing into unconsciousness again.

Determined to carry out what seemed very likely to be Charlie's dying wish, Frank left him in the care of his parents and the other neighbors and went outside. As he left the house he ran into his sister Lena, who had finally found her nerve and come to see for herself what had happened. Pale and wiping away tears, Frank knew that she wasn't ready for the scene he'd just left. "Don't go in there," he snapped as he darted past. "If you see what's in there, it'll kill you." Running on, he hurriedly hitched up his horse and buggy, leapt into the seat, and snapped the reins.

Under the circumstances, Frank reckoned that finding a doctor was a higher priority than locating a brother-in-law. Charlie Cortimiglia would forgive him if he briefly delayed his errand. The first doctor he called on was not at home. Having better luck with his second choice, Dr. G. W. Rossner, he begged him to hurry to the Cortimiglias: "People are dying down there!"

After the doctor promised to head right over, Frank turned his buggy in the direction of Amesville, a small farming community about three miles up the river from Gretna. Setting his horse to a brisk trot along the dirt track running next to the Southern Pacific Railroad line, he thought unhappily of news he had to deliver: that the Cortimiglias had been cut up and robbed. For that, reasonably enough, was what he assumed had happened. Perhaps the thought flitted across his mind that they had been victims of the "fiend"—that's what the newspapers called him—from across the river. But no, he had never struck in Gretna, always in New Orleans itself. Frank flicked the reins to make the horse go faster.

Dr. Rossner arrived at the Cortimiglias' to find a houseful of people milling about the bedroom. He took one look at the figures on the bed and realized he could do nothing for them. What they needed was Charity Hospital, and as soon as possible. Fortunately, Manny Fink had already realized that.

Emmanuel Fink—"Manny" to his neighbors—engineer, machinist, businessman, and city councilman—was an energetic man used to taking charge. Living only half a block from the Cortimiglias, he had been one of the first to be roused by Hazel's cries. After seeing that Rosie and Charlie were still alive, he left the bedroom and grabbed Tony Winters, the first person he met on his way out of the house, and ordered, "Come back here; these people are all chopped up." He stationed Winters at the bedroom door with orders not to touch anything and not to let anyone else touch anything.

Fink then telephoned everyone he could think of: the sheriff, the chief of police, a couple of doctors, and the Charity Hospital ambulance. Charity Hospital was not as helpful as he had expected. The big-city hospital, he was informed, did not extend their ambulance service to his side of the Mississippi. The unpaved roads of little Gretna were so bad that the hospital was afraid of the ambulance getting stuck on the far side of the river. *For God's sake*, Fink insisted, *two people are dying here. Well*, the hospital offered, *we could have the ambulance meet you at the foot of Jackson Avenue. You just have to get them to the ferry and across the river.*

Fink wasn't left with much choice. He returned to the Cortimiglias' to find the police chief and deputy sheriff. He reported the hospital's response and then went home to get his own horse and wagon. Hitching up his horse as quickly as he could, Fink drove back to the Cortimiglia place.

There, someone had found a thin mattress to use as a stretcher. Gingerly, Rosie was placed on the mattress and numerous hands gently lifted her into the wagon. But what about Charlie? Fink looked around, not seeing another potential stretcher. Then someone had the clever idea of using the bathroom door. Someone else grabbed the axe—covered in congealed blood—that had already been found underneath the house and knocked the door free of its hinges. As Charlie was carried out of the room, Fink glanced back to see two pieces of skull lying on the bed. Shaking off the sight, he snatched up the reins and sent his horse as fast as he dared down the dozen blocks to the ferry.

Little Mary Cortimiglia's body was left lying on the bed. A neighbor put a blanket over it. Someone else called Fred Leitz's undertaking parlor.

Dr. Henry Leidenheimer strode down the wide hallways of Charity Hospital toward the Accident Room. As the surgeon on duty, new cases were reported to him first. At thirty-nine, he was an experienced surgeon. And Charity, despite the name, was a good hospital. Established for the poor in the early eighteenth century, it was one of the oldest public hospitals in the country and a well-regarded teaching hospital for Tulane Medical School. The main building dated from 1832; the very solidity of the imposing three-storied brown structure, lateral wings flanking both ends of the central corridor, was reassuring. Overcrowded and chronically short of funds, Charity nevertheless managed to provide a fairly decent standard of care for the city's needy, both white and "colored," by the standards of the time. The Cortimiglias would need all the expertise Charity and Dr. Leidenheimer had to offer.

In the treatment room, Leidenheimer examined the couple, now lying on clean white metal hospital beds instead of their makeshift stretchers. Axe wounds didn't particularly surprise him; the presence of axes and hatchets in most homes for chopping firewood made them obvious weapons of choice in domestic disputes; irate people in New Orleans periodically took a swing at each other. Only last year, a man had gotten himself shot when he took after a friend with a kitchen axe. But these were particularly bad cases. A quick glance told him that Charlie probably wouldn't live: two severe cuts had sliced through his head, fracturing his skull and cutting into the soft tissue and brain beneath; his traumatized brain had swollen, oozing through the fractured bone like mud through the slats of a chicken crate. Dr. Leidenheimer shook his head. All he could do for Charlie was clean his wounds with antiseptic, dress them, and hope for the best.

By then Dr. Jerome Landry had come on duty and taken charge of Rosie. She had several gashes on her head and one on her left ear. Much more serious, a blow to the left side of the head had left her with a depressed fracture, pressing in on her brain. Dr. Landry didn't think Rosie was likely to survive, but he could perform a craniotomy, a procedure to relieve the pressure on her brain. Without much optimism, he ordered her wheeled into the surgical amphitheater. He didn't bother with anesthesia; Rosie's injuries made it unlikely that she would wake up during the surgery. Besides, he wanted to avoid the risk of oversedating and accidentally killing her. Rosie survived the operation, but afterward, still without much hope, Dr. Landry, as he later put it, "sent her back to the ward to die."

Which she stubbornly refused to do. By Monday morning her relatives—parents, sister, brothers, brother-in-law, and niece—were pouring in from surrounding parishes and gathering at the hospital, waiting for any sign of improvement. Charity had no waiting room in which to confine them. They were a nuisance for the nurses, crowding about, begging to see Rosie and Charlie, and demanding to know who was responsible for the attack. Her niece Anna implored hospital authorities to let her see her aunt. *I can speak to her in Italian*, she insisted. *She'll tell me who did this*. While Anna pleaded, Rosie's stepbrother John threatened: "I must see her! She will tell me who did this and then something will happen!" He made such a fuss that the police had to step in to persuade him to listen to the nurses and leave.

Rosie's parents were the only ones allowed to see her. Mostly, she slept quietly, as her pulse and color gradually improved. From time to time, she mumbled in Italian or murmured her daughter's name; at times she seemed vaguely to recognize her parents as they sat by her bedside.

Charlie was still supposed to be dying. That's what the doctors kept telling his in-laws. But, also not very cooperative with his physicians' dire predictions, he hung on.

Neither parent was in any condition to be told Monday when Rosie's parents arranged for the funeral of their granddaughter. Children were buried in white, the color of innocence. Wealthy people could try to mitigate their grief with a grand display of a white coffin in a white hearse pulled by white horses in a white harness. The Cortimiglias could afford no such extravagance, even for their only child. On that dismal, rainy March day, relatives and neighbors clustered around a modest white casket as the little girl was entombed in one of the whitewashed vaults of the Hook and Ladder Cemetery. Almost certainly Frank Jordano and his parents were there. What must he have thought as he stared at the pathetic little casket? That little Mary had played in his parents' store countless times? That she had called his own father "Grandpa"? Now she was dead, an ugly, violent, incomprehensible death. Who would bash a toddler in the head with an axe? Everyone in the cemetery must have asked themselves that, over and over. And as they listened sobbing to the final words said over the body of the little girl, no one would have disputed the *New Orleans Daily States*' description of it as "one of the saddest funerals ever held in Jefferson Parish."

Mary wouldn't be the Axeman's only Gretna victim. That Saturday-night attack would damage her father's business, ruin her parents' marriage, and endanger the lives of the friendly neighbors who had only tried to help.

Only thirty-one years after Jack the Ripper terrorized London and presented the world with a new kind of killer, fifty years before the term *serial killer* even existed, the police were ill-equipped to deal with serial murder. Jack the Ripper lives forever as the ghostly fiend of Whitechapel, and his five victims are among the most famous unsolved murders in history. But he is hardly the only one who got away with such crimes. Killers who target strangers and have no obvious motive are always difficult to catch. In the 1970s Ted Bundy killed over twenty young women before he was finally apprehended, despite over a dozen detectives in three states looking for him. The BTK killer of Wichita was caught after thirty years only because of DNA evidence and his own arrogance. The Zodiac killer of northern California evaded a forty-year manhunt, never to be captured or even identified with certainty.

In the early twentieth century the difficulties of catching a serial killer—even identifying serial murders—were even greater. It was the dawn of a new age: police forces were becoming professionalized as they began wriggling free from the taint of corruption and patronage. While police procedures and investigative techniques were rapidly developing, the science of homicide investigation was still in its infancy. The art of profiling was unknown. Scientists had only learned how to distinguish human blood from animal blood in the last twenty years; detectives could now conclusively prove whether a pinkish stain was blood. Fingerprinting had only recently been introduced as a crime-fighting tool. Toxicologists in New York City's coroner's office were just beginning to systemically develop the discipline of forensic chemistry as a way of detecting poisoners. In Vienna, Freud was still unpacking the unconscious motives of the human mind. Detectives still operated mainly on legwork, gut feeling, common sense, their knowledge of their community, and the surprising willingness of suspects to confess.

In New Orleans, where the killer struck first, some recognized that they faced no ordinary criminal. The city was blessed with two police superintendents who realized that they were stalked by a Jack the Ripper of their own, a different kind of murderer against whom traditional methods were . . . well, if not useless, at least limited. What they weren't blessed with was luck. One, an experienced homicide investigator, met his own tragic end. The other was a well-meaning bureaucrat defeated by office politics.

Gretna was a small town, living in the shadow of its better-known neighbor across the river. Its murders were tragically mundane, arising from drunken brawls, jealous rivalries, and clumsy robberies. Crimes like these can usually be solved the old-fashioned way. With a serial killer, the police need to know what they are looking for. The authorities of Gretna, unwilling to face the reality that they couldn't solve this appalling murder, convinced themselves that Frank Jordano and his father—a teenage boy and an old man—attempted to hack their neighbors to death over a rental dispute. Through their ignorance (which they couldn't help), their willingness to bend the law in pursuit of an end (which they could), and perhaps their malice toward Italian immigrants, the Gretna authorities made the tragedy of Mary Cortimiglia's death worse.

Unrecognized by them, the attacks of the serial killer who had come to terrorize New Orleans had actually begun on a hot summer's night some nine years earlier.

2

The Cleaver

3 AM, Saturday, August 13, 1910

HARRIET CRUTTI WOKE FROM a sound sleep to find the shadowy figure of a man standing over her with a meat cleaver. The apparition, holding up the mosquito netting with one hand, and waving the bloody cleaver at her with the other, came sharply into focus as he demanded her money: "Or I'll do to you what I just did to your husband!"

Panicking, Mrs. Crutti looked down and saw her bloodied husband lying still across the foot of the bed. "You've murdered him!" she screamed. Terrified, she did the only sensible thing: she reached under her pillow for the box containing eight dollars (a significant sum in 1910) and handed it over.

It wasn't enough to satisfy the man with the cleaver: "Is that all you got? I want all of it!" *Yes*, she insisted. *Just take it.* Mrs. Crutti was too frightened to mention the more substantial amount of money under the mattress. Fortunately, the intruder believed her. He turned around and strode out of the bedroom, and through the Cruttis' combination grocery/bar/residence, snatching up their pet mockingbird in its cage as he went. Tossing aside the meat cleaver in the yard, he retrieved the shoes he'd taken off and climbed over the back fence, leisurely walked a block down Lesseps Street until he reached the corner, and sat down on a doorstep. There he flipped open the latch on the birdcage and freed the bird. Then he deliberately rolled a cigarette, leaned back against the

Harriet Crutti.

stoop, and smoked it. Afterward, he pulled on his shoes, stood up, and sauntered down Dauphine Street.

At the same time, Mrs. Crutti, afraid that her husband was dead or dying, was desperately trying to shake him awake. Groaning, he tried to rise, only to fall semiconscious off the bed. One of the Cruttis' young sons added to the chaos by waking up and starting to cry, panicking his mother even more. Frantic, Mrs. Crutti left her husband on the floor and ran out into the street. She pounded on her neighbors' doors. *Please! Open up! My husband's hurt!* No response. Some slept through the commotion. Others looked through their windows to see what was happening. But all the doors remained shut. For an agonizing fifteen minutes Mrs. Crutti lurched desperately along the dark and deserted street, running from house to house, pleading for help. She finally managed to rouse Officer Gus Albert, a policeman who lived nearby. Officer Albert, still in his nightclothes, grabbed his revolver and rushed after the assailant, now long gone.

Grocer August John Crutti,
the Axeman's first victim.

The injured grocer was taken to Charity Hospital while the police arrived to investigate. They soon discovered that earlier that night the assailant had stolen the meat cleaver from a butcher's stall six blocks away. As the police reconstructed the crime, at about three o'clock on that Saturday morning, the shoeless intruder had removed a pane of glass from the Cruttis' kitchen door (presumably to reach in to the bolt) but had ended up using a railroad shoe pin (a thin, curved steel bar used to couple railroad cars and a common burglary tool for prying doors and windows open) to force the door. Their small business was typical of its time: a small grocery and bar attached to the family's living quarters. Moving noiselessly, the intruder passed through the kitchen, through the grocery store, and on into the bedroom. There he pulled back the mosquito netting that protected sleepers in subtropical New Orleans from the harassing insects, raised the stolen meat cleaver, and struck the sleeping grocer twice.

But why?

The forty-year-old son of an Italian immigrant, August Crutti and his twenty-nine-year-old wife Harriet had opened their store on the corner of Royal and Lesseps Streets only a month before. It was located in the Bywater District of New Orleans, a block from the Mississippi River, just over a mile and a half east of the French Quarter. Crutti had been in the ice business, but he had worked hard to save the money to buy his own grocery, a modest establishment in a modest neighborhood. August and Harriet shared the small house with their two young sons, Jake and August Jr., and eighteen-year-old Arthur, Crutti's stepson. What could they have done in just a month to provoke such an attack?

Once the blood was cleaned off, Crutti's injuries turned out to be far less serious than they'd first appeared. He'd been cut on the head and chest, but neither wound was life-threatening. By Saturday afternoon he was sitting up in his bed at Charity Hospital, smoking a cigarette and patiently answering the police's endless questions about the evening's events. He remembered going to bed at midnight but then having an attack of heartburn. Thinking that a cool drink might make him feel better, he got up to get a glass of water and then walked about the house for a bit before going back to bed. The bed was crowded by the presence of his seven- and eight-year-old sons, so Crutti lay with his head toward the foot of the bed, where he fell asleep about an hour before the assault. He remembered nothing about the attack itself; as far as he knew he'd been fast asleep when the first blow fell.

No one could come up with any reason for the attack. Neither Crutti could think of anyone who would harm them. August Crutti admitted to an enemy from his days in the ice business but scoffed at the idea that he would have been capable of such an assault.

Besides, his milquetoast enemy didn't match the description that the police had put together based on the accounts of Mrs. Crutti and a neighbor who'd happened to look out of the window in time to catch a glimpse of the assailant. The police were looking for a man thirty-six or thirty-seven years old; about five foot six inches tall; broad shouldered and clean shaven; with dark hair, thick nose and lips, and a rough, husky voice. He'd worn dark trousers, a loose blue workingman's shirt, and a black derby hat.

The man in charge of investigating this puzzling crime was Chief of Detectives Jim Reynolds. The forty-two-year-old policeman hailed from Algiers, right across the river. Joining the police force at age twenty-five as a supernumerary clerk, he'd rapidly been promoted to plainclothes officer, detective, and finally chief of detectives. Portly, with a fleshy face that became almost cherubic when he smiled—as he often did—Reynolds was easygoing and likable, a chain-smoking joker who liked good company and good stories. Popular with the men under his command as well as the reporters assigned to the police beat, he was intelligent and sensible, with a reputation for hard work, a detective who would work a case as long as was necessary. As a seasoned veteran of robbery, kidnapping, and murder investigations, he shouldn't have been stumped by a simple robbery and assault.

Chief of Detectives James Reynolds.

But Jim Reynolds was as mystified as anyone. He walked slowly through the house and grocery, surveying the crime scene. He assumed that the incident at the Cruttis' home and grocery was just a robbery, although an odd one to be sure. If he was after money, the robber must have checked the grocery first and, finding nothing, realized that all the cash was probably in the proprietor's bedroom. But why attack the sleeping grocer? Had Crutti stirred in his sleep, frightening him? Why did the assailant take the risk of talking to Mrs. Crutti? Why take the bird? And given that he had just committed a hanging offense—for that was what assault with a deadly weapon was—for what possible reason did he take his time leaving the crime scene?

The most common supposition was that the attacker was plain mad. After crawling all over the little grocery examining the evidence, hearing the Cruttis' story, and interviewing the neighbors, most policemen were inclined to shrug their shoulders and dismiss the criminal as "drunk or crazy." Not much else made sense. August Crutti's own idea was that "some half-witted fellow" did it for the money.

The description of the attacker, and the description of two strange men seen hanging about the grocery on the night of the attack, gave detectives enough evidence to question a "well-known police character." A couple such characters were brought to Mrs. Crutti for identification. *No*, she said both times, *not the man I saw with the cleaver.*

Finally, after about two weeks, detectives got lucky. Chief Reynolds had decided, quite reasonably, that a criminal who acted as oddly, even irrationally, as the Crutti assailant did, was probably either mentally ill or drug addled. And he'd instructed his men to be on the lookout for such a person. So when a known burglar who had spent time in a mental hospital came to the attention of detectives, they leapt on him.

John Flannery was an addict—a cocaine and morphine "fiend" the newspapers called him. He also was a petty criminal with a history of burglary to support his drug habit, a previous arrest for assault, and features that roughly tallied with the description of the Crutti assailant. When he was caught breaking into a grocery two weeks after the attack on August Crutti, Mrs. Crutti was called down to police headquarters.

There she unhesitatingly identified him as her husband's attacker. Police were also able to connect Flannery with a series of other burglaries in which a railroad shoe pin similar to the one left in the Cruttis' grocery had been used. The case against him seemed clinched.

But it wasn't perfect. At age twenty-five, Flannery was a bit younger than the mid-to-late-thirties man described by witnesses. And he vehemently denied the crime, even after hours of interrogation by Reynolds and St. Clair Adams, the district attorney. But Harriet Crutti's identification was positive, Flannery fit the physical description of the attacker, and he was the kind of criminal the police had suspected all along; the case appeared likely to close in short order.

On September 9 John Flannery was indicted for feloniously breaking and entering into the Crutti residence and assaulting August Crutti. But he never went to trial. Doubts about his fitness to stand trial led to a commission to assess Flannery's mental condition. The commission consisted of two doctors, E. M. Hummell and Joseph O'Hara, a neurologist who was also coroner and city physician of Orleans Parish. The doctors concluded that Flannery's mental state had been compromised by drugs and alcohol, that he was suffering from disorganized schizophrenia, and that he was "insane and irresponsible [and] . . . a permanent menace" to society.

O'Hara and Hummell recommended that Flannery be placed in an insane asylum. He was not committed immediately, however, for he was still in Orleans Parish Prison, the city jail, almost a year and a half later, when Dr. O'Hara reported that his mental condition had improved considerably, and he now appeared perfectly sane. Under normal circumstances the correct procedure would have been to take Flannery to trial. But by that time District Attorney Adams had reason to doubt Flannery's guilt and declined to prosecute, arguing even if he were guilty of the Crutti attack, Flannery had been irresponsibly insane at the time of the offense.

Yet the end of August 1910 seemed to bring the Crutti case to a gratifying conclusion. Reynolds was satisfied that he'd found the culprit. Crutti went home to his family after only one night in the hospital.

Even the liberated pet bird made its way home and was spotted on the roof of the grocery.

A month later the attacker struck again.

A man crept up to the grocery and residence of Joseph and Conchetta Rissetto shortly after 1:45 AM on the morning of September 20, 1910. Tonti Street and London Avenue (now A. P. Tureaud Avenue) was a rundown, crime-ridden part of town, mostly poor and black. This sparsely populated neighborhood on the outskirts of New Orleans hardly seemed part of a proper city at all, littered as it was with pigpens and cowsheds and barely passable dirt roads.

The Rissettos, both children of Italian immigrants, had done well in spite of their impoverished neighborhood. Their business among the local "Negro" population was so successful that five years earlier they had been able to build a new grocery and barroom and add a poolroom. The cottage they built alongside their business was bigger than those

Conchetta and Joseph Rissetto.

of many other small grocers; it had the extravagance of both a parlor and a dining room, as well as a bedroom and kitchen. At forty-two and thirty-six years old, Mr. and Mrs. Rissetto had been married for seventeen years. With no children, they had only each other for company and were a devoted and loving couple.

The man quietly approaching the Rissettos' home and business early that Tuesday morning probably cared about none of this. He carried a stolen meat axe, similar to a butcher's cleaver but, at three pounds, a little heavier. From the cowshed in the back he stole up to the kitchen and climbed through an unlatched window. Inside the house, he walked past the open door leading into the grocery. Entering the bedroom, the intruder went over to the woman's side of the bed and with a knife sliced open the mosquito netting, exposing the sleeping couple. He raised his weapon. He brought it down purposively on the helpless woman. The first blow hit her in the face, breaking her right cheekbone. As she reflexively twisted away from her attacker, he struck her again, and again, cutting deep into the left side of her face and slashing her neck. He moved around to the other side of the bed and struck her husband twice in the face, one blow slicing cleanly though the cartilage of his nose. The assailant then dropped his meat axe into the tangled, bloody strands of the mosquito netting. He didn't stop to take anything but made his way out of the house, going through the poolroom behind the kitchen, opening the door leading out into the yard, and heading toward the fence in the front yard.

Awake now, Joseph Rissetto felt something warm running down his face. He tried to get up, but, blinded by the blood in his eyes and stunned from two blows, all he could do was fall out of bed. Frantically crawling around on the floor on his hands and knees, feeling blindly around for matches, hurting badly and unable to see, he painfully managed to light a lamp. Still barely able to see, he groped his way to a dresser where he grabbed a revolver and staggered to a side porch to fire two shots into the air.

Help came fast. Hearing the shots, Bartholomew Pratts, one of the Rissettos' black neighbors, ran over to investigate. He found Rissetto sitting on his bedroom floor, his bloodied face in his hands, barely able to speak. Pratts immediately raised the alarm, sending for an ambulance and the police. As word spread that something horrible had happened down at the Rissettos' place, neighbors and relatives made their way in the dark down to the grocery where they could do little but wander through the house in shock and confusion, sickened by what they found. The Rissettos' bedroom resembled, according to one newspaper, a "slaughtering pen." Blood soaked the bed and was smeared all over the floor. Traces of Mrs. Rissetto's hair, cut by the blows of the axe, lay bloody on the bedclothes. She still lay in her own blood, unrecognizable, in great pain, pleading for help. Her distraught husband begged someone to help her. There was, however, little anyone could do except attempt to comfort them and wait for the ambulance.

But the Charity Hospital ambulance couldn't reach them. The cratered and rutted roads were impassible. Charity had only just replaced its horse-drawn ambulance with a motorized one, which wasn't up to the neighborhood's mud and potholes. Rescuers had to carry the victims by stretcher four blocks from their home to the waiting vehicle. Joseph and Conchetta were then taken to the hospital, he permanently blinded in one eye and disfigured for life, she with injuries so severe that surgeons didn't expect her to live.

A mounted policeman, Harry Gregson, who'd heard the gunshots, was the first to gallop over the rough terrain to the Rissetto place. He was the beginning of an impressive police response. Chief Reynolds and District Attorney Adams were awoken from their beds, and city officials, detectives, and uniformed policemen descended on the grocery in the early morning hours, newspaper reporters not far behind.

Chief Reynolds found his policemen scouring the house and neighborhood as best they could in the dead of night. Even by candlelight, they could trace the intruder's movements through the manure and mud tracked into the house and the doors left open as he departed. Joining his detectives in their search, Reynolds took careful note of the fact that nothing in the grocery appeared to be disturbed; the cash register had twenty-three dollars in it; the safe, which held several hundred dollars, had not been tampered with. Valuables in the bedroom were also untouched: Joseph Rissetto's gold watch and chain were still in the drawer where he'd left them; thirty-five dollars sat on the dresser. Reynolds knew very well that John Flannery was sitting in the parish prison; he also noted how similar this crime scene was to that of the Crutti grocery.

Once he'd been thoroughly through the crime scene, Chief Reynolds went with several of his detectives and District Attorney Adams to the hospital. Joseph, in much better condition than his wife, had the most to say. But even Conchetta, as badly wounded as she was, did her best to whisper answers to the detectives' questions.

Other than a romantic rival he had had for his wife years earlier, Rissetto couldn't think of any enemies. He knew of people who disliked him—mostly customers who'd been refused credit and threatened him from time to time—but he didn't believe any of them would actually try to kill him. Both the grocer and his wife assumed that the crime must have been committed by someone bent on robbery. But this bloody attack was so unlike the type of crime usually associated with the poor, black population of his neighborhood that Reynolds doubted the explanation was so simple.

Once daylight came, Reynolds's men searched the Rissettos' home and grocery again. Assistant Chief of Detectives Dan Mouney combed over the yard outside the grocery, meticulously making note of all the footprints crisscrossing the property and trying to identify to whom they belonged. Investigators traced footprints leading into the pigsty and footprints leading from the cowshed. Two sets of tracks were spotted outside the kitchen window, leading to speculation that two people were involved. Impressions of bare feet led some investigators to argue that the assailant had been shoeless.

Over the next several days, the police questioned suspect after suspect, without making any progress. Most were black; all were dismissed as possible assailants. Investigators remained thoroughly baffled.

Meanwhile, Reynolds uncovered a curious fact. The meat axe used in the attack had been stolen from a butcher's stall in a local market several weeks previously. And a large butcher knife stolen from the stall at the same time had turned up a week or so ago at a burgled grocery less than two miles from the Rissetto grocery. This made the crime even more puzzling. The criminal appeared to be a thief who had robbed one grocery without hurting anyone, as well as an assailant who viciously attacked the Rissettos without stealing anything. The chief of detectives shook his head. None of this made any sense.

As they had done after the Crutti incident, the newspapers debated a range of possible motives: robbery, revenge, drug-induced mania, even "domestic strife." To some, the previous assault on the Cruttis did not rule out a vendetta as a motive. Both couples were, as more than one paper deliberately noted, "of Italian descent." The implication that the families had run afoul of some Italian criminal gang was clear.

Reynolds's own view is hard to discern in the pages of the newspapers. Three days after the attack, the *New Orleans Item* quoted him as insisting, "I am certain that burglars did the work." The *Times-Democrat*, on the other hand, was convinced Reynolds believed the attacker was no ordinary criminal, with no ordinary motive, but someone who simply delighted in the sight of blood. But rumors also circulated that the chief leaned toward the "revenge theory." Reynolds may well have found it prudent to keep his views to himself, leaving reporters to infer them as best they could. But the *Times-Democrat* was likely nearer the mark. Both the Crutti and Rissetto crimes were too unlike the handiwork of any ordinary burglar. That much was clear to almost everyone. The "meat axe fiend" theory seems to have been the most popular: that the assailant was motivated by "a fiendish thirst for blood"—a desire to draw blood, perhaps to actually see the blood. Newspaper headlines spoke of "Jack the Axeman" and speculated about New Orleans's own Jack the Ripper, all of which contributed to what the *Daily News* called the "dime store novel flavor" of the affair.

The main benefactor of all this speculation was John Flannery. His trial was scheduled to begin at the end of the month, and it was becoming increasingly clear that, drug addict or not, he hadn't assaulted August Crutti. It was also increasingly a matter of concern that the attacker would strike again if he wasn't stopped. And no one knew how to stop him.

At the end of the week, Chief Reynolds again assured the public that "the trail is very warm and we expect to capture this man shortly." But the investigation had petered out, although Reynolds was loath to admit it publicly.

The episode did have a happy ending, of sorts. From the beginning the doctors at Charity Hospital had thought Joseph Rissetto, while badly scarred and blind in one eye, would live but that his wife probably would not. Yet Conchetta held on, day after day, despite constant pronouncements in the papers that she couldn't last much longer. If she did survive, the surgeons said, she would probably be permanently paralyzed on one side of her face. Her husband, injured and in the men's ward, waited anxiously for news about his wife's condition and asked frequently how she was and when he could see her. She lay in the women's ward pleading to see him. After a week, he was finally permitted to leave his own hospital bed and go to his wife's bedside. As badly scarred as both were, they were each delighted to see the other. Their affectionate but brief reunion over, he returned to their home, alone. How long he had to wait for her to join him is not known, but join him she undoubtedly did, for she lived to a good age, dying only in 1940. Joseph, however, died only two years later, in 1912. While the newspapers said that his death wasn't a direct result of the injuries he'd sustained, he was never the same after that September night, and it's hard not to suspect that his wounds contributed to his long decline. Perhaps Joseph Rissetto was another, unacknowledged fatality of the Axeman.

According to the *Daily Picayune*, Mrs. Crutti had described her husband's attacker as having "murder stamped on his countenance." She was right. For if "the Cleaver," as he would soon be known, hadn't yet actually managed to kill anyone, that would change in the summer of 1911.

3

Dagoes, Sugarcane, and Muffulettas

THE AXEMAN'S VICTIMS—JOSEPH AND Conchetta Rissetto, August and Harriet Crutti, the Cortimiglias, Frank Jordano and his entire family—represented a particular niche in early twentieth-century New Orleans: the Italian grocer. Italians, especially refugees from the rocky soil of western Sicily, came to Louisiana as laborers, but many quickly became businessmen. How? And why would anyone want to kill them?

The dusty little Sicilian town of Campofiorito didn't have much to offer Iorlando Guagliardo, and he knew it. Slight but handsome, with a full, dashing mustache, he was also illiterate and unskilled; all that lay ahead of him was a lifetime of poverty, confiscatory taxation, rapacious bandits, endless vendettas, and constant labor in someone else's fields. Still, at age twenty-one, Iorlando had another option. In 1873 he packed everything he could carry into a canvas bag, kissed his mother good-bye and hopped on a cart that jostled him twenty-five miles north to the port of Palermo. There he boarded a ship and sailed to America, joining the vanguard of what would become a flood of Sicilians into Louisiana.

Louisiana plantations had always run on the sweat and blood of black labor. But after the Civil War many former slaves were anxious to get as far out of Dixie as they could, and they migrated in large numbers up north and out west. Many who did stay in Louisiana preferred day labor in New Orleans or Baton Rouge to hoeing weeds in a cane field, for them an echo of times best forgotten. For their part, white planters heartily disliked dealing with freedmen and looked around for another, more amenable source of cheap labor for Louisiana's rapidly growing sugarcane industry. It was this need that led to the great influx of Sicilians into the state and the city in the later nineteenth century and explained the journey of many young men like Iorlando Guagliardo.

The Sicilians turned out to be just what the sugar planters of Louisiana needed, for they were industrious, dependable laborers—a "hard-working, money-saving race, and content with . . . few of the comforts of life." The trickle of Sicilians in the 1860s and 1870s became a torrent by the 1880s and 1890s. They dominated Italian immigration into Louisiana.

For the city's inhabitants, the new arrivals presented a strange and exotic sight—swarthy men in their fur caps, close-fitting black velveteen jackets and trousers, booted to the knee, and sporting earrings; stout women with their heads tied up in brightly colored kerchiefs, earrings dangling to their shoulders. Newspaper reporters covering the arrivals smiled condescendingly at the strange sight of bearded men rushing into each other's arms and kissing each other. The men were "like school girls," reporters wrote of the un-American emotion with which relatives and friends welcomed the newcomers: "The meeting between the immigrants [and] their friends, who had preceded them to this country, was in accordance with the manners and customs of the passionate, warm-hearted people of the Southern climes. . . . All talked and chattered as only Italians and Spaniards can."

Sicilian traditions only added to their alien air, traditions that had developed to make bleak lives bearable. Saint Joseph was a favorite in some Sicilian towns. He was the patron saint of workers. Tradition held that once during a famine farmers became so desperate that they ate the fava beans they'd been feeding their cattle. With the help of Saint Joseph, they survived. In gratitude, every year on his feast day the devout created an altar loaded with breads and pastries that they shared with the poor.

By the time immigration was shut down in the 1920s, over 100,000—and perhaps as many as 290,000—Italians, over 80 percent of them Sicilians, had passed through New Orleans into Louisiana. Most of these arrivals came with families, but many were single men like Iorlando. Most of these were temporary "birds of passage" making the journey to work and return home with their savings. Others, like Iorlando, stayed. By 1900, at least 8,000 Italians—and possibly as many as 15,000 to 25,000 if children of immigrants are counted—made New Orleans their home, making it the largest such colony in the South.

How Iorlando actually got to Louisiana isn't known. He might have sailed into New York Harbor and made his way from there. Or he may have boarded a ship loaded with lemons and figs and sailed from Palermo to New Orleans. He might have been recruited by padroni—labor agents—who were sent to Europe to sign up workers for Louisiana plantations. Possibly, having heard about jobs in Louisiana, he traveled to New Orleans on his own, hoping to find work when he arrived. If he arrived in New Orleans alone, speaking little English, wondering what he should do next, he would have been relieved to have a padrone welcome him in Italian and offer to arrange work.

The New Orleans that greeted Iorlando was dirty and smelly, with few paved streets and no proper sewage; it was also a cultured and sophisticated city, more indulgently Latin than American, although the Americans west of Canal Street had come to dominate the city, to the chagrin of the Creoles of the Vieux Carré. The elegant white and orange stucco Creole townhouses with their pitched roofs and lacy wrought-iron balconies lined the narrow streets of the Vieux Carré and the Faubourg Marigny. In the American sector, along broad Saint Charles Avenue, Italianate and Greek Revival mansions on expansive grounds proclaimed the presence of American banking and merchant wealth. Fashionable cafés and fine French restaurants catered to a sophisticated crowd. The French Opera House hosted international theatrical stars. Visiting Europeans preferred New Orleans to the "foggy cities of the North," because of its "sunlight, its festal air, its all-pervading cheeriness and gaiety."

The city dwarfed Iorlando's hometown of Campofiorito. And it was expanding. New arrivals were pouring in at a brisk pace and had done so throughout the nineteenth century. With a mere 8,000 souls in 1803, by 1810 the population had jumped to over 24,000. By 1840, 102,000 residents made New Orleans the third largest city in the nation. On the eve of the Civil War, the population stood at 174,491. When Iorlando arrived in 1873, the population was 191,418. By the end of the century the city would reach well over a quarter of a million people.

Most of the new arrivals were, like Iorlando, European. Nothing is less original than observing that the United States is a nation of immigrants, but of few places is this truer than New Orleans, especially in the nineteenth and early twentieth centuries. Founded by the French, ceded to the Spanish, sold to the Americans, influenced by Creole, European, Caribbean, African, and South American elements, New Orleans was a genuinely multicultural stew of peoples, languages, and cultures. As he absorbed his new surroundings, Iorlando may well have had the reaction of the mid-nineteenth-century German visitor who marveled at the "Americans, Brazilians, West Indians, Spanish and French, Germans, creoles, quadroons, mulattoes, Chinese and Negroes . . . Mexicans, Spanish and Italians" who were to be found swirling together on the city streets.

Despite the city's glamour, Iorlando wouldn't have remained in New Orleans. Like so many later Sicilians, he was bound for the "Sugar Bowl," the sugarcane parishes surrounding the city, and eventually he found himself forty miles up the river in the flat, green, mosquito-infested fields of Saint James Parish. Here, in all likelihood, he went to work in the brutal cane fields.

Life in the cane fields was a constant, hard slog. Sugarcane production was labor intensive, much more so than growing cotton. Iorlando would have worked long hours during the planting season in the spring and hoeing back weeds under the punishing Louisiana sun in the summer. The *zuccherata*—the grinding season—arrived in October when the gold-green stalks had deepened into a mature purple and the cane was ready for harvest. For three months, Iorlando and others like him worked to exhaustion, cutting and loading cane seven days a week as long as there was light to see, and probably putting in an evening shift in the sugarhouse, turning the stalk cane into sugar and molasses.

For Iorlando, this arduous life was better than anything he could have hoped for in Sicily. Swinging a cane knife, chopping weeds—all this gave him what most Sicilian immigrants wanted: the chance to save money. Working as an ordinary laborer, he might have earned seventy-five cents a day; as an experienced cane cutter, perhaps as much as $1.25 or $1.50 a day. As little as it sounds, such wages were twice what he could have made in Sicily, and Sicilians often carefully hoarded their wages—some managed to save fully half of theirs.

Despite the hardships, workers flocked to Louisiana during the zuccherata, when planters had to hire large numbers of temporary workers. In these months, the presence of Italians may have swollen by tens of thousands. For a time, Iorlando probably joined the circuit of migrant agricultural workers, harvesting sugarcane in southeastern Louisiana during the zuccherata from late fall to early winter, laboring in the cotton fields of central and northern Louisiana in the boiling summer months, and scattering to larger cities—New Orleans, Chicago, New York—to find work in the months in between. Much of the temporary help arrived in Louisiana for the harvest and went home to Italy with their cash afterward. Not Iorlando. He stayed in Saint James Parish.

Like so many destitute, illiterate Sicilians, Iorlando wanted security and respect. He wanted to be his own boss, more possible here than at home. So, like many other Sicilian laborers, Iorlando, hacking at cane and weeds under the murderous Louisiana sun, made up his mind to become a businessman. By working hard and saving his money, Iorlando could squirrel away enough to leave the cane fields and go into business for himself. This was the one problem with Italian workers as far as their employers were concerned. Planters grumbled that they couldn't keep Italians in the field because in only a few years they would save a little money. Then, as one sugar planter put it, they "are ready to start a fruit shop or grocery store at some cross-roads town. Those who do not establish themselves thus strap packs and peddle blue jeans, overalls and red handkerchiefs to the Negroes." This was no exaggeration; by 1900, Italian-owned businesses had sprung up all over Louisiana.

The commercial success of Sicilian immigrants didn't protect them from the racial prejudices of the American South. Italians never entirely replaced black labor in the Louisiana cane and cotton fields but worked alongside blacks and the occasional Spaniard or Filipino. While Italians found nothing shameful about working in the fields with black workers, for native whites their willingness to do so made them no better than "Negroes," Chinese, or other "nonwhite" groups. Because of the work they did, the small, swarthy Sicilians were often considered not white at all, nothing but "black dagoes." It wasn't lost on an observer that even "Negroes made unabashed distinction between Dagoes and white folks and treated these alien fellow tenants with a sometimes contemptuous, sometimes friendly, first-name familiarity."

The notion that "dagoes" were no better than "Negroes" helps account for growing prejudice against Italian immigrants in the 1870s and 1880s. Iorlando arrived in the earliest stage of southern Italian and Sicilian immigration that began in the 1870s. The handful of Italian immigrants before 1870 hailing from northern Italy weren't primarily laborers: they included skilled craftsmen, artists, musicians, importers, cotton brokers, accountants, and physicians, as well as merchants, shopkeepers, and fruit dealers. But most of those who arrived after 1870 were peasants from southern Italy, especially Sicily. As numbers of the uneducated and unskilled newcomers mounted in the 1880s, prejudice grew, and Sicilian immigrants in Louisiana faced suspicion and the occasional lynch mob. In 1924, a Tulane University thesis expressed a common view of the "filthy paupers" from Sicily, decrying their "viciousness, ignorance, debauchery, and crime."

Such attitudes didn't prevent men like Iorlando Guagliardo from climbing the ladder from day laborer to merchant. We don't know exactly what route he took, but in 1892 Iorlando paid $200 cash for a small store in Convent, the seat of Saint James Parish. In 1883 he'd married another immigrant, Rosalie Lillian "Lillie" Billa. Over the next fifteen years, they produced a succession of children: two girls, two boys, and two babies who died at birth, a sadly common occurrence at the time. Then Iorlando left Saint James Parish, moving his family for a few years to Saint John the Baptist Parish, before settling in Gretna, the growing settlement across the river from New Orleans, about 1910.

Perhaps Iorlando left Convent for the New Orleans area because he wanted a larger city with more opportunities for his children. With its relaxed cosmopolitanism and Latin Catholic heritage, the city absorbed new arrivals relatively easily. The Italian community in New Orleans was less segregated than in any other city in the United States. In New Orleans, ethnic ghettos simply didn't exist, as Italians, Germans, Irish, Chinese, Jews, Greek, French, Russians, African Americans, and nonimmigrant whites frequently shared the same streets and neighborhoods. Still, ethnic clusters could be found. African Americans dominated the area near the marshy backswamp known as back-of-town. A small Chinatown developed around the 1100 block of Tulane Avenue. A strip by the river between Magazine and Tchoupitoulas Streets was known as the Irish Channel after its inhabitants. The Faubourg Marigny was home to "Little Saxony."

The oldest section of the city, the French Quarter, or Vieux Carré, had become the Italian neighborhood. By the early twentieth century, so many Sicilians congregated in the lower French Quarter near the river that the area from Jackson Square to Esplanade Avenue, between Decatur and Chartres, was known as "Little Palermo."

Despite sporting an elegant European atmosphere with narrow streets, vaulted passageways, and iron lacework balconies overlooking tropical courtyards, the Quarter didn't have the cache it had had in the French and Spanish periods, or that it would regain by the end of the twentieth century. As the Creole gentry abandoned it in the late nineteenth century to move uptown to join their American rivals along Saint Charles Avenue and toward Lake Pontchartrain along Esplanade Avenue, the oldest section of the city became a squalid Sicilian slum. Multiple families of the city's poorest immigrants were crammed into decrepit Creole townhouses. Whole families, including four or five children, shared a single room and a lone bed. Drying laundry hung from balconies, courtyards were full of rotting garbage; ventilation was bad; sanitation was worse. The disapproving author of the Tulane thesis probably wasn't exaggerating much when she described the Italian sector's pervasive "filth and . . . intolerable stench . . . [and] deafening clatter and chatter."

Many of the inhabitants of Little Palermo, like their countrymen on plantations, were determined to start their own businesses as soon as they could. Usually these were small enterprises needing a minimum of investment. Tiny shoe shops were everywhere; eventually, 75 percent of shoemakers in New Orleans were Italian. Barbershops, too, were on every block. They were particularly popular as start-ups because it was easy enough to turn one's own parlor into a barbershop: all one needed was a straight razor, a mirror, a chair, and a steady hand.

But the real Italian niche was food.

One of the most common upward trajectories for an ambitious Sicilian was that from plantation worker to truck farmer and peddler to grocer, probably the route Iorlando took. Many in New Orleans followed the same path. Much of the area on the outskirts of New Orleans was still quite rural. Dairy cows, chickens, hogs, and horses could be found in the sparsely populated Carrollton neighborhood west of the French Quarter, Amesville across the river, and Marigny, just outside the Quarter across Esplanade. From these locations truck farmers set out to furnish the city with its fruits and vegetables, or its milk and eggs, loading their produce onto horse-drawn wagons. They drove into town, selling to markets and groceries or hawking their goods on the street, the "humble, loud-voiced vendor, driving his cart . . . along the streets and calling out the different varieties [of produce] in English impossible to understand."

Most Italian enterprises remained fairly modest. By the early twentieth century, corner grocery stores were expanding all over New Orleans, multiplying until they were ubiquitous; by 1910 when Iorlando and his family moved to Gretna there was one on practically every corner.

This is one reason Italians were scattered all over the city. In the early decades of the twentieth century, no one had refrigerators. Iceboxes were stocked with big blocks of ice bought from the ice wagon. Most houses were modest, with small kitchens and very limited storage space. Housewives often shopped twice a day: once for the noon meal and again in the afternoon for supper. A grocery down the block, even a small one, was often more convenient than a central market. Corner groceries flourished, and Italian grocers flourished with them. In 1880 only 7 percent of grocers were Italians. By 1920 Italians owned half of all groceries in New Orleans.

Iorlando shunned cramped Little Palermo and settled his family across the river in Gretna, a growing suburb of New Orleans. There, at the corner of Second and Jefferson Streets, he ran one of the little neighborhood groceries that sold all the basics: canned goods, fruits and vegetables, cheese and bread, and multiple varieties of pasta. When a customer entered the unpretentious wooden building, she was greeted with the briny smell of olives overlaying the sharp, pungent smell of cheese; Italian sausage added a peppery flavor to the air. Canvas bags of fava beans sprawled on the concrete floor. Cans of tomatoes and tins of sardines were stacked on the shelves that lined the walls, stretching up almost to the ceiling. During the summer, watermelons were piled neatly outside the store. The shopper was usually greeted by Iorlando or his wife; Iorlando was an old man by this time, gray and slightly stooped, but still slim with a full mustache, speaking with a thick Italian accent—"Good-a morning. Nice-a day." No doubt, many of his lady customers thought him charming.

For modern tourists, the legacy of the New Orleans Italian groceries is the muffuletta, a daunting combination of salami, capicola, ham, provolone, emmentaler cheese, and olive salad on bread. Its invention is most often attributed to Salvatore Lupo, owner of Central Grocery, which still stands on Decatur Street, across from the French Market. According to tradition, the sandwich originated in the early 1900s with the lunches of the Sicilian truck farmers who provided the French Market with its produce. Day after day Lupo watched the Sicilians sit on crates, balancing their trays of bread, cheese, ham, salami, and olive salad on their knees as they ate. Finally, Lupo took all the ingredients, put them together in round Sicilian sesame bread, and New Orleans's most famous sandwich was born. Today it's not longshoremen from the sugar wharves or peddlers from the French Market who get their lunches from Central Grocery, but tourists waiting for a muffuletta and a Dixie Beer who endure long lines that spill out into Decatur Street.

The people who gave New Orleans the muffuletta—hardworking, self-reliant, frugal, and ambitious—these were the Axeman's targets. Despite the odds against them, Italian immigrants managed to carve out a slice of the American Dream for themselves. But for some, their success created resentment. And someone wanted to take it away.

Iorlando Guagliardo and his family would pay a high price for the Axeman's crimes. Iorlando and Lillie prospered in Gretna as their business flourished. They were successful enough to put a little money away for the future. At some point the family had taken the name Jordano—*Guagliardo* was too easy for Americans to trip over. Iorlando Guagliardo became Iorlando Jordano; his eldest son, Frank Jordano. With the murder of Mary Cortimiglia, their American dream appeared to be over. Iorlando and Frank would be accused of murdering the little girl.

4

The Davi Murder

Wednesday, June 28, 1911

JOSEPH DAVI TOOK THIRTY hours to die.

The doctors at Charity were astonished at the amount of fight still in the young grocer. His brains were seeping out of his head, having been bashed out of his skull. He should have died more or less on the spot. Perhaps being a newly married husband and expectant father made him reluctant to give it all up. And resist his fate he did. For over a day the doctors at Charity could do nothing but admire his struggle against death. But in the end the trim, handsome twenty-six-year-old was no match for his injuries. He slipped away without regaining consciousness. No one told Mary Davi that she was now a sixteen-year-old widow.

In those days, the New Orleans coroner didn't fuss with invasive autopsies—no opening of the chest cavity, measuring of organs, or toxicology reports. Assistant Coroner Charles Groetsch's job was limited to getting a good look at the body after all the blood had been scraped off and deciding what had killed him. In Davi's case, this wasn't hard. He had sustained repeated blows to the front of his head that smashed his skull and pulped his brain.

A clerk in the Coroner's Office called the police to notify them that they were now in the midst of a murder investigation.

Joseph Davi, the Axeman's first fatality.

In Baltimore, New Orleans inspector of police James Reynolds tore open the envelope the messenger handed him and read it without much surprise. His fears had been realized. The Cleaver was back.

When Jim Reynolds had been appointed inspector of police only four months earlier, he had a force of fewer than 250 to police a city of 339,000. Fortunately, the serious crime rate in New Orleans was relatively low. Robberies and burglaries were common; murders, mercifully, were not. New Orleanians did have a murder rate considerably higher than most other southern cities and comparable northern cities such as Chicago. Nevertheless, New Orleans wasn't a particularly dangerous place for ordinary citizens as long as they stayed out of barroom brawls and conducted domestic spats well out of reach of guns and knives. The murder rate in New Orleans in 1911 was much lower than it would be a hundred years later. And it was considerably lower than it had been in the 1880s when murder was so common it couldn't even be used to sell newspapers.

New Orleans murderers at the turn of the century were not an exceptionally clever lot. In 1910, the city had fifty-two murders, and the police immediately identified the killer in almost all of them. Most homicides were easy to solve for the simple reason that most murderers committed their crimes in front of witnesses. The majority of these killings were intensely personal—a domestic argument, a fight over a woman, a barroom brawl over an imagined insult. Death in the course of a robbery was unusual. Murders like that of Joseph Davi were exceptionally rare.

But the people of New Orleans were only just beginning to suspect how unusual the killing of Joe Davi was.

The police world was in the midst of a revolution of procedure and professionalism that would turn a badly paid, poorly trained, low-status force into an efficient law enforcement organization. In 1911 modern policing was still less than a hundred years old. New Orleans was hardly on the cutting edge of this trend, and in the early twentieth century only just starting to catch up.

In the years after Reconstruction, New Orleans police officers were known for their corruption and incompetence. The financially strapped city had one of the worst-paid police departments in the country so, not surprisingly, it didn't attract the highest caliber of applicants. Poorly paid, haphazardly trained, often inexperienced, New Orleans policemen were almost as much a menace as the criminals they pursued. They routinely broke the law against carrying concealed weapons. Worse, when they drew their revolvers, they were lousy shots, usually missing the criminals at whom they aimed and frequently hitting innocent bystanders.

Why did the residents tolerate such incompetence? Because of the nature of city politics. After Reconstruction, New Orleans was dominated by the Regular Democratic Organization, a political machine generally known as the Ring or the Choctaw Club (named for the social club on Saint Charles Avenue where its members met). This city machine operated by systematically getting out the vote on Election Day, rewarding its members with city jobs and contracts, and engaging in a bit of ballot-box stuffing when necessary. By the early twentieth century the Ring was led by Martin Behrman, one of the great city bosses in an era of city bosses. Pudgy, mustached Behrman looked like the German grocer he had been. The son of Jewish immigrants, Behrman began as a ward worker in his neighborhood of Algiers and quickly climbed the hierarchy of the Ring to become mayor in 1904. One of the most gifted politicians of his generation, he was to control the machine—and the city—for the next twenty years.

The New Orleans Police Department, like most United States police departments at the time, ran on patronage. After 1877, New Orleans mayors had the power to appoint police officers, and they used that power to reward supporters and punish opponents. Policemen were therefore not hired or promoted on the basis of ability or job performance, but because of political and familial ties. For politicians, the advantage was both the ability to give jobs to supporters and a loyal police force with which to harass political opponents. The disadvantages for the people of New Orleans are obvious.

The police department that Jim Reynolds joined was loaded with bribery, kickbacks, abuse of authority, and a general lack of discipline. Patronage wasn't the only culprit responsible for these faults. The conditions under which policemen worked were also to blame. Successful police work—tracking stolen property, locating a suspect—often meant a thorough knowledge of the criminal world. Counting criminals among one's acquaintances often led to temptations that a poorly paid policeman would find hard to resist. They enforced laws selectively, arrested people solely in order to meet quotas, and took bribes from criminals. The New Orleans Police Department had developed an entirely deserved reputation for corruption.

When James Reynolds became the police chief in February 1911, he was a popular choice, a career policeman rather than a politician, and was free from the taint of corruption. He could hardly have been chosen without being a Behrman ally, but Reynolds publicly promised to "keep the police force entirely out of politics."

He did his best to enforce training and discipline, cracking down on lazy and delinquent policemen. But there were limits to what the police inspector could do. Reynolds could no more stamp out the petty graft of day-to-day life than he could banish prostitution or illegal gambling. He had to police the city with the force he had.

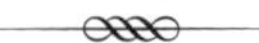

Monday, June 26, 1911

It was a perfectly ordinary day for Joe and Mary Davi. They woke up early, had their grocery store at Arts and Galvez Streets open by 5:30 AM, and spent a long day waiting on customers. The Davis were still newlyweds, married only five months, and the routine was not yet old. Mary usually handled the business of the store while her husband ran

The Davi grocery and home, where Joseph Davi was killed.

the saloon. Italian immigrants who had come to the United States as children, they made an attractive couple. Mary was pretty in a plump, youthful way, with masses of thick, light brown hair, brightened by a hint of gold and radiating with the glow of her first pregnancy. Joe was a good-looking fellow with a handlebar mustache whom everyone thought a "steady, sober and good young man."

Usually, Mary closed the shop with Joe and they went to bed together. But tonight she was unusually tired and retired early. Joe closed up by himself about 10 PM. After counting his receipts for the day, he took the cash with him into the bedroom. The bedroom door didn't fasten properly, so Joe propped up a makeshift alarm on the top of the door—several empty seltzer water bottles that would clatter to the floor if anyone entered in the night. He also kept a loaded revolver on the table next to the bed. If he faced any burglars, he planned to be prepared. He finally slipped under the mosquito netting and crawled

Mary Davi, pregnant and widowed at sixteen.

into bed next to his sleeping wife at about 11 PM. One imagines that Joe leaned over, kissed Mary good night, and, tired from his long day, quickly fell into a deep sleep.

Some time later, something woke Mary. At first she wasn't sure what it was. Then a movement caught her eye. She looked up to see a stranger in the bedroom. By the dim light of the oil lamp burning in a corner of the room, she saw a man near the wardrobe. She shook her husband: "What is that man doing here?"

Joe only moaned in response. Hearing a voice, the intruder turned to her: "Where is your money?" he wanted to know. Mary simply stared, too frightened to reply. Apparently infuriated, the intruder grabbed a heavy porcelain mug and hit her hard on the side of the head. She fell back on her pillow, unconscious. When she could look around the room again, the man had disappeared. Mary didn't yet realize the extent of her wounds, but she had cuts on her face and her right hand and arm, and she could feel the blood dripping down her face. Panicky questions flashed through her head. Who was he? Where was he? Was he robbing the grocery? Would he come back to kill her and Joe if she screamed for help? Perhaps if she remained perfectly still, he wouldn't return. Mary lay frozen, paralyzed with fear and shock, listening to her husband's ragged breathing, as the hours dragged by.

5:30 AM, Tuesday, June 27, 1911

Standing in front of the Davi grocery in the postdawn glow, Ernest Boyer, a young bartender, was puzzled. And he was getting impatient. He needed two loaves of bread, but the grocery was locked and ghostly silent. That was strange. He pounded on the door again, and again he got no answer. He went around to the side of the building, the side where the Davis lived, and rapped on the bedroom window, hoping to rouse someone.

After a moment, Mary Davi appeared at the window and peered hesitantly at him though the blinds. He asked for some bread, but she told him the store wasn't open.

"Call your husband," he insisted.

"I can't," she replied. "He's asleep."

Boyer knew immediately something was wrong. Mary Davi was acting very oddly. She seemed confused, even frightened. As he continued to study her through the blinds, he noticed blood on her face. *Why is your husband asleep? What's the matter?* Dazed, almost unwillingly, the young woman finally admitted that she couldn't wake her husband because he was bleeding. Would Boyer go fetch Benjamin Gallin, a close friend of her husband's?

When Gallin, Boyer, and a few other concerned neighbors entered the house a short time later, they discovered Joe lying on his blood-soaked bed with a badly fractured skull. His breath came in gasps, as his brain, swelling as a result of trauma, pressed against the respiratory centers in his brainstem. Mary was in shock, herself cut and bleeding. Disoriented and shaking, the young woman gave every sign of not having really absorbed what had happened in the night.

The Fifth Precinct Station, only a mile and a half away, got a telephone call just after 6 AM Tuesday morning. A man and a woman had been injured at Arts and Galvez Streets, said the caller. Could they send someone right away? A sergeant with a detail of patrolmen was sent to investigate. He took one look at the dying man and traumatized girl and immediately alerted police headquarters. Soon afterward, after the couple had been taken to Charity Hospital, detectives were on the scene.

Inspector Reynolds was out of town. He had gone up north to attend the annual conference of the International Police Chiefs Union. In his absence, George Long, the new chief of detectives, took charge of the investigation. By ten o'clock, over half a dozen investigators crowded into the grocery and its tiny living quarters to take an inventory of the crime scene.

The Davi place was a small grocery store at Arts and Galvez Streets. Business was good, considering that it was in a sparsely populated area at the edge of the city. It was only a little over a mile from Joseph and Conchetta Rissetto's store, and not far from the swamp and woods that defined the city's boundary. A rough partition sectioned off part of the grocery for use as a saloon. The residence was behind the store and consisted of a dining room, kitchen, and bedroom. The building was fairly isolated. Overgrown, grassy lots lay behind and to the side of the grocery.

The intruder had pried open a window with a railroad shoe pin and climbed into the saloon. Once he made his way into the store, he had raised the hinged section of the grocery counter to gain access to the door leading up two or three steps into the residence. He then had gone through the dining room to the bedroom door. The investigators found the seltzer water bottles deliberately placed next to the door. The homemade alarm hadn't worked.

In the bedroom, it was clear that the intruder had hammered the grocer mercilessly, smashing his skull and drenching the bed and the bottom half of the mosquito netting in blood. Joe Davi had been attacked while he was asleep, with no chance to fight back; the revolver still lay on the side table, untouched and useless. He'd been hit with such force that the impact of the blows had collapsed the top of the moss-packed double mattress in at a fifteen-degree angle. Skull fragments and bits of brain littered the sheets. On Mary's side of the bed, detectives could see the bloody print left on the wall where she'd put out her hand to steady herself as she'd staggered to the window in response to Ernest Boyer's knock. The mug that had hit her in the face lay on the floor.

After assaulting Mary, the assailant left by the door opening onto Arts Street. As far as the detectives could tell, nothing had been stolen. Despite his demand for money, the man hadn't tried to take the sixty-four dollars in cash hidden under the pillow—an obvious place for a burglar to look. Contents from the wardrobe and a trunk were scattered about, but Mary's jewelry was undisturbed. Small amounts of money were still in drawers. Nothing indicated that the attacker had robbed the place.

The police found no weapon other than those belonging to the Davis at the scene. The nature of Joe Davi's wounds—and the similarity of the attack to the Crutti and Rissetto crimes—made everyone assume that it was a cleaver of some sort. Davi's wounds, the inquest would later show, were caused by "a blow with a sharp-edged though heavy blade almost in the center of the head, crushing through scalp and bone . . . just such an injury as would have resulted from a blow with a butcher's cleaver."

Some never had any doubt about who had viciously attacked the young grocer. On Wednesday morning the *Daily Picayune* screamed, FIENDISH CLEAVER ABROAD AGAIN.

After inspecting the crime scene, District Attorney St. Clair Adams went to the hospital to interview the victims. There, the doctors told the district attorney that Joe Davi was beyond help and certainly beyond interviewing. Adams turned his attention to Mary, but he didn't get far. All the shaken young woman could get out coherently was that the attack took place around 1 or 1:30 AM and the attacker was a white man. A more in-depth interview would have to wait until she recovered from the shock.

Investigators at the scene were interviewing friends, neighbors, family—anyone who happened to be there. Warren Doyle, an assistant district attorney, tried to question Peter Davi, Joe's older brother. When Peter, having just seen the bloody mess that had been his brother's bedroom, ignored Doyle and insisted on seeing his brother immediately, he was arrested and forcibly taken to the district attorney's office.

The next day Chief Long made his own attempt to interview Mary. He found her recovering in the women's ward. She lay pale and still in the white hospital bed, her eyes still reflecting the pain of her wounds. Bandages covered her face and cheek where she'd been cut; under the bandages her bruised face had turned a deep bluish-purple. She had cuts and bruises on her right arm and hand as well, presumably from the same weapon that had injured her husband.

Mary repeated the story she'd first given detectives, a little more coherently this time. She'd heard nothing until she woke to see the man ransacking the wardrobe. She remembered very little after having been hit. She was clear that he spoke English.

"Are you sure about the man speaking English?" asked Long.

"Positively he spoke English," she replied. Unaccented English, she insisted, so she knew he wasn't an Italian.

Even though she had only glimpsed him by the light of the single taper burning in the bedroom, Mary was able to provide a description of the man. He was white, clean-shaven, about five foot eight or ten, and not especially strong looking. He wore a blue jumper—a workingman's shirt—and black pants, but no hat. He'd moved soundlessly across the floor, so she thought he must have been barefoot.

The chief thanked Mary for her help and left. What he had not told her was that earlier that day her husband had died. No one else told her either. She was allowed to believe that he, too, was in the hospital, gravely wounded but expected to recover. Because of her youth and prettiness and pregnancy, discreetly referred to in the newspapers as her "delicate state," the girl inspired a great deal of sympathy among the press and the public. Her physicians advised against telling her about Joe's death just yet, arguing that the shock, on top of her injuries and the trauma of her experience, would be too much for her. It's likely they were concerned about the baby she was carrying.

That night a wake was held in her parents' parlor, and the funeral service took place there the next day. The black-clad procession then accompanied the casket to the cemetery. As Joe Davi was laid to rest, his wife lay in her hospital bed wondering when they'd finally let her see him.

Chief of Detectives George Long had almost no technology with which to catch a killer. The New Orleans Police Department mostly investigated crimes with shoe leather and gut instinct.

Nevertheless, the science of investigation had progressed rapidly in the late nineteenth and early twentieth century. In the late 1870s, Alphonse Bertillon, a clerk with the Sûreté in Paris, developed a system for classifying criminals based on measurements of various body parts. Each person had a unique collection of measurements that could be collected and used for identification. In the 1880s *bertillonage,* as it came to be called, spread over Europe and the United States.

Bertillon's system arrived in New Orleans in 1897, and by 1911 Inspector Reynolds had two Bertillon operators. For each criminal the Bertillon expert painstakingly took eleven measurements and recorded the information on a card, along with a more general description of the arrestee—hair color, eye color, identifying scars—and two mug shots, both a profile and frontal view. Mostly, the New Orleans police used the Bertillon cards for criminals who originated elsewhere—that is, criminals who might be wanted in other jurisdictions. The police knew their homegrown felons by sight.

The Bertillon system, as clever as it was, was soon overtaken by an even more accurate system of identification when Frances Galton published *Finger Prints* in 1892. Police departments, however, were sometimes slow to be convinced of the superiority of fingerprinting over bertillonage. Not until 1911 was fingerprint evidence used for the first time in an American courtroom. Only in 1918 did fingerprints begin to be added to Bertillon cards in New Orleans.

In the late nineteenth and early twentieth century, great strides were also being made in criminology. In 1893, Hans Gross, an Austrian judge, published *Criminal Investigation: A Practical Handbook for Magistrates, Police Officers, and Lawyers,* the first textbook of scientific criminology. Gross's handbook was a thousand pages of advice on how to examine witnesses, behave at crime scenes, handle the press, deal with hair, blood, and fiber evidence, preserve footprints, make use of experts, and handle dozens of other tasks that could be brought to bear on solving crimes.

There is little evidence that anyone in New Orleans read it.

The Bertillon operator did take photographs of the crime scene for the New Orleans Police Department, and the city chemist could determine if rust-red stains were blood, but otherwise it was a decidedly low-tech organization.

Many detectives probably preferred it that way. They didn't put their faith in science. They trusted intuition and a lifetime of dealing with criminals. Jim Reynolds himself said that to be a good detective a man didn't need to be Sherlock Holmes. "All he needs is to use his eyes, and have the widest circle of acquaintances he can get," Reynolds shrugged, "and exercise the horse sense God gave him." Horse sense could take investigators a long way. Detectives were expected to know the local criminals, where to find them, and who their associates were. When a crime was committed, the investigation usually started with "a well-known police character."

Homicide investigation as a specialization didn't exist. Inspector Reynolds, Chief Long, and their detectives investigated whatever came their way—robberies, assaults, blackmail, and murder. The nature of homicides in New Orleans meant that most of them didn't require much investigation. The big question was often not "Who did it?" but "Was it self-defense?" as many barroom killers claimed. But even with a mysterious death in which the perpetrator wasn't immediately obvious, Long and his men proceeded much as they did with any other crime.

In the case of murder, a detective would talk to people, figure out who benefited from the death, and proceed from there. The inspector's detectives knew that "motive is the clew [*sic*] which leads to the solution of half the crimes committed." If there was no motive, that, too, could be a clue. One reason Reynolds hauled in the drug-addicted Flannery for the Crutti attack was that he couldn't imagine what sensible criminal would commit such an odd—and pointless—crime.

When detectives found a likely suspect, they grilled him. Without the luxury of fingerprint or DNA evidence, and especially if there were no witnesses, detectives relied on sweating suspects until they confessed. Policemen found that the pangs of conscience were a marvelous thing. Most people feel a natural impulse to feel guilty when they've done wrong, and they have an equally natural impulse to relieve their guilt by telling someone. Investigators have always exploited this to clear their caseloads. This is why Assistant District Attorney Warren Doyle's reflexive response was to arrest Peter Davi immediately and take him in for interrogation. As a relative of the victim, Peter was bound to be interviewed anyway, and even the mere appearance of wanting to avoid an investigator's questions was enough to get him arrested.

As natural as the urge to confess is, sometimes detectives gave nature an assist. If a few hours of questioning didn't work, detectives might resort to the "third degree." This innocuous-sounding term covered a range of interrogation techniques from intense psychological pressure to physical torture, limited only by the imagination of the interrogator. Documented instances of the third degree include sleep deprivation for days on end, withholding food and water, sticking the suspect in a sweatbox, hanging the suspect out of a third-floor window, forcing the accused to spend the night in a room with the dead body of the victim, and for the unimaginative, a thoroughly old-fashioned beating. Sometimes the mere threat—a detective taking off his jacket, rolling up his shirtsleeves, and flexing a rubber hose—would be enough to induce a confession.

The use of the third degree was widespread in the early twentieth century. Some policemen denied it happened; others boasted about it. Illegal in Louisiana, it was used anyway. Some policemen made it quite plain that they found such intense interrogation a useful professional tool: "I've forced confessions," bragged one, "with fist, blackjack and hose—from men who would have continued to rob and kill if I had not made them talk." In the course of their careers as detectives both George Long and Jim Reynolds were accused of employing the third degree. A murder defendant (later acquitted) once testified that Chief Long had stuck a revolver in his gut and threatened to shoot him unless he confessed to the crime.

Without a doubt, some in the New Orleans Police Department used these sorts of tactics, and it's very likely that Reynolds or Long themselves applied them in one form or another. The *Daily Picayune* praised Reynolds as a cop who "knew the effect of moral suasion and the weight of a blow." This suggests that Reynolds could get rough—and that the *Daily Picayune* approved. At the conclusion of one murder investigation, the *Times-Democrat* thought it worth noting that District Attorney Adams obtained two confessions "through persuasion and without the slightest use of force."

Even if their methods didn't spill over into physical or psychological mistreatment, they certainly did bring intense pressure to bear during interrogations. Chief Reynolds had once shaken an iron dumbbell in the face of the accused in an attempt to make him look at the murder weapon. If New Orleans detectives did slap a suspect around from time to time, they almost certainly did so with a clear conscience when convinced of his—or her—guilt. In his own case, Long probably felt justified in using rough methods to get a confession since the defendant had been caught with the victims' diamonds.

Reynolds and Long didn't beat confessions out of any of the Cleaver suspects. They wanted the guilty party, not a warm body coaxed into confessing; they questioned suspects and released most of them. John Flannery never admitted to assaulting August Crutti, and after the Rissetto attack the authorities dropped charges against him. Frank Armistead, a black suspect in the Rissetto attack, was questioned and released. Peter Davi, dragged protesting into the patrol car, wasn't in custody long.

When Reynolds and Long got hold of a questionable character but had no way to connect him to a particular crime, they used the "flim flam" technique. New Orleans police called it that too, writing "flim flam" on the suspect's Bertillon card. That is, they could charge a suspect with being a "dangerous and suspicious character" and get a judge to throw him in the parish prison for a few weeks. This was a routine practice with known troublemakers and a useful way of keeping a suspect on ice without having to worry about the niceties of evidence.

Whatever their deficiencies in technology or respect for constitutional rights, Jim Reynolds and his detective force were determined to find the midnight intruder with a grudge against grocers.

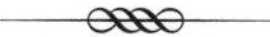

After Joe Davi died, the governor of Louisiana posted a $500 reward for information leading to the capture and conviction of the killer. In the meantime, Chief Long had over half his detective force working the case, including his "Italian Specialist," John Dantonio. Dantonio was himself

John Dantonio, the "Italian" detective.

the son of an Italian immigrant, a tailor who had come over from Palermo. He was the only Italian on the force. Joining the police department in 1896 and promoted to detective in 1902, Dantonio had a reputation as a smart and resourceful officer. He had been involved in the Crutti and Rissetto cases but was to play an especially large role in the Davi murder.

The investigators worked out of police headquarters, housed in the First City Criminal Court Building, at Saratoga Street and Tulane Avenue, where the New Orleans Public Library is now located. The court building was a three-storied, redbrick, neo-Gothic affair, its turrets and Romanesque arches a strange contrast to the tropical flavor of most of the city's architecture. The high ceilings lent elegance to the building while having the practical effect of keeping it cool. The summer heat was eased when breezes off the river blew through the high rectangular windows, ventilating the offices. Pictures from the period present patrolmen in belted woolen tunics and rounded helmets, detectives in suit coats and tightly knotted ties. No one willingly dressed like that in a New Orleans summer. More likely, when Chief Long, Assistant Chief of Detectives Daniel Mouney, and Detective Dantonio gathered in the Detectives' Office to consult and send their investigators out with fresh instructions, their ties were loose, their white shirts sweat stained, and their useless coats flung over their chairs.

By Wednesday—a day after the attacks were discovered—most of the investigators were working on the case from before dawn until late into the night. For days they did nothing else. While everyone else in New Orleans tried to stay out of the sweltering July heat, they tramped up and down dusty streets, canvassing neighborhoods, asking the same questions over and over. *Did anyone see anything suspicious that night? Were there any strange men in the neighborhood? Did Davi have any particularly troublesome customers? Did he have any enemies? Had he quarreled with anyone recently?* They talked to neighbors, friends, relatives, housewives who shopped in the grocery, men who hung out in the saloon, and peddlers who delivered produce in one-horse carts. They picked up known police "characters" and shadowed possible suspects. They searched the dank, roach-infested shacks near the woods close to Davi's grocery, terrifying the destitute residents. Every lead, no matter how trivial, was pursued.

Amid all the activity at police headquarters Wednesday evening, Joseph Rissetto entered the building and asked to speak to one of the detectives working the case. He badly wanted to help the investigation however he could. No one had to ask why. The vivid scar across his nose and his blind right eye explained all. But he could tell the detectives nothing that would lead to Joe Davi's killer.

At first, what baffled the police was that no one seemed to have any reason to kill Davi. His family assured them that he had no enemies. Investigators didn't turn up any. Frustrated, Dantonio told a reporter: "There is no apparent motive here."

The detectives kept digging.

By the end of the week they thought the tedium of their repeated questions had paid off. They finally had a promising suspect.

Joe Davi's friend Ben Gallin told police about Sam Pitzo, a Sicilian truck farmer who had come to see Joe in his saloon about a week before his murder. They got into quite an animated conversation, Gallin recalled. Gallin couldn't tell what they were saying since they spoke in Italian, but the conversation seemed to take an angry turn and ended when Joe took two dollars out of the cash drawer and shoved it at Pitzo to get rid of him.

After the truck farmer left, Joe told Gallin that the man had hit him up for cash with a hard-luck story of a sick wife. Pitzo wanted more than Joe was willing to give him, and he didn't take being turned down graciously. Joe told Gallin that he was worried the man might be trouble.

Detectives immediately brought Sam Pitzo in for questioning. At first, he didn't give them enough information to warrant holding him. But the officers didn't let up. They asked neighbors about the truck farmer, who turned out to have an unsavory reputation. His real name was Sam Parieno. He regularly went around the neighborhood spinning stories of bad luck and pleading for money. The police also found evidence that he had lied to them about how much time he had spent in Davi's neighborhood. They didn't have the evidence to move against him just yet, but Long ordered his men to keep an eye on the shady truck farmer.

On Friday, four days after the attack on his brother, Peter Davi showed up at police headquarters and told the doorman he'd like to speak to a detective. Directed to Dan Mouney's desk, he sat down across from the detective and pulled out a year-old letter.

About a year ago, he told Detective Mouney, he and his brother Joe had run a grocery just outside of the Vieux Carré. One day Joe had received a letter warning him that unless he paid $200, he'd be killed. The letter included detailed instructions about where to deliver the money in Carrollton. His brother had ignored the letter, but a week later another arrived. When Joe still didn't respond, he received a third communication. This was the letter Peter had found in a trunk after his brother's death and now handed over to Mouney. Mouney turned the cheap notepaper over in his hand. The unsigned letter was written in Italian and dated May 24, 1910. The letter threatened Joe, Peter told Mouney. The writer warned that since Joe had ignored previous communications, he could expect retaliation.

Why didn't Joe take the letters to the police? Mouney asked. Peter said that he and his brother talked about it but put it off and never got around to it. Nothing ever came of the threat so, eventually, they forgot about it. It was only after Joe's murder that Peter dug out the letter. And, Peter told the authorities, that wasn't all.

The combination of the blackmail letters and Sam Pitzo's history had made Peter and Ben Gallin even more suspicious of the truck farmer. They had gone to Mary and asked her if she knew Pitzo. She said, yes, he had delivered figs to the store. Did he look like the man she had seen in her bedroom? Well, she admitted, he might resemble him. This was enough to convince both Peter Davi and Ben Gallin of Pitzo's guilt.

Mouney went straight to the chief of detectives' office and told him Peter Davi's story. They decided now was the time to bring Pitzo in. They snatched him from the steps of his Carrollton shanty, also pulling in Pitzo's employee, Philip Daguanno, caught wearing a shirt with tiny bloodstains on it.

Saturday afternoon Long, Mouney, and Dantonio interrogated the two men for hours. *How well did you know Joseph Davi? Did you ever try to blackmail him? Where were you Monday night?* Neither suspect was very helpful. Pitzo made no effort to cooperate, often merely shrugging his shoulders in answer to a question. Daguanno's English wasn't very good, and he had to be questioned by Detective Dantonio. Both men denied knowing anything about who had battered in Joe Davi's skull.

Long and his men were starting to get frustrated when a neighbor of Pitzo's showed up at the police station. Sam Constanza, a grocer in Carrollton, accused the truck farmer of attempting to extort money from him. Pitzo, he told detectives, had come to his grocery and demanded ten dollars, promising to "beat his brains in" if he didn't pay.

Now the detectives had what they needed—a plausible motive for murder. They knew Davi refused to be blackmailed; they knew he had quarreled with Pitzo; now they knew Pitzo was a blackmailer. Perhaps he'd tried to victimize Davi, and when he refused to pay, Pitzo made good on his threat. The self-congratulation must have been palpable. The pieces fit.

Late Saturday afternoon George Long, Dan Mouney, and John Dantonio marched both suspects down the whitewashed halls of Charity, past the starched nurses in white uniforms, down to the women's ward. They pulled white screens around Mary's bed to block the stares of other patients on the ward and planted the shabbily dressed workmen in front of her.

Mary looked warily at the suspects. Pitzo was about forty years old, short, sturdily built, with black hair and a thick, bushy black mustache. Yes, she said, she'd seen him before; he delivered figs to the store. She had also seen him when he'd come asking Joe for money. Pitzo resembled the assailant because he had a similar build. *But*, she added, *I am almost certain the man who hit me had no mustache.*

Next Long pointed to Daguanno. Had she seen him before? He was short like Pitzo but thin and nervous, a ferret-faced man, clean-shaven with brown hair. She shook her head without hesitation: *No, I don't recognize him.*

Disappointed, the detectives returned to the police station. Without eyewitness testimony, they couldn't make a case against Pitzo. Their other witnesses that day were equally disappointing. August and Harriet Crutti and Joseph and Conchetta Rissetto all came in that afternoon. None of them had ever seen Pitzo before. Harriet Crutti, the only one who'd gotten a good look at the attacker, shook her head. "The man who attacked my husband was about the same height, but he was a little broader," she said.

Sunday night, morale in the Detectives' Office must have been low when, to everyone's surprise, Jim Reynolds walked in unannounced. He hadn't been expected back for almost a week, but when he heard about Davi's murder, he hastily caught a train from Baltimore. Now the inspector sequestered himself with Chief Long to be brought up to speed on the investigation.

Before he left for the night, Reynolds walked across the hall and into the pressroom. Reporters would have been there well into the night, anxious to get the latest word on the investigation, and they weren't willing to leave as long as a detective's light was on. Most of the writers on the crime beat spent so much time at police headquarters that the inspector knew them almost as well as he knew his own officers. Some crime reporters, young men like Andy Ojeda of the *Daily States*, never seemed to go home. They spent their days—and frequently their nights—hunched over their typewriters in the Press Office, tapping out stories of theft, blackmail, accident, and murder. When the telegraph operator or Reynolds's secretary posted an emergency bulletin, they'd heave themselves into their jackets, tighten their ties, grab their hats, and be out the door after the story.

The press and the police had a clubby relationship. Reynolds tried to make reporters' jobs easier, personally updating them on developments in major stories, giving them whatever information he felt he could, even occasionally offering them a lift in the patrol car on the way to a crime scene. The reporters identified with the police, some even going so far, as one admitted, to think of themselves as "closely allied to the [police] department, and likewise working for its advancement in [our] own way."

Now Reynolds needed to use the press to reassure the people of New Orleans:

"I came back early because I am deeply concerned about the Davi affair. This murderer must be captured. Neither men nor money will be spared in bringing the fiend to justice. Not only will public funds be available, but I mean to go into my private purse if necessary. He must be captured and we are going to do it."

Whether or not Reynolds actually felt such confidence, with his arrival the investigation took off in new directions.

The first thing he did Monday morning was to interview Pitzo and Daguanno. Reynolds came away convinced neither had anything to do with Joe Davi's murder, but he and St. Clair Adams decided to hold both men for a few more days. Who knew what evidence might turn up in the meantime?

Monday afternoon Reynolds went to see the Davi residence for himself. He arrived to find a gang of prisoners from the parish prison cutting the tall grass growing in the vacant lots behind and next to the grocery. It was the latest effort to find the murder weapon. Dripping with sweat in the humidity, the prisoners were searching the lots on the chance that the murderer might have tossed his weapon there as he fled. So far, they'd found nothing but snakes and weeds.

Reynolds spent several hours going over the crime scene with Long and the others. This would have been a good opportunity for the detectives to outline their respective theories of the crime; with more than one theory floating around, there must have been some lively discussion as first one and then another tried to persuade the inspector of the viability of his view.

John Norris, the Bertillon operator, was also there. He had presumably been summoned to the grocery as soon as the injured couple had been discovered. But the crime scene hadn't been searched thoroughly, as Assistant District Attorney Doyle had just discovered what he thought was an additional print that needed to be photographed. The handprint of Mary Davi had been noted immediately, but Doyle had spotted what appeared to be another bloody print near the window of the bedroom. This print, investigators surmised, was that of the murderer, since it was too high to have been made by Mary.

Norris disappointed the detectives by telling them that the "print" was nothing more than a smear and would be useless in identifying any suspect. But the bloody smudge should have been noted earlier. This wasn't the only evidence that had been overlooked. Ben Gallin had found a bloody print on an outside door that the police had missed. This, and the search for the weapon on adjoining lots almost a week after the attack, suggests that New Orleans detectives relied too much on their gut and not enough on evidence catalogued at the scene. And, of course, no one had even thought about preserving the crime scene.

The police at least were now keeping away the morbidly curious wandering by in hopes of getting a glimpse inside the now-famous grocery.

Monday night Inspector Reynolds was up until midnight discussing the case with his detectives. Everyone agreed that the Cruttis, Rissettos, and Davis had been attacked by the same person. The attacks were too similar to think otherwise. But there was disagreement about motive. Despite the lack of actual theft, some detectives believed that all of the attacks were burglaries gone wrong. Chief Long was the leader of this faction. He argued that nothing was taken from the Rissetto and Davi groceries because the thief was frightened away. He could point out that the intruder who attacked their husbands took eight dollars from Mrs. Crutti and demanded money from Mary Davi. *Look*, he could say, *this fellow is nothing more than a burglar who got interrupted.*

None of this convinced John Dantonio, who led the second camp. He insisted that they weren't dealing with an ordinary burglar. No attempt had been made to rob either the Rissetto or Davi groceries. The "thief" was interested in something very different. Dantonio was outspoken, telling a reporter, "I do not believe any of these jobs were the work of a burglar. I believe the guilty man took the $8 Mrs. Crutti gave him to throw the police off the scent. A fiend committed these crimes."

During the week after Reynolds's return, perhaps at his urging, Dantonio took several other detectives to consult with a medical expert to learn as much about sadism as they could. Perhaps if they learned what motivated the fiend, they could catch him. Reynolds was careful to remain open-minded and publicly noncommittal. He kept his men working all aspects of the case. But he, too, seems to have inclined toward the sadistic "fiend" theory. As first one and then another line of investigation played out, nothing else made sense.

Without any evidence to connect Pitzo to the Davi murder, Inspector Reynolds and DA Adams decided to charge him with what they had. Pitzo faced a count of attempted blackmail, and Daguanno was charged with being a "dangerous and suspicious character." Pitzo found someone to sign for his bond; Daguanno could not. Pitzo walked out, leaving Daguanno, arrested only because he worked for the other man, in the parish prison.

In the excitement of the investigation, two people had almost been forgotten, two other innocent people whose lives had been changed by the Cleaver.

Mary Davi left the hospital on Wednesday, July 5, just over a week after having been admitted. Finally, she learned that her Joe was dead, and the blow was worse than any cuts inflicted on her by the Cleaver. She had almost collapsed and was still in a very emotional state when her parents came to take her home. In the months ahead the young widow would dream of her dead husband, dream that he visited her, but the most constant reminder of Joe was the son she gave birth to early the next year, named Joseph P. Davi for his father.

John Flannery still sat in the parish prison, waiting to be shipped off to East Louisiana Hospital for the Insane as a drug addict, even though the DA had dropped charges for the assault on August Crutti. He wrote to St. Clair Adams from his cell, insisting again that he was innocent of any violence. The murder of Joe Davi was more proof of this, he argued. Flannery pleaded for Adams to send him to the Louisiana Retreat, a private Catholic hospital in New Orleans, rather than to the state insane asylum in Jackson, Louisiana, over a hundred miles away. That was where the state sent the criminally insane. Perhaps he wanted to remain closer to his family in New Orleans. Perhaps he was terrified of the conditions in a state asylum. But he desperately wanted to be free from the stigma of criminal insanity. Whether the DA ever responded to his plea is unknown, but five years later Flannery was shot dead during an attack on a teenaged boy.

Despite continued assurances from Reynolds that Joe Davi's killer would be caught, two weeks after the attack the public began to realize that the police weren't going to find the murderer. The case was rapidly getting cold. The Italian community was particularly unnerved by the police failure. This was the third attack on an Italian grocer in a year, and the police seemed powerless to put a stop to them. And on the morning of July 7, nine days after the Davi murder, an attempt had been made to break into another Italian saloon "in very much the same manner in which the store of Crutti, Davi and Rosetti [*sic*] were broken into," reported the *Daily Picayune*. Fortunately, something had scared off the intruder. Nervous grocers securely fastened their doors and windows each night, praying to Saint Joseph that they wouldn't be the Cleaver's next victim.

While Chief Long looked for a murderous burglar and Inspector Reynolds looked for a crazed maniac, there was a third possibility. All the attacks had been on *Italian* grocers. What was the significance of this? Why not German or French or American grocers? When Joseph and Conchetta Rissetto were attacked, the *New Orleans Item* suggested they were the victims of "vengeance"—i.e., the Italian vendetta. "Both families," the paper deliberately noted (referring to the Cruttis and Rissettos), "are of Italian descent." After Joe Davi's death, the *Daily Picayune* opined that the "fact that all the victims were Italians of the small tradesmen class should point the direction in which the clews [*sic*] are to be sought." Everyone in New Orleans knew what this meant. As the case was dissected over dining tables or in saloons, the same question was asked all over the city: Did the Mafia kill Joe Davi?

5

The Black Hand

Around midnight, October 15, 1890

THE STREET WAS QUIET, except for the soft brush of light rain. New Orleans police superintendent David Hennessy and Captain William O'Connor of the Boylan Protective Police paused at the corner of Rampart and Girod.

Hennessy turned to his companion. "It's not necessary for you to go any further. You go on and look after your business."

Superintendent Hennessy usually worked late into the night, and since the threats had started, one of his friends usually insisted on accompanying him home. The chief (as most people called him) didn't give much thought to his own safety and didn't like making his friend go any farther out of his way on this dreary night. Besides, he was only a block and a half from home and the Boylan officer who'd been hired to watch his house. The two men said good night, and Hennessy turned down Girod Street toward the cottage he shared with his mother. O'Connor took off in the opposite direction.

O'Connor had only gone two blocks when he heard the bang of a shotgun from the direction he'd just come. He spun around to see a bright flash and hear the loud crack of another shot. Almost immediately, three pistol shots rang out. Instinctively, O'Connor took off at a dead run in the direction of the gunfire. Firing continued as he ran.

O'Connor raced past the spot where he'd left Hennessy. As he neared the corner of Girod and Basin Streets he heard someone call his name. Glancing down Basin Street, he could make out the chief's form, slumped on the steps of a house fronting the street. O'Connor rushed over and knelt beside his friend. Even in the dim light he could see Hennessy was covered with blood.

"They've given it to me," Hennessy grimaced. "I gave them back the best I could."

"Who gave it to you, Dave?"

The dying Hennessy motioned his friend closer. O'Connor leaned toward him. The chief whispered one word: "Dagoes."

The Mafia had struck again. Or so everyone said.

Francisco Domingo was the Mafia's first victim in New Orleans. In 1855, the story goes, the Sicilian truck farmer received a note threatening to kill him if he didn't come up with $500. The note was signed with the ominous imprint of a black hand. Unimpressed, Domingo laughed at the threat as nothing to worry about. A few days later, the luckless immigrant's throat was slit and his body dumped on the bank of the Mississippi River. The next several years saw six more murders—each complete with a black hand note. In 1861 the New Orleans *Daily True Delta* reported on bands of Sicilian thieves and counterfeiters, some of whom, the paper claimed, were probably the "black hand" murderers. The legend of the New Orleans Mafia was born.

Unfortunately for Mafia aficionados, large parts of this legend are completely bogus. A Francisco Domingo was killed in New Orleans in 1855. But he was from Manila, his throat was not cut, and there was no great mystery about the identity of his killer. An argument at the dinner table escalated into a fistfight, and Guillermo Ballerio grabbed a knife off the table and plunged it into Domingo's chest. Later writers spun the mundane murder into the more dramatic tale.

In the 1860s, New Orleans newspapers did warn against gangs of Sicilian robbers and counterfeiters active in the city. Sicily was a violent, poverty-stricken backwater in the nineteenth century, with the highest murder rate in Europe. There, the vendetta survived well into the twentieth century. Since New Orleans itself was a turbulent, vice-ridden, and often lawless town, it isn't exactly surprising that some immigrants were drawn to crime, and that some Sicilians were among them.

The question of when the "Mafia" arrived in New Orleans is a messy one. Historians of crime can't seem to agree, and more than one criminal has been credited with establishing the organization in the city. John S. Kendall, a historian writing in the 1930s, gave the honor to Giuseppe Esposito, a notorious black-haired, black-bearded Sicilian outlaw. According to Kendall, in the 1860s and 1870s Esposito belonged to a criminal gang that terrorized western Sicily, robbing and kidnapping at will. Eventually he fled Sicily and made his way to New Orleans. But the law caught up with him. In 1881 Esposito was nabbed in Jackson Square by New Orleans police officers—one of whom was the good-looking, twenty-three-year-old David Hennessy. Esposito was extradited back to Sicily, and Dave Hennessy became famous.

Kendall argued that while he was in New Orleans, Esposito led a handful of desperadoes who set up an extortion business, preying on local Italian merchants. This racket continued to flourish after Esposito himself was back in prison in Italy. And that, pronounced Kendall, "was in essence the Mafia."

Except that it wasn't. Esposito as Mafia boss was a later invention. At the time, no one described him as anything other than a bandit or brigand. Such fantasy is typical of the myths surrounding the Mafia in New Orleans, most a mixture of exaggeration and outright fabrication.

The citizens of New Orleans, however, didn't realize that. For many—perhaps most—people in New Orleans at the turn of the twentieth century, the Mafia was a deadly reality. The gunning down of David Hennessy that rainy night cemented for many New Orleanians—and much of America—a firm belief in the Mafia, a secret criminal organization that could reach out of the shadows and strike down anyone who dared stand up to it, even one of the country's most famous policemen.

Dave Hennessy had had an eventful career after becoming the great hero of Esposito's capture. Shortly after that episode, he and his cousin Mike (also a policeman) stood trial for the murder of another police officer in a shootout and won controversial acquittals. Leaving the police force, Hennessy then became successful as a private detective and what would now be called security consultant, but his police career effected a remarkable comeback when Joseph Shakespeare ran for mayor as the Reform Democratic candidate against the regular Democratic—the Ring—candidate in 1888. Mayor Shakespeare was serious about rehabilitating the city's corrupt and incompetent police force. After his election to office, he appointed David Hennessy superintendent of police and instructed him to turn the demoralized, corrupt police department into a professional police force.

The capture of Esposito had made him famous, and his charisma made him many friends. At thirty-two, Hennessy was a handsome fellow, with a luxuriant black handlebar mustache, his hair fashionably oiled and parted in the middle. The premature gray in his black hair only added distinction to the young chief; his steely gray eyes gave a hint of the toughness and cool nerve for which he was known. He was curiously abstemious for a tough crime fighter: He didn't drink, didn't gamble, and at thirty-two still lived with his mother. A supremely confident man, the chief got his way by reputation and force of personality. If that wasn't enough, well, he had his fists and the revolver tucked into his waistband.

Hennessy had a reputation as a crackerjack detective, but great detectives don't necessarily make good administrators; Hennessy proved gifted in both roles. In only two and a half years, he shaped the New Orleans Police Department into a better disciplined and more efficient police department.

An affable and sociable man, Hennessy belonged to the Red Light Social Club, a social organization in the Vieux Carré that welcomed the middle-class Irish and Italians kept out of the city's more exclusive clubs. There he became friendly with successful Italian businessmen like Joseph Macheca (suspected by some later writers as the real founder of the Mafia in New Orleans), a wealthy steamship owner and fruit importer, and Joseph and Peter Provenzano, owners of a stevedore firm.

If Dave Hennessy was a man of many friends, many years in police work had given him equally many enemies. Ironically, it may have been one of his friendships that killed him.

Along the waterfront, Irish and African American longshoremen monopolized the loading and unloading of rice, cotton, and sugar. Italians, however, had seized control of the fruit business. By the 1880s, the Provenzano brothers—Joseph, George, Vincent, and Peter—ran a successful stevedore firm of longshoremen who wrestled crates of coconuts, bananas, limes, pineapples, and mangoes off ships from Latin America. But their business began to suffer when brothers Charles and Tony Matranga elbowed their way onto the waterfront in 1886 and began taking contracts away from the Provenzanos.

After this business rivalry turned violent, Hennessy got the two sides together and tried to broker a truce, but on the night of May 5, 1890, gunmen fired on a wagonload of Matranga workmen as it jolted down Esplanade Avenue. After the gunsmoke cleared, Tony Matranga was left writhing in agony, his leg so badly mangled by buckshot that it had to be amputated. Two others were also wounded.

When the ambush victims identified Joe Provenzano, his brother Peter, and four of their men as the shooters, Hennessy duly arrested his friends, and in July, the six men went on trial for the shooting. The trial was noteworthy for the numerous policemen who provided alibis for the defense and for the defense's accusation that the Matrangas were members of the Stoppagliera, an offshoot of the Mafia. The jury ignored the policemen's testimony and the Mafia accusation and promptly convicted the defendants. The trial judge just as promptly vacated the verdict as contrary to "the law and the evidence."

Many suspected that Hennessy had extended his friends a lifeline. After the trial, rumors about the chief's chumminess with the Provenzanos were rampant, and his officers were widely suspected of perjury. Hennessy's friend Joe Macheca was also very unhappy with him. Macheca, who'd testified against the Provenzanos, feared them. When he'd confided his anxiety to Hennessy several months before, the chief had reassured him that he would protect him. But now Hennessy appeared to be siding with the Provenzanos. Macheca was afraid, and he was angry, and he said so.

Hennessy had three months until the retrial. He'd developed suspicions about Italian criminals in New Orleans, suspicions that some of them were connected to Giuseppe Esposito, the bandit he'd captured and extradited nine years earlier. The Provenzanos later claimed that he hoped to impeach several of the witnesses against them and prove that the Matrangas were indeed involved with the Mafia. Hennessy wrote to a police official in Rome, Louis Berti, and requested information about men in New Orleans who had been friends with Esposito. What specific names he inquired about isn't known, but he asked for photographs and facts about their criminal past. In September, Berti responded politely, promising to send photographs and criminal histories in the near future.

The Provenzanos' second trial was scheduled for October 22, 1891; rumors swirled about that this time Hennessy would appear for the defense. When he was shot dead that rainy night, a week before the trial was slated to begin, it was easy to conclude that the chief had been killed to prevent him from testifying and that the Matrangas were behind it.

The police were after Italians from the start—not without reason. Hennessy had identified his murderers as "Dagoes," and a block and a half from the scene of the shooting a private watchman had spotted five Italians, two of whom were trying to hide sawed-off shotguns under their coats. But the authorities showed little discrimination about which "Dagoes" they arrested. Before the chief was even dead, Mayor Joseph Shakespeare gave the order: "Scour the whole neighborhood. Arrest every Italian you come across, if necessary, and scour it again tomorrow morning as soon as there is daylight enough." On the day after Hennessy's funeral, Shakespeare made it clear what he planned to do about the Italians: "We must teach these people a lesson that they will not forget for all time."

And indeed he did.

Nineteen Italians were eventually charged with the assassination of David Hennessy, including Joseph Macheca and Charlie Matranga. The first lot of nine went on trial in mid-February 1891 at Saint Patrick's Hall on Lafayette Square. The evidence against them consisted of a theory of the crime—that Macheca had masterminded a plot to get rid of the chief before he could testify at the Provenzanos' retrial—and a series of problematic eyewitness identifications. The case against the accused was so weak that at the end of the two-week trial, the judge ordered a directed verdict of "not guilty" for two of the defendants, including Charlie Matranga. And after deliberating for less than a day on the fates of the remaining seven, the jury deadlocked on three and outright acquitted four more.

With the pronouncement of "not guilty," a collective gasp of dismay rippled through the courtroom. How could the killers of Hennessy walk free? In the hysteria that had washed over the city, few doubted their guilt. The crowd gathered outside of Saint Patrick's Hall was stunned by the verdict. Then they became angry. "Who killa de chief?" chanted the outraged mob. "Who killa de chief?" Accusations of jury tampering flew around the city.

The next morning the fury erupted. A lynch mob of some eight thousand vigilantes stormed the parish prison where the Italians were still being held on another charge. Shouting "Hang the Dago murderers!" they battered down a side gate, surged into the prison, and murdered eleven of the accused Italians, including five who had not yet been tried. Charlie Matranga survived, but Joseph Macheca was among those murdered.

To this day nobody knows for certain who killed Dave Hennessy. But in the minds of most New Orleanians, there was little doubt that he'd been brought down by the "Mafia."

This was the beginning of New Orleans's—and America's—obsession with the Mafia. Previously, few Americans had been familiar with the term. But Dave Hennessy's murder and the lynching of the Italians splashed the misdeeds of the "Mafia" on the front pages of newspapers all over the country. Before 1890, most violence involving Italians was attributed to the "vendetta." After 1890, New Orleans papers that had rarely referred to the Mafia now blamed the mysterious organization for almost any crime committed by an Italian.

So did a Sicilian Mafia terrorize the city?

The question of whether the many crimes attributed to it were committed by the Mafia revolves around the question of what is meant by *Mafia*. While the origins of the Sicilian Mafia are shrouded in mystery, the phenomenon appears to have originated in response to specific social and economic conditions in western Sicily and the south of Italy. The government wasn't much interested in the welfare of those working the land, who were often at the mercy of brigands or rapacious landowners. So peasants turned to local patrons for protection. In nineteenth-century Sicily, such a protector had to be a brave, swaggering sort of man who didn't hesitate to do what was necessary to get what he wanted—burn a neighbor's field, kill his cows, threaten his family, slit his throat. A man who had the guts and nerve and brains—and luck—to do this successfully could become a mafioso, a "respected man," who became the patron of a large number of locals. He provided protection; he did favors; he mediated disputes; he "found" stolen goods. And each time he managed to extract a share of the rewards, a sort of unofficial tribute for his services. The natural consequence of this is obvious. Offering protection evolved into insisting on it. Turning to mafiosi for help evolved into mafiosi collecting payments simply for not causing harm. It was blackmail by another name.

A successful mafioso not only built a network of clients grateful for his patronage, but also created for himself a *cosca*, literally "artichoke"—"family" in American Mafia jargon. This small group of henchmen generally came to do the dirty work, allowing the most successful mafioso—the *capo mafioso*—the luxury of pretending not to be a thug. The more established his reputation, the more deference a "man of respect" could command and the less effort he had to put into the exhausting business of coercing compliance. People fell into line because they dared not risk otherwise.

Originally, then, *Mafia* referred not to an organization but to "a form of behavior and a kind of power." It's more accurate to say that there wasn't any Mafia as such—that is, there was no organization at all; there were only capo mafiosi and their cosca. Another way of putting it is that there were numerous mafias, independent organizations, based on client-patron relationships, scattered throughout western Sicily. By 1900 these extralegal client-patron relationships—"part armed criminal gang, part commercial enterprise, and part political clique"—were functioning as a parallel form of government, involved in both legal and illegal activities. It was confused outsiders, baffled by the situation in Sicily, who wrongly surmised that the term *Mafia* referred to a single organization.

Some of these extralegal entities stretched their tentacles as far as the New World. Most Sicilian criminal gangs in the United States were simply that—garden variety hoodlums. But some crime syndicates had Mafia connections. A capo mafioso would have been too well-protected to ever need to flee Sicily, but without a doubt a scattering of low-level Mafia henchmen crowded the decks of ships bound for America.

To survive in a strange new country, they naturally turned to what they knew best. Giuseppe Morello, born in Corleone, Sicily, boarded a ship to America in the 1890s to avoid a murder charge. Born into a Mafia family, he established a successful extortion and counterfeiting ring in New York City and became the most powerful Mafia boss of his day. Gangs like Morello's could retain ties to Mafia cosca in Sicily, but they always operated independently; no Mafia boss in Corleone ever called the shots in New York or New Orleans.

Sicilian gangs in America acted in a social context considerably different from that of Sicily. In Sicily, Mafia networks were embedded in society; they performed an important social function. In the United States Mafia bosses were just gangsters. *Mafia* might be convenient shorthand for referring to Italian criminal gangs in the United States. It's more accurate, however, to see the American version merely as gangs of criminals who were, by the way, Italian, rather than true Sicilian Mafia. And in neither case did they form a large, overarching organization.

But in the late nineteenth and early twentieth century New Orleans *was* plagued by a very real threat: Black Hand crime. A type of petty extortion, the Black Hand racket was straightforward: The victim usually received a note, often signed with a grim black handprint (or sometimes skull and crossbones) demanding payment of a specified sum. If the cash was not forthcoming, the target was warned, there would be consequences. Sometimes the victim and his family were threatened with death; sometimes the blackmailers threatened to burn the family business to the ground. These warnings were often taken seriously: insurance policies could be canceled if word got out that the owner of a business had received a Black Hand note. The specter of the Black Hand generated genuine fear. (The apocryphal story of Francisco Domingo probably reflected the early existence of this kind of crime.)

Sicilian immigrants offered natural targets for this kind of extortion. Their well-developed distrust of government made them reluctant to go to the police. By the 1880s, such blackmail was prevalent among southern Italian communities all over the United States. By the early twentieth century, Black Hand crime was rampant in New Orleans, where *Mafia* and *Black Hand* came to be used more or less interchangeably. *Black Hand* was used to designate an organization, as well as a particular method of crime, and a mysterious "Black Hand Society" was often blamed for extortion attempts. But no Black Hand Society ever existed in New Orleans or anywhere else. Instead, opportunistic individuals or gangs sent Black Hand notes to anyone they thought could be terrorized into paying them off.

This, then, was the "Mafia" that in some quarters was suspected of the Axeman's work: the Crutti and Rissetto attacks and Joe Davi's murder. For some, it was the obvious suspect. An editorial in the *Daily Picayune* immediately after the Davi killing accused the Black Hand, noting that the "fact that all the victims were Italians of the small tradesman class should point the direction in which the clews [*sic*] are to be sought."

Some New Orleans police officers clung to the theory that Joe Davi's murder was a Black Hand crime. The letters Davi had received a year before his death were typical Black Hand missives, a strange mixture of graciousness and menace: "Dear Friend," the first one politely began. "Pardon us that we are going to bother you, because we are in need and we ask you to favor us with $200." But it concluded with a definite, if vague, threat: "Be careful and do what we ask you. Otherwise you will suffer the consequences." Joe Davi had shrugged off the letter and those that followed as just a bluff.

Maybe that had been a mistake. This is why Pitzo made such an appealing suspect. He had a history of cadging money from Davi and others. He'd been accused of attempting to blackmail Sam Constanza. He'd been seen in the neighborhood of a grocery that had mysteriously burned. He'd argued with Davi over money. For some investigators, it wasn't such a stretch to see Pitzo as a Black Hand operator who'd carried through on a threat.

John Dantonio, the Italian expert, wasn't convinced. He reasoned that the Black Hand wouldn't have left August Crutti and Joseph Rissetto alive; it was pretty efficient at killing people. There were other arguments against the Black Hand: The attacker, witnesses said, wasn't an Italian. Who'd ever heard of a non-Sicilian mafioso? Plus, neither the Cruttis nor Rissettos hailed from southern Italy or Sicily. And they didn't move in immigrant circles; their friends and associates were all Americans. Black Hand crime was an almost exclusively Sicilian and immigrant phenomenon. And the Black Hand stabbed, shot, and bombed; no one in New Orleans could recall another case in which it had resorted to an axe.

So while it might not be accurate to talk about a New Orleans Mafia in a strictly technical sense, there were certainly criminal gangs in New Orleans who engaged in blackmail, kidnapping, and extortion, preyed primarily on the immigrant Italian population, and were known to use violence, including murder. Given this context, when the Axeman attacks began in 1910, suspicion that the Black Hand or Mafia might be involved was not entirely unreasonable. People believed in an

Italian criminal conspiracy that targeted even modest people such as owners of a grocery store and was known to threaten people reluctant to pay them off.

Joseph Mumfre was just the kind of garden variety Black Hand operator who tormented successful immigrants and fueled fears of a vast, powerful conspiracy. His square head, crooked nose, and scarred face gave him a threatening presence, but Mumfre had none of the sinister glamour of the stereotypical mob gangster. His rough braggadocio revealed him for the low-level thug that he was. Mumfre gave his profession as "labor agent"; his nickname—"Doc"—came from the patent medicines he sold on the side. The knife and bullet scars on his body, however, testified to the type of life he led. He had emigrated from Italy in his twenties and spoke heavily accented English. His background was varied: soldier, city employee, magazine salesman, money lender, letter writer for illiterate Italians, mule stealer, and horse thief. Black Hand extortion was his latest trade.

One fall day in 1907, grocer Camillo Graffagnini received a letter in Italian that began with the familiar "Dear Friend." Graffagnini owned a grocery a few blocks east of the Vieux Carré. He'd done well, invested in property, and was proud of his success. He could easily have paid the $1,000 the letter requested. But he tossed the letter aside.

A few days later, Joseph Mumfre entered the store. He looked around the grocery and swaggered his way up to the counter.

How is business? he inquired.

The grocer shrugged his shoulders modestly. *It's fairly well.*

Dear friend, said Mumfre. *Do you have anything to give me?*

Graffagnini knew what this meant. He hesitated. Then he picked up a cigar from one of the cigar boxes sitting on the counter and offered it to Mumfre. *Here*, he said. *Have this.* Mumfre took the cigar but looked at Graffagnini and asked again. *Are you sure you have nothing else for me?* Graffagnini shook his head. Mumfre turned toward the door, shaking his head as he walked out; this grocer was going to be trouble; he would need more encouragement.

Not long after, Graffagnini received another "Dear Friend" letter. This one warned him to comply, "Otherwise your family will fare badly." Mumfre showed up a few days later and again left empty-handed.

Graffagnini saw Joe Mumfre one more time, about a month later, when he came by to have a drink in the saloon. Then the next night, just after midnight, a loud explosion outside their residence jolted the sleeping Graffagnini and his family out of their beds. When the stupefied grocer staggered outside to investigate, he found that he shouldn't have dismissed the Black Hand so cavalierly. Someone had tried to throw a bomb into his family's living quarters, up on the second story. Luckily, telephone wires had intercepted the bomb and it had dropped to the sidewalk. There it had exploded, gouging out a hole in the sidewalk next to the grocery and shattering every pane of glass in the building's door and windows.

An investigation quickly resulted in Mumfre's arrest, along with four others. Witnesses had seen him near Graffagnini's store the night of the bombing. The police must have been relieved. They suspected him of being the ringleader of a Black Hand group and of involvement in several other crimes. A jury convicted him in fifteen minutes, and Mumfre was sentenced to twenty years in the penitentiary.

"Doc" Mumfre was in the purgatory of the Louisiana State Penitentiary when Joe Davi had his head smashed in. But the Black Hander would come to be associated with the Axeman's murders in a way no one could have anticipated.

6

The Cleaver Returns

After Joe Davi's murder, Jim Reynolds fully expected another attack in the coming months. The Cleaver already had struck three times without being caught, without leaving any real clues to his identity. If he was a "fiend," as Reynolds suspected, he would strike again soon; he wouldn't be able to help himself. So the city waited. Especially the Sicilian shopkeepers, who looked nervously up and down the street when they shut up their stores in the evening and wondered when the Cleaver would make his next appearance.

But nothing happened. The months slid by without any sign of the Cleaver. Reynolds had plenty to keep him busy: weeding out corrupt policemen, putting more patrolmen on the streets at night, and making the city safe for Carnival. He handled robberies, suicides, run-of-the-mill homicides, and the occasional mysterious murder. But no midnight marauder split open the head of an Italian grocer in the dead of night. Gradually, in the face of daily life, fear of the Cleaver slipped away.

The killer disappeared for six years.

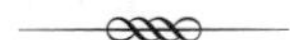

Where was the Cleaver, or the Axeman as he would become known, after Joe Davi's murder in June 1911? It's not unknown for serial killers to take a long break, especially between their first and second kills, but the most likely answer is prison; the Cleaver probably went away for burglary or petty larceny. The railroad shoe pin he used was popular with thieves because it was so useful for prying open doors and windows, and the Cleaver handled one with ease. The Crutti job was almost certainly not his first. His practice of removing his shoes so as not to make noise on the wood floors also suggests some experience in housebreaking; the Cleaver knew what he was doing.

Perhaps that is how he got his start. Perhaps he didn't set out to harm anyone. Perhaps August Crutti, the first victim, stirred in his sleep, startling the burglar whose original object was the week's cash. When he hit the grocer out of fear, he discovered that he enjoyed it. It made him feel powerful, like nothing he'd ever felt before. For a moment he didn't feel like a loser, an insignificant day laborer and freelance burglar. So he attacked Joseph and Conchetta Rissetto, viciously cutting both of them with his meat axe, producing plenty of blood. That they escaped alive was just luck. But with Joe Davi, the Axeman became a killer, a success in his own mind, luxuriating in a feeling of dominance and control as he bashed the young man's brains onto his pillow.

Not long afterward, he was probably arrested for something else—burglary most likely—and shipped off to prison for a term. The Louisiana State Penitentiary was set up for punishment, not rehabilitation, so time spent there wouldn't cure the itch to kill. Murder is addictive, and when the Axeman returned to New Orleans, he slunk around the city, like a demon choosing his next soul.

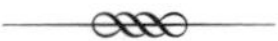

3 AM, December 22, 1917

The Cleaver returned one chilly December night.

Shrieks—hysterical, high-pitched shrieks—shattered the still winter air. Sixteen-year-old Mary Andollina was startled out of her sleep by her mother's cries. Instantly awake, she darted from the room she shared with her four younger sisters into her parents' bedroom to find her father sprawled on the floor, covered with blood and moaning in pain. Her first impulse was to go to her father, but her mother screamed at her: *Get the children out of the house! Someone tried to kill your father! Get the children out of the house! They'll be murdered!*

Obediently, Mary turned back into her own bedroom. She shook the younger girls awake and hurried the sleepy, protesting children out of the house. Mrs. Andollina, with her infant daughter in her arms, soon followed Mary out into the street, screaming for someone to call an ambulance.

The neighbors responded, the ambulance came, and the police were called. Not only did Epifanio Andollina need to be taken to Charity Hospital, but so did his sons: the two boys—ages thirteen and fourteen—had minor injuries, but their father had several serious head wounds.

As the sun came up and the cool night air warmed into a mild winter day, the police settled down to unwinding what exactly had happened. Interviewing the family, they were able to patch together an account of the night's events.

Epifanio and Anna Andollina, both Sicilian transplants, had for five years run a small grocery and saloon at the corner of Apple and Dante Streets in Carrollton, about four miles west of the Vieux Carré. The large family lived in a building attached to the grocery, the parents in one room with their infant daughter, the two boys in a back room, and the five girls in the third room.

Mrs. Andollina told the detectives that she had awoken to see a man standing on her husband's side of the bed, a revolver in one hand and a hatchet in the other. Seeing her eyes open, the intruder leveled his pistol directly at her and commanded, "Shut up!" She froze in terror. The man then hit her husband four or five times with the hatchet. That, apparently, was what he had come for because he then turned and walked out of the room. That's when Mrs. Andollina began screaming.

On his way out of the house, the assailant ducked into the room of the two boys. As they struggled awake at the sound of their mother's screams, the intruder stunned fourteen-year-old John with a blow to the head and whacked the younger Salvatore with his pistol butt on the arm. Then he slipped out through the kitchen, dropping the hatchet on the kitchen floor.

John Andollina shows off the wound he received from the Axeman; Detective Arthur Marullo demonstrates how the Axeman entered the Andollina grocery.

Detectives closely questioned the family, but no one could describe the assailant. Mrs. Andollina, who'd seen the man only by the dim light of an oil lamp in the bedroom, couldn't even tell if he was black or white. "It was too dark," she explained, "and I was so excited at the time."

Later, from his bed in Charity, Epifanio Andollina was no more help. He couldn't describe the assailant because he'd been asleep when the first blow fell and had tried to protect himself by pulling the bedclothes up over his head. He denied knowing anyone who had it in for him. "I have no enemies," the grocer declared. "I don't know why anyone should make an attempt on my life."

The hatchet man, as the press called him, had come in through the back door, chiseling out a large panel of the heavy wooden door. Nothing had been stolen. No one had seen a suspicious character hanging around the grocery. It was a puzzling crime, and some of the detectives were openly skeptical of the family's story. Were they sure it wasn't just a domestic spat that got out of hand? Or maybe they'd quarreled with a neighbor and knew the assailant?

No! the family insisted. *That is not what happened.* Well, perhaps it was a Black Hand crime. But the Andollinas denied ever receiving blackmail demands. They could only recall a previous incident about five years before when someone had knocked out a door panel and entered the house. He stole some money from the grocery but was frightened off as he was trying to break into the family's quarters. Were the two cases connected?

Almost certainly the Andollinas' attacker was the Cleaver of 1910 and 1911. That another assailant would target specifically Italian grocers in the same manner is extremely unlikely. If Jim Reynolds had been investigating the break-in, perhaps he would have made the connection with similar attacks on other Italian grocers six and a half years before. But Superintendent Reynolds was not on the case. He'd been murdered five months before.

On August 2, 1917, Terrance Mullen, a patrolman known to have mental problems, entered the crowded First City Criminal Court Building. He walked upstairs to police headquarters and in front of several of the department's most senior officials shot Chief Reynolds in the eye, piercing his brain and killing him instantly. In the ensuing firefight, bullets flew in all directions, drilling into the courthouse walls and crashing into the tall glass windows as Mullen fired and ran, shooting until his revolver clicked empty. Policemen opened fire, some taking aim at the assassin as he retreated down the hallway; others, rattled, fired at random. For what seemed an eternity, chaos and confusion washed down the corridors of one of New Orleans's most important government buildings.

Terry Mullen's ten-minute rampage through the First City Criminal Court Building left a shattered police department in its wake. The most popular superintendent since Dave Hennessy was dead; several other officers were wounded, one mortally. The careers of several of the officers who'd failed to protect Reynolds were ruined, forced to take early retirement or resign. Terry Mullen spent the rest of his life locked up in a state asylum.

Mayor Martin Behrman was stunned and genuinely grieved by the death of his friend. And he was furious. He couldn't understand, he said to one reporter, "how a man could be shot down in his own office surrounded by a number of men, who were there to protect him."

Who could be trusted to take charge of the police department? Anger over the department's apparent incompetence may well have played a role in the selection of the next superintendent. Instead of choosing from within the department, Behrman and the city's Commission Council unanimously selected Frank T. Mooney, superintendent of terminals for the Illinois Central Railroad.

This appointment made more sense than it might appear. Even if his manners were a bit unrefined, Frank Mooney was a capable manager; he knew how to handle big projects and large numbers of men. He was familiar with city hall, the people in it and how it worked, and he already knew many of the officers in the police department. He was a loyal Democrat, and that he wanted the job there was no question; he'd been up for it before, in 1911, when he was beaten out by Jim Reynolds.

Superintendent of Police
Frank T. Mooney.

Running the Illinois Central Railroad—one of the most important of the nine rail lines that snaked their way into New Orleans—was a complicated business. While much of Mooney's time was spent in necessary but dull public relations—attending Red Cross lectures, demonstrating the safety of the railroads to women's clubs—he also had to pacify unhappy laborers, lobby the legislature, and hammer out agreements with other railroads, as well as be responsible for the over 200,000 IC railroad cars that went in and out of New Orleans each year. All this required tact, organization, and public speaking skills. To be in charge of the Illinois Central in the city of New Orleans was a tremendous responsibility, just the kind of challenge a man like Frank Mooney relished. What it didn't require was police experience.

At forty-seven, Mooney had the solid frame of a man who'd been an athlete in his youth but put on flesh in his middle years. A photo of

Mooney in his thirties projects a picture of rectitude, an upright, honorable man who believed in duty and service and the efficacy of hard work. All that had certainly worked for him. Frank Mooney was a self-made man. The son of an Irish immigrant, he'd begun his career as a thirteen-year-old flagman in the Illinois Central and risen higher and higher because of his industriousness and gift for finding efficiencies. He planned to apply the same businesslike formula to the police department; what the department needed, he was sure, was a firm hand and a few new ideas. Reynolds had tightened discipline in the force, to be sure, but Mooney knew there was much more to do. The chief had been too much one of the lads, too indulgent of his men, and too lax in enforcement of moral legislation. The new superintendent planned on shaking the department up.

But Mooney hadn't been involved in the investigations of the 1910–1911 attacks on Italian grocers. John Dantonio, the Italian detective who'd helped investigate those crimes, was also gone from the force by this time. Dantonio had retired in October 1917. He was only fifty-three, but he'd fallen sick with the illness that would kill him three years later. Besides, he was an early victim of Superintendent Mooney's new economizing. By 1917 Dantonio was chief of the night detective bureau, and one of Mooney's first acts was to abolish it. Dantonio reckoned that this would be a good time to retire. After twenty-one years on the force, he was eligible for a pension, and he took it.

He was replaced as the Italian expert by Arthur Marullo, an Italian immigrant who'd been a detective in New York City before joining the New Orleans Police Department in 1915. Marullo investigated the Andollina case, but of course since he hadn't been on the force then, he may well have not known about the earlier attacks. Chief of Detectives George Long had been one of the investigators of the Davi murder, but he'd been of the opinion that it, as well as the other attacks, was simple robbery gone wrong. At any rate, no evidence suggests that anyone made the connection between Epifanio Andollina's assailant and the killer of six years before.

What interested detectives was the connection between the Andollina case and similar attacks in the same section of the city. This was the third assault on this side of the city in a mile and a half radius in the last year.

On a moonless Saturday night seven months earlier, a French-born dairyman, Vincent Miramon, had been sleeping soundly in the hayloft above his cow barn at 4131 Washington Avenue. About 1 AM, May 19, someone took Miramon's hammer from its resting place on a shelf in the barn and crept up the stairs to the Frenchman's cot. With the first blow, the prowler bashed in Miramon's head, fracturing his skull. He hit the unconscious dairyman at least six more times, hammering his face into a broken, swollen, bloody mess. The assailant then descended the stairs without taking the $150 in cash Miramon carried in his pocket. He dropped the bloodstained hammer on his way out.

The police developed only a handful of suspects in the attack: several black truck farmers who'd threatened Miramon because he didn't keep his cows out of their cornfields. Eventually, they narrowed their focus to one, Cornelius Jones. But the quarrel over the roaming cows was the only evidence they had against him. It wasn't much of a motive, and everyone knew the police didn't have much of a case.

At Charity Hospital, Miramon appeared to be recovering when meningitis set in. He died five days after the attack.

The other case was eerily similar to the Andollina attack. Just before 4 AM on a warm, rainy night ten days after the attack on Vincent Miramon, a man entered the residence of Joseph Girard, grocer and ice dealer at 3429 Fern Street. The area was rural and thinly populated, grassy lots dotting the racially mixed neighborhood. The thirty-seven-year-old Louisiana born son of French parents ran a tiny grocery in the front room of his house; in the back two rooms he squeezed his wife and seven children.

Two small flimsy wooden latches proved no obstacle to the prowler who easily forced his way past the kitchen door. He moved directly into the bedroom of Girard and his wife Adele. By the light of the lamp, he could see the man, his wife, and the toddler between them in the bed; an older child slept across the foot of the bed.

Gripping a hatchet with a large blade and small handle, a type sometimes used by butchers, the intruder approached the husband's side of the bed. Standing above the sleeping figure, he delivered two hard blows, slicing Joseph Girard across the face and through the nose.

Adele Girard was woken by the sound of her husband gurgling for air. She rolled over to find herself staring straight into the face of the man with the hatchet. He hit her once, and then again. He was swinging at her for a third time when his hatchet became entangled on the mosquito bar.

By this time, eight-year-old Helen had woken up, taken in the situation, and started screaming. The hatchet man punched her in the face and slashed her once on the forehead. When Mrs. Girard saw her daughter slump bloody on the bed, she forced herself off the bed and leapt into the side gallery (or porch) off the bedroom hollering, "Murder! Murder!" The assailant escaped back through the kitchen.

This was just the kind of straightforward case that made a policeman's life easy. When Chief Reynolds interviewed Mrs. Girard later that morning at Charity Hospital, she immediately told him that it was John Wesley Sumner, a rival ice man with whom she and her husband had clashed only two days before. She and her daughter had both seen him. Three months later, a jury took twenty minutes to convict Sumner for breaking and entering with a dangerous weapon and assault and sent him to the Louisiana State Penitentiary for life.

The Andollina case six months later offered no such easy solution for detectives. Most of them probably didn't believe the family anyway and dismissed it as one of those mysterious "Italian" crimes that were nearly impossible to solve. No one much noticed when Epifanio Andollina died ten months after the attack. He died in the influenza epidemic that struck the city, his constitution perhaps weakened by the serious injuries he'd sustained in the nighttime attack. Perhaps, like Joseph Rissetto, he was another unknown victim of an unknown killer.

That unknown killer had vanished into the darkness. But this time, not for long.

Thursday, May 23, 1918

The voice on the phone that rang at the police station just before dawn was frantic with grief and shock. "Come at once!" the caller pleaded. The anguish in the man's voice was palpable. "My brother and his wife have been killed!"

Captain John Dunn of the Seventh Precinct ordered a squad to come with him. The patrol wagon was hitched up, the policemen climbed aboard, and they headed north across Saint Charles Avenue toward Carrollton. The patrol wagon bumped down the dirt road, passing by grazing horses, fields of sprouting corn, and vacant grassy lots. This section of New Orleans was as much country as city, with dairies and stables and small truck farms. It was very similar to the Andollina neighborhood and not far from it, less than two miles distant; the Miramon attack had taken place just over a mile away. It was also a high-crime area. Captain Dunn knew that only three months earlier a bandit responsible for a string of drug store and grocery holdups had shot and killed a policeman nearby.

When the officers arrived at the corner of Magnolia and Upperline, they found the usual small grocery and saloon with a residence in back. Pale and shaken, brothers Andrew and Jacob Maggio came out to meet them and motioned them toward the back room. Entering the bedroom, Captain Dunn came upon one of the most gruesome scenes he'd ever encountered: the proprietors of the grocery store, Joseph and Catherine Maggio, appeared to have been hacked with an axe. Dunn was surprised to see that Joseph was still—just barely—alive. The ambulance from Charity Hospital had already been called and pulled up at the grocery store just after the police detail arrived. The interns didn't even have time to put the dying man in the ambulance. They entered the bedroom only to watch with Captain Dunn as Joseph Maggio choked out his last breath. His wife had been dead for several hours. The ambulance returned to Charity empty.

Captain Dunn quickly hustled Andrew and Jacob Maggio down to the Seventh Precinct station where he took their statements. The brothers were still in shock, but they managed to pour out their story.

Twenty-eight-year-old Andrew Maggio had not wanted to go into the army. On his draft registration form in answer to the question "Do you have a father, mother, wife, child under 12, or a sister or brother under 12, solely dependent on you for support?" he had written "Mother." This wasn't true. Not only did his mother live with his sister in Arkansas, but he also had three older brothers, all successful businessmen, to share in the support of their mother. Surely Andrew, a barber, wasn't expected to do so alone. He didn't even have his own home; he lived with Joseph and his wife. No, clearly Andrew wanted to duck military service. But now the army expected him to defend his classification as "exempt because of dependency." He'd received instructions to report to the exemption board office next week. Later he claimed to have been out drinking that Wednesday night. Perhaps he needed to steady his nerves for the coming interview. That would explain why he'd slept so deeply that night.

About 4:30 that morning something woke him from his sleep. At first he couldn't tell what it was. Then he heard it. A low groan coming from the other side of the wall, from Joe and Catherine's room. Andrew sat up in bed and listened again. He heard nothing. He rapped on the wall. No answer. Andrew wasn't sure what to do. He had a feeling that something was very, very wrong. But he wasn't used to barging into his brother's bedroom. And he was afraid of what might be on the other side of the wall. As the youngest of four brothers, Andrew was used to following, not leading. So he pulled on some clothes and ran down the block to the house of Jacob, another of his older brothers. Waking him, Andrew told Jake that he was afraid something terrible had happened.

The two men returned to the house and went around the back to enter by the kitchen door. What they saw there made them even more apprehensive about what they'd find inside. The kitchen door stood open; one of its panels lay on the ground. Anxiously, the two brothers went through the kitchen, past the bathroom, and stood at the door of the bedroom. Jake tapped on the door. There was no answer. Slowly, Jake pushed open the bedroom door to reveal the horrific scene. Reeling from the discovery, they immediately called the police and ambulance and waited for help to arrive.

After the brothers finished their statements, Captain Dunn kept them at the station, using the handy excuse that they were "material witnesses." He knew Chief Long and Superintendent Mooney would want to talk to them.

Back at the Maggio grocery, Bertillon Operator John Norris flashed away with his camera. Superintendent Mooney, Chief of Detectives George Long, and a handful of other officers inspected the bodies. This wasn't Mooney's first big murder case. Most of the others, however, had been straightforward shootings that didn't require much detective work to determine who the shooter was. None had been anything like this. Even if he was new to police work, Mooney planned to apply the same systematic thinking that had always served him so well to this murder case.

Joseph was on the bed with his feet hanging off the side. Catherine lay on the floor at his feet, sprawled on her back, a gaping wound on the right side of her neck. Both were drenched with blood. An axe stained with blood had been discarded in the nearby bathroom, dropped into the bathtub; it was the couple's own axe, last seen lying in their backyard. Blood on the bed, blood on the floor, and blood spattered seven feet up the wall testified to the ferocity of the attack.

A few hours after the bodies had been removed to the morgue, Dr. O'Hara's autopsy showed that both had had their throats cut. In addition, Joseph had been hit twice with the axe, fracturing his skull, and cut a couple of times on his face and neck. Catherine hadn't actually been hit with the axe at all but had died an even more horrific death. She had gotten out of bed, the police speculated, to defend her husband from his killer. But he'd slashed her seven times—on the face, on the shoulder, on the hand, the last probably a defensive wound received

Joseph and Catherine Maggio and the grocery where they were murdered.

as she attempted to protect herself from the deadly razor. The killing stroke had cut deep into the right side of her neck, slicing through the muscles, internal jugular vein, and carotid artery and cutting into her airway. Such a stroke must have immediately dropped her to the floor, where her gasps for breath would have sucked the gushing blood into her airway, drowning her in her own blood as she simultaneously bled to death.

The means of the killer's entry they'd seen before at the Andollina grocery: he had chiseled out a panel in the kitchen door and then reached through to the lock. Once inside, he went straight through to the bedroom.

"Robbery was the motive," announced the *New Orleans States*, reporting what the police were telling the public. The small safe in the bedroom was open; likely it had been left unlocked because Joe Maggio had deposited $650—several days' receipts from the grocery—in the bank the day before. A tin strongbox had been forced open and fifty dollars taken. The jewelry box hadn't been tampered with, although it contained jewelry worth much more than the money stolen. Dresser drawers had been pulled out and clothes strewn about.

After Dr. O'Hara took charge of the bodies and sent them off to the morgue, Superintendent Mooney had the house and grocery locked and put under guard. The half-dozen detectives assigned to the case spent the rest of Thursday interviewing neighbors and family members and finding out as much about the Maggios as they could.

Investigators didn't systematically search the premises immediately. Before the development of scientific crime scene analysis, such things were less important than tracking down witnesses—and suspects—as quickly as possible. Even neophyte policeman Frank Mooney knew that the way to solve a case was to find a suspect and sweat a confession out of him as soon as possible. A time-consuming search of the residence and grocery could wait.

There were few surprises in the information the detectives gathered. The Maggios were typical Sicilian immigrants, small-time businessmen. Forty-year-old Joseph was the eldest of the four brothers. Andrew, the youngest, had a barbershop down in the Central Business District. Jacob, thirty-six, owned a shoe repair shop only about a block (or a "square," according to New Orleans vernacular) away. A fourth brother, Salvatore, thirty-three, ran another grocery. Joseph took over as the head of the family when their father died years before. He had been the first to leave Sicily, immigrating to America and sending for the rest of his family as soon as he could.

Joe had married Catherine in 1903. A photo of them on their wedding day shows a sober groom, his dark mustache curling upward, and a self-conscious Catherine, still radiant in her wedding finery. Except for the unusual circumstance of having no children, they were an ordinary, happily married couple, working seven days a week to build a business that served both black and white customers who affectionately knew them as "Mr. and Mrs. Joe." The Maggios were careful with their money, as Sicilian immigrants usually were, investing their small excess funds in

Liberty Loan bonds. And patriotic as only new Americans can be, the Maggios tucked away their Red Cross pledge cards among their other important documents. They were the "right sort" of Italians, the detectives discovered, hardworking merchant *petite bourgeoisie* who had no enemies or questionable associates. No one had any reason to harm them.

In the course of his inquiries that morning, Detective Theodore Obitz stumbled across a bizarre message chalked onto the banquette—the sidewalk—a block away. What the message actually said is uncertain. Police records that might have preserved the message are lost. The *Times-Picayune* reported it as "Mrs. Joseph Maggio is going to sit up tonight just like Mrs. Toney." The *States* had a slightly different version: "Mrs. Joseph Maggio is going to sit up tonight. Just write Mrs. Toney." The *New Orleans Item* carried a third variant: "Mrs. Joseph Maggio will sit up tonight—just write. Mrs. Tony." That all of the newspapers carried a different version of the message suggests that the reporters didn't see the writing themselves but relied on secondhand accounts muddled in the retelling. The versions in the *Item* and *States* are closer to each other, but the one in the *Times-Picayune* makes the most literal sense.

Was it a clue? What did it mean? None of the various versions made much sense. The newspapers bandied about explanatory theories about the message ranging from its having been left by the deranged killer to it being the work of an accomplice warning the Maggios to be on their guard, to a practical joke of unusually bad taste. No wonder that Captain Dunn's statement to the press on Thursday evening could only say that this was an "unusually mysterious" case.

While detectives were still puzzling over the chalk message Thursday afternoon, another murder weapon turned up. A black woman the newspapers designated a "colored girl" working next door noticed a straight razor sticking out of the rose trellis on the lawn of the house next to the Maggio property. She alerted the owner of the property, who notified the police.

Chief of Detectives George Long turned the tortoise shell–handled razor over in his hand. The stainless steel blade was only three inches long, but it was deadly sharp. Dried blood clung to the blade and the black and yellow handle. *If we can find the owner,* Long thought as he folded the blade into its handle, *we'll have the killer.*

Long immediately sent Captain Dunn to Andrew's barbershop to interview his employees. Under questioning, one of them, Estaban Torres, conceded that he had seen Andrew take a similar razor from the shop a few days before, saying that it needed to be honed.

This was just the piece of evidence that Long and Mooney needed. From such minor details cases could be solved. The blood-smeared razor was almost certainly the murder weapon, and now the investigators might be able to connect it to one of the chief suspects, someone familiar with the house and grocery. Andrew had aroused suspicion from the beginning because he claimed to have slept through two people being hacked to death in the next room. It also seemed odd that Andrew hadn't inspected the sounds in Joe's bedroom himself but instead had gone to get Jake. He was either a coward, the detectives thought, or else something more sinister.

Optimistic that they were on their way to solving the case, Mooney let Jake go home Thursday night. But not Andrew. Less than twenty-four hours after the murders, the investigators had zeroed in on a suspect.

Now they were ready to thoroughly search the crime scene. Perhaps they could turn up more evidence to support a charge against Andrew. On Friday, Superintendent Mooney, Chief of Detectives Long, Captain Dunn, Detective Obitz, and Obitz's partner, Detective James P. Ford, returned to the Maggio grocery where they went through the premises room by room. In the murdered couple's bedroom, they found a blood-spattered suit of clothes in the corner, a pair of blood-stained socks, a bloody footprint, and a loaded revolver.

A search of Andrew's room turned up three more straight razors, not very surprising since he was a barber, none with blood on them. Of more interest was a shirt found in his bathroom—a stiff-bosomed white dress shirt spotted with faded dark stains that someone had tried to wash out. Were they bloodstains?

The search was as thorough as the investigators could make it. Detective Obitz even wedged himself uncomfortably under the house looking for evidence. In the backyard, one of the investigators found a screwdriver matching the marks in the door panel. Like the axe and razor, this tool had been abandoned by the killer. In the grocery, footprints of stocking feet were spotted on the bar's newly varnished counter, indicating that the killer hadn't worn shoes. Perhaps, someone speculated, he had climbed on the counter to switch on a light.

Once they completed the search, the detectives returned to their witnesses. Yes, some remembered that on the day before the murders, Andrew had worn dark clothes, similar to the blood-stained ones found in his brother's bedroom. The case against the youngest brother seemed to be tightening.

Then investigators suffered a setback. When they reinterviewed Estaban Torres, he looked carefully at the three razors found in Andrew's room. He pointed to one of them, saying that it looked like the one Andrew had taken from the shop. Now, there was no evidence of any connection between Andrew and the bloody murder weapon. Nevertheless, he remained the only suspect.

As rumors spread that he would be charged soon, Andrew begged to be allowed to attend his brother and sister-in-law's funeral. Mooney refused to release him, citing "the unsettled state of the case."

On Friday afternoon, two services were held to accommodate the many mourners. The first was at the funeral parlor on Toulouse Street, where the overflowing crowd spilled out into the street, blocking traffic. A second service was held at Saint Mary's Italian Church, the parish church for Italian immigrants in New Orleans, situated at the site of the old Ursuline Convent in the French Quarter. Here the tearful young nephews and nieces of the childless couple trudged by the caskets to say good-bye to their aunt and uncle. After the funeral mass, pallbearers loaded the flower-laden caskets into two hearses. The melancholy procession then slowly made its way down Esplanade Avenue the two short miles to Saint Louis Cemetery No. 3, where Joseph and Catherine Maggio were interred in the same vault. Meanwhile, Joe's youngest brother sat in the parish prison, suspected of their murder.

On Saturday morning, accompanied by Assistant District Attorney Ben Daly and Dr. O'Hara, Superintendent Mooney made a final examination of the Maggio residence and grocery. It was an opportunity for Mooney to show Daly and O'Hara the crime scene, outline his theory of the crime, and listen to their views. Mooney told them he was inclined to think that Andrew was their best suspect, but a lot would depend on the interview and how Andrew answered the investigators' questions. The case could go either way.

Finally prepared to confront him with evidence, Mooney had Andrew Maggio transferred from the Seventh Precinct to police headquarters on Saturday afternoon, where he was ushered into the superintendent's office. The young man was seated in front of Mooney's desk; Superintendent Mooney stationed himself on one side of Andrew; Assistant District Attorney Daly came at him from the other direction. For four hours Mooney and Daly grilled Andrew, pelting him with question after question and flinging his brother's bloodstained clothes in his face. Hour after hour Andrew repeated his story, insisting again and again that he did not kill his brother and sister-in-law. The bloodstained razor wasn't his; he'd never seen it before. He didn't know who it belonged to. The bloody clothes in the room belonged to Joseph. He'd slept through the noise of the murders because he'd been drinking the night before and was soundly asleep. The stains on his white shirt were from wine, not blood. He'd spilled a glass of wine over himself at a wedding. Over and over again Andrew protested his innocence.

Finally, he could stand it no longer: "How could you think I could kill my own brother?" he demanded, his voice choking on tears. "He sent us the money to come to America. He supported us after our father died in Sicily. Joe was like a father to me since I was eleven years old. I know a man isn't supposed to cry but . . ." and slumped over, his face in his hands, sobbing.

Mooney sat back in his chair and looked on thoughtfully as the distraught young man finally got control of himself and wiped his eyes. He had planned to charge Andrew, but now the case against him didn't seem strong enough. Mooney couldn't claim to have a policeman's long-honed skill in interrogation. But his career so far had taught him to be a judge of character, and his instinct told him he should look elsewhere for the murderer.

When Andrew was released Saturday night, Superintendent Mooney made a statement to the press: "Up to the time we conducted a rigid cross-examination of Andrew Maggio, I suspected strongly that either he committed the crime or had knowledge of the identity of the person or persons who did so. Andrew, however, explained so readily and clearly some of the puzzling threads of evidence that we gathered, and which we thought might be binding on him, that Mr. Daly and I concluded that the doubt as to Andrew's guilt was so strong that we were compelled to give him the benefit of the doubt."

Mooney promised that the investigation would go on, declaring, "Our hope for a solution is still bright."

Privately, however, he may have felt much less optimistic. But it was important to bolster public confidence in the police force. Having the public frightened of a razor-wielding maniac who killed with impunity could only complicate the police superintendent's job.

One step Mooney took to inspire confidence at the beginning of the investigation was to announce that he had assigned Chief of Detectives George Long to take charge of the case. The New Orleans public had faith in Long; he had a reputation as a clever detective who could solve difficult cases. The Reidel murder, a few years earlier, had been one such case.

In the fall of 1910, the bloated, decomposing remains of a middle-aged man sown into coffee sacks bobbed up in the Old Basin Canal. While the body was quickly identified as that of Franz Reidel, a German immigrant and watchmaker who'd gone missing with his life savings, investigators didn't have much to go on, except that the victim had died of blunt force trauma. Jim Reynolds, chief of detectives at the time, had little else in the way of clues or suspects. "We don't know where to start," he conceded to a newspaper reporter. "There is absolutely nothing to give us any idea of what to do." The *Daily States* was calling it "one of the criminal mysteries of the year."

Captain George Long unearthed the clue that broke the case. At the time, Long wasn't even in the Detectives' Office. But he had a flair for investigative work and kept his eyes and ears open, as Reynolds advised his officers to do. Long's patience was rewarded by a tip that Reidel had been seen entering a door at 630 North Rampart Street, on the edge of the French Quarter. More nosing around revealed that this was the address of an unsavory character named Eugene Bescanon, a tall, fish-eyed French immigrant with a criminal past, who had been an acquaintance of Reidel's. Further probing led to a squalid apartment in a dilapidated building on North Rampart Street (only two blocks from the Old Basin Canal) where investigators found bloodstained floors and rags.

This discovery quickly led to Bescanon's arrest, confession, and implication of his accomplice, a fellow Frenchman named François Rodin. The unsuspecting Reidel had been lured to Bescanon's apartment, where he was battered to death and robbed. The recovery of Reidel's watch chain, a distinctive one with a horse head locket, confirmed the men's guilt. The investigation had solved the mystery of Franz Reidel's murder and produced two culprits to hang—all because of a tip that might have escaped a less vigilant officer than George Long.

And Chief Reynolds wasn't stingy about sharing the credit. Captain Long's part in unraveling the mystery was publicly celebrated, with one newspaper editorial "award[ing him] the first honors in the quest." The case was a triumph for the New Orleans Police Department, showing that with thoroughness, perseverance—and a little luck—apparently hopeless cases could be solved.

Mooney only hoped Detective Long could accomplish a similar turnaround with the Maggio murders.

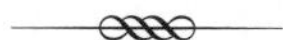

By May 1918, the United States had been in the First World War for just over a year. For months the New Orleans papers had carried stories about Red Cross fund drives, violations of the Espionage Act, and the first military conscription in America since the Civil War. But for the people of New Orleans the war was far away compared to the immediacy of the Maggio murders. The city was no stranger to violent death, but not since Joe Davi's death had it seen this kind of butchery. Newspaper accounts of the investigation into the murders of Joe and Catherine Maggio inspired far greater interest than stories of Zeppelin attacks or U-boat warfare.

As they drank their chicory coffee and contemplated the grisly murders, New Orleanians couldn't help but wonder whether all the attacks on Italian grocers were related. The Crutti and Rissetto attacks, the Davi murder, the Andollina case, and now the Maggio murders. Were they all connected? And who was targeting these people? And why?

Another name cropped up again and again in discussions as alert readers of the New Orleans papers thought back to another murder of another Italian grocer six years before.

Less than a year after Joe Davi's murder, another Italian grocer died in the middle of the night. Superficially, the crime was similar to the attack on Davi—a young grocer brutally murdered as he slept next to his wife. Yet the two murders were dissimilar in one crucial way, a way that indicated a different kind of criminal and a different type of motive.

At twenty-seven, Tony Sciambra was already a success. He'd learned the business as a boy in his father's Carrollton grocery and now ran his own grocery and bar at the opposite end of town, on France and Villere Streets in the Bywater District. The hard work and frugality that came as naturally to first-generation Americans as it had to their immigrant parents had allowed him to pay cash for the property. A personable young man, Tony was married to "Mrs. Tony" as the locals called her—pretty twenty-three-year-old Johanna. They were well on their way to producing the hoped-for houseful of children: married not quite two years, they had one son—eleven-month-old Jake—and another baby on the way. So, as Tony slept in his bed on the morning of May 16, 1912, he had reason to be pleased with himself, and with life.

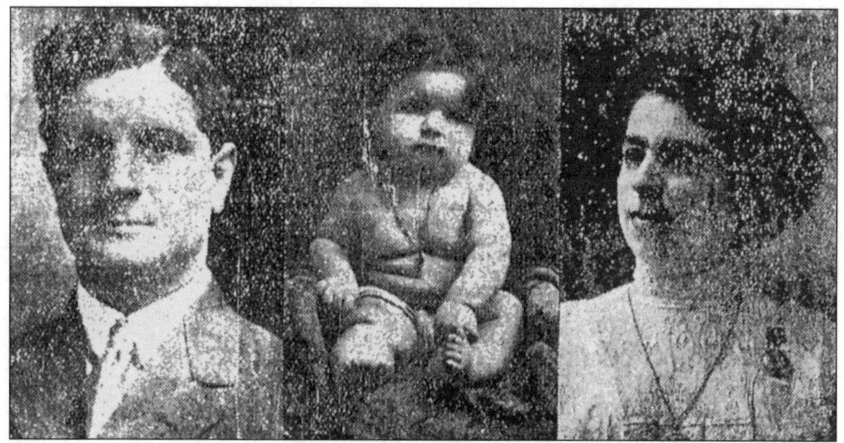

Tony, Jake, and Johanna Sciambra.

But not everyone, apparently, was pleased with Tony Sciambra.

About 2 AM on that morning, an intruder stacked a couple of soapboxes on top of each other and climbed up to reach a kitchen window at the back of Tony and Johanna's house. Opening the shutters, then raising the unlatched window, he crawled into the kitchen. Once inside, he paused and listened; no one in the house stirred. One door off the kitchen led into the grocery. He chose the other door, the one leading through the small dining room to the room where the young couple and their son were fast asleep. Entering the bedroom, the intruder attacked Tony, killing him almost instantly and inadvertently wounding Johanna; the baby sleeping next to them was unharmed.

How was this crime so different from the murders of Joe Davi or Joe and Catherine Maggio?

Tony Sciambra was shot to death.

In the bedroom the assailant walked up to the bed, pulled the mosquito netting out of the way, pointed his .38 caliber pistol at the sleeping grocer, and pulled the trigger. Again and again he fired. He unloaded five shots into Tony before turning around and slipping out through the kitchen door, giving no thought to the jewelry in the wardrobe or the cash in the till.

The Sciambra grocery and home, where Tony Sciambra was shot to death.

The first three bullets entering Tony's back caused him to jerk involuntarily so that the next two hit with less accuracy, wounding him in the side and the arm. But it didn't take long for internal hemorrhaging to kill him. Tony was dead by the time the ambulance arrived.

Johanna was killed accidentally. One bullet shot right through her husband's body, struck her in the hip, and penetrated her abdomen. At first everyone thought she would live, but the wound went septic, and she died of peritonitis ten days after her husband, leaving little Jake to be raised by his grandparents.

New Orleans vibrated with speculation over the assault on Tony Sciambra, yet another Italian grocer. People whispered to one another that it must be connected to the Davi murder less than a year before, and the Crutti and Rissetto attacks before that. There was no shortage of theories: it was the vendetta or the Black Hand; newly arrived Sicilians were trying to take the grocery business away from "local Italians"; the attacks were revenge for mistreatment by Italian grocers; the killer was a fiend.

The most popular notion was that the Black Hand was at it again. An indignant editorial in the *New Orleans Item* demanded that "the better class of Italians"—i.e., those not criminal—"take active measures . . . to induce their own people to tell what they knew regarding these crimes." It was only in this way, the editorialist continued, that Tony Sciambra's murder could be solved and "the authorities will be able to discover and punish the guilty."

The writer may well have been right. But he, like most commentators at the time, didn't recognize the significance of the choice of murder weapons. A gun and a blade are both lethal, but they kill in very different ways.

Many aspects of the Crutti, Rissetto, Davi, and Sciambra (and later the Andollina and Maggio) attacks were similar: targeting a successful grocery and bar in an unfashionable, isolated part of the city (the Sciambra grocery was less than a mile from the Crutti place) and breaking in during the dead of night. Robbery was never the motive. The assailant usually targeted the man first, if he attacked the woman at all. Harriet Crutti, Mary Davi, and Anna Andollina escaped relatively unscathed. Only Joseph and Conchetta Rissetto were attacked with equal ferocity. And perhaps Catherine Maggio wouldn't have died if she hadn't attempted to defend her husband.

All of these attacks were made with a blade of some kind—a meat cleaver, hatchet, axe, or razor—something that would draw blood. That's what the Axeman craved.

If all the Axeman wanted was the death of Italian grocers, he could have used a gun. He had one when he entered the Andollina home. It would have been less trouble—cleaner, more efficient, deadlier. But he never fired it, using it only to terrorize the victim's wife. The survival of several victims attests to the fact that an axe or cleaver wasn't as sure a method of killing as a revolver.

So, why choose such an insecure weapon as a blade? Because guns are impersonal. Killing a man by standing over him and bashing his head with a hatchet or cleaver is a much more intimate affair. A blade is an intensely personal weapon, requiring the killer to actually touch his victim and risk being splattered with blood and gore. A killer who chooses this kind of weapon wants more than his victim's death; he wants the power that comes with holding a man's life in his hands and then choosing to spill his blood and brains out on the bed.

Amid all the speculation after the murders, the *Times-Democrat* was closest to the mark, recording that many people attributed the killer's actions to a "lust for blood." The Axeman was willing to take the chance that his victims might actually survive.

Tony Sciambra's killer wanted something else. He only needed Tony dead. He didn't need to enjoy it. He didn't need to derive psychological pleasure from it. He didn't require the satisfaction derived from bringing an axe down on a helpless, sleeping man and spattering his blood and brains over the bed. Tony Sciambra was murdered with a weapon meant to be used at a distance, one that didn't require physical contact between the killer and his victim.

So, if Tony Sciambra and his wife weren't victims of the Axeman, who was responsible for their deaths? A clue may be found in a business transaction involving Tony's brother, Henry. After Tony's death—it's unclear how long—Henry Sciambra sold his own thriving grocery business at Marigny and Dauphine. The neighbors, the *Times-Picayune* said, shook their heads, puzzling over why the young man would sell a business that had been doing so well.

The man Henry Sciambra sold out to was Vito Di Giorgio.

Di Giorgio was reputed to be a major figure in the local "Mafia," the New Orleans gangsters who thrived on blackmail and counterfeiting. He'd been arrested in 1908 as the ringleader of a gang of Black Hand extortionists who'd tried to blow up a dry goods store when the owner refused to pay, but the police couldn't make the charges stick. He also had connections to a local counterfeiting ring and to New York crime boss Joseph Morello.

Was Tony Sciambra's death connected to the sale of his brother's store? Was it meant to serve as a warning? Or had Tony offended someone, someone who resorted to the vendetta and took a merciless revenge?

That wasn't all. Notorious Black Hander Joseph Mumfre—the man convicted in 1908 of trying to bomb grocer Camillo Graffagnini's home—may, possibly, have been mixed up somehow with Di Giorgio and the Sciambras.

Mumfre knew Di Giorgio; that was certain. Police suspected Mumfre—out on bond before his trial for dynamiting the Graffagnini home in December 1907—of involvement in the Black Hand bombing of another grocery in June 1908, for which Vito Di Giorgio was also arrested.

After Tony Sciambra's death, as Chief Reynolds, Detective Dantonio, and the other investigators began probing into the couples' background, trying to find a motive for the gunning down of the young grocer, neighbors whispered that Tony Sciambra had heard that relatives of Mumfre—who had begun serving his twenty-year prison term—lived in the neighborhood, and this had frightened the young grocer enough that he'd considered selling his store. He'd gone as far as lining up a prospective buyer when he changed his mind.

The would-be buyer, however, wasn't to be put off and had shown up at the store with a companion in tow, to persuade Tony to sell. One woman confided to detectives that a few months previously Johanna had been "considerably worried because of an Italian who looked dangerous . . . [and] had been to the store."

Reynolds and his men followed up on these leads, without any result. They questioned the two men who'd been in to see Tony. They also questioned Johanna Sciambra, who was well enough to be interviewed the morning after the murder. No, she hadn't seen the shooter. No, she and her husband had known nothing about Mumfre relatives in the neighborhood. No, they'd never received any Black Hand letters. Yes, her husband had considered selling but only because he hadn't gotten along with the landlord.

To add to the mystery, George Musacchia, the same grocer whose store had burned down just before Joe Davi's murder, came forward to claim that someone had also tried to break into his house the night of the Sciambra killing, using much the same method. He'd discovered a barrel sitting under one of his windows; someone had broken some of the slats in the blinds in an apparent attempt to get in. Reporters noted that Musacchia's grocery sat next to a vacant lot, just like the Davi, Rissetto, and Sciambra businesses. Why had the intruder abandoned the break-in? What connection—if any—did it have to the Sciambra case?

The different threads of the investigation never came together to form a coherent picture for the detectives. The murders of Tony and Johanna Sciambra were added to the list of the city's unsolved crimes. But contrary to the belief of most in his city, Chief Reynolds had concluded that the killing of the Sciambras and the murder of Joe Davi (and so presumably the attacks on the Cruttis and Rissettos) were products of very different minds: the Sciambras were, he thought, yet more victims of the Sicilian vendetta, still an all too common occurrence in the city. But Reynolds was convinced that Joe Davi's murder was not the work of a criminal gang but "bore all the earmarks of the acts of a degenerate." He never heard the term *serial killer*, but Chief Reynolds had clearly grasped the concept.

If he'd lived, Chief Reynolds presumably would have agreed that the Maggio case had more in common with the Davi than the Sciambra murders. But most people didn't think that way. Most people only remembered that some Italian grocers had died mysteriously under similar circumstances. The person who chalked the mysterious message onto the sidewalk—"Mrs. Joseph Maggio is going to sit up tonight just like Mrs. Toney," or something similar—was probably only doing what many in New Orleans were doing that warm May morning of 1918, as news of the slaughter of the couple swept through the city—linking the murder of one innocent Italian couple with the other.

The police weren't in a position to tell them anything different. Less than a week after the Maggio murders, the investigation was flailing. The most obvious suspect had been released and no obvious leads presented themselves to Superintendent Mooney and his detectives. The investigation suffered another blow when Detective Theodore Obitz, one of the officers investigating the case, was himself murdered. Obitz had spent the Saturday after the murders running down clues, but at

3 AM on Sunday morning he was cut down by a bandit he was chasing through the deserted streets of the city.

The Italian community might have been understandably jittery, but the rest of the city was resigned to the likelihood that the Maggio murders would in all probability not be solved. Confusion as to what kind of killer the city faced—a bloodthirsty fiend or a criminal gang—only unsettled people more.

Then another grocer was attacked.

7

A German Spy?

All of New Orleans was uneasy in the wake of the Maggio murders. The Italian community, especially, stirred apprehensively. Memory of the first two attacks in the fall of 1910, the subsequent murder of Joe Davi, and the assassination of the Sciambras created an undercurrent of anxiety, a worry that Italian grocers had special reason to fear. Gossip about a new and lethal Black Hand gang or a fiend with a grudge against Italian grocers was whispered up and down Little Palermo as the city struggled to make sense of the latest killing.

Then, just a month after the Maggio murders, when the police still had hopes of stumbling upon a Reidel-case-like clue and running it to ground to find the killer, an axeman struck again. This time, however, the victims were not Italian.

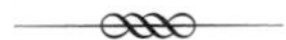

6:50 AM, June 26, 1918

Thursday morning dawned hot and humid. It was going to be another sweltering New Orleans summer day. But John Zanca wasn't thinking about the weather when he stopped his delivery wagon in front of the People's Cash Store, a grocery owned by an Eastern European immigrant named Louis Besumer.

The Besumer grocery.

Zanca stared at the shuttered store, puzzled. It was his usual time, but the little yellow grocery sat closed and bolted shut. Who was going to accept his bread delivery?

He jumped out of his wagon and knocked on the door. No answer. He knocked again, more forcefully. Nothing. He hammered on the door. When he still got no reply, Zanca walked from the store entrance on North Dorgenois Street around the corner to a door facing Laharpe Street that led directly into the grocer's residence.

Rapping on the door, at the same time he called out, *Is anybody home?* Finally, he heard footsteps on the inside shuffling toward him.

But the door still didn't open. Zanca strained to make out the muffled words from the other side: *Come around to the front.*

Zanca turned and walked again to the store entrance. The door of the grocery finally opened a crack, and Louis Besumer's unshaven face peered out. Usually a distinguished-looking man who tried to exude a sophisticated, European air, this morning the grocer looked aged and haggard. Zanca was startled to see that his face was streaked with blood.

"My God, what's happened?" gasped Zanca.

Grimacing slightly as he dabbed at his bloody head with a sponge, Besumer replied, "Nothing. Don't worry about it. There was an accident."

Has your wife been hurt? asked Zanca, concerned for the attractive black-haired woman who lived behind the store with Besumer.

The old man didn't know. When Zanca pressed him, Besumer brusquely told Zanca to check on her himself. Brushing past the grocer, Zanca hurried through the store into the residence and made his way down the hall to the second bedroom. There he found the woman lying blood-soaked and nearly unconscious in her bed. When she opened her eyes to see the young man leaning over her, she whispered, "I'm cold." Despite the hot day, Zanca looked around the room, grabbed some clothes off the floor, and tucked them around her as best he could.

Returning to the grocery store, Zanca told Besumer that he was going to call the Charity ambulance.

No, don't do that, Besumer responded hastily. *Just fetch a doctor.*

But she's cut up pretty bad!

Besumer gave up. "Suit yourself," he shrugged. He was pale and drawn, without the energy to argue. Zanca later told police that he seemed weak.

You should go lie down, Zanca suggested as he sped away to alert the nearest policeman.

Besumer was lying on his bed when a squad from the Fifth Precinct arrived at the grocery a few minutes later and entered the scene of what would later be called "one of the queerest [mysteries] in the annals of New Orleans crime."

The store fronted a two-bedroom residence with a hallway and a small, screened back porch at the end of the hall. On the porch, fresh blood pooled around a woman's hairpiece. The wooden handle of an ancient short-handled axe lay nearby; its rusty blade sat a good five feet away. Both were bloodstained. Bloody footprints led from the porch through the hall, into the bedroom, and right up to the bed where the woman still lay, covered in blood.

Realizing that he had another axe attack on his hands, the corporal in charge immediately notified his commander, who informed the superintendent of police. Before the morning was out Frank Mooney, Assistant DA Ben Daly, Coroner O'Hara, and a handful of detectives had congregated at the small grocery and residence.

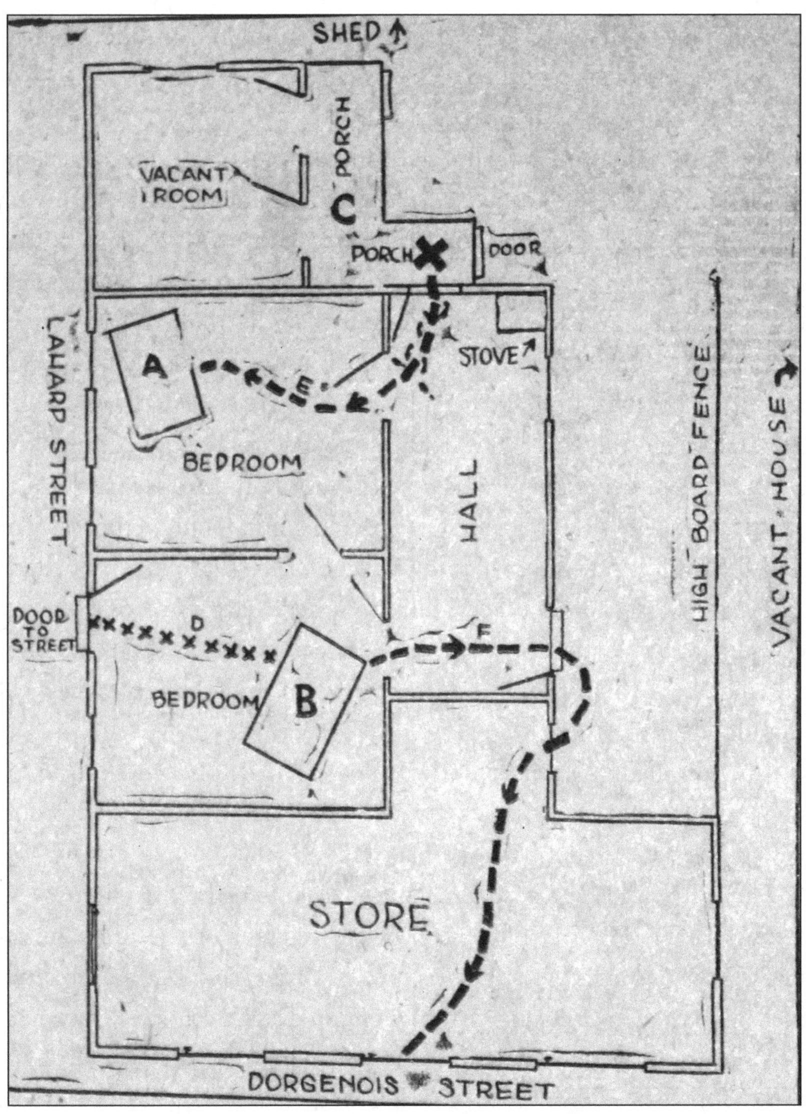

Sketch of the Besumer crime scene.

One of the first things investigators noted was the fresh blood: The attack must have occurred only a short time before, perhaps an hour before John Zanca's delivery wagon pulled up to the grocery. Its basic outline could be reconstructed without much difficulty: The woman had been struck on the porch so violently that the axe blade had flown off its handle. Somehow she'd managed to stumble from the porch to her room and collapse on her bed.

There was no sign of forced entry.

As the Bertillon operator busied himself fingerprinting the axe and photographing the bloodstains, detectives considered Mrs. Besumer's bedroom. (Later Louis Besumer explained that he and his wife had separate rooms because the noise of the electric fan that he ran all night kept Mrs. Besumer awake.) They noted that the room's windows sat right on Laharpe Street and were well lit by a nearby streetlight; anyone passing by on the busy street could see straight into the bedroom. If this attack, like the other axe attacks, had begun in the bedroom, the assailant risked being seen by passersby. And if an intruder had broken into the grocery, the policemen wondered, didn't the victims scream for help? And if they did, why didn't any of their neighbors hear them?

Next, investigators checked Louis Besumer's bedroom. Someone had gone through the contents of his dresser and wardrobe and left them scattered about the room, but nothing seemed to have been taken. The only blood in the room was on the pillow.

Robbery hadn't been a motive. No one had touched the grocery safe, and Mrs. Besumer's jewelry was still in the dresser; the cash in her pocketbook remained where she had left it.

James Reynolds was dead and John Dantonio had retired, but several of those inspecting the crime scene were veterans of the previous axe attacks. Dr. O'Hara was still the coroner, and George Long remained chief of detectives. Ben Daly, the assistant district attorney, had been at his job since 1909. The experience of men who had seen the Axeman's work before would no doubt prove valuable to the new police superintendent.

Leaving his capable detectives to untangle the scene at North Dorgenois and Laharpe Streets, Superintendent Mooney went to Charity Hospital to check on the injured couple. Both victims had head injuries. Besumer had a single wound, a long cut over his right eye. The blunt, rusty axe blade may have fractured his skull, but it was not, house surgeon Hiram W. Kostmayer assured police, a life-threatening wound.

The woman's injuries were much more serious. In addition to several gashes on her arms and chest, she had been hit twice on the head, cracking her skull. Severe brain trauma can damage the body's ability to regulate itself, which explains why earlier she had been so cold on such a hot day.

The seriousness of Mrs. Besumer's injuries made the police even more anxious to question her. Senior Captain Thomas Capo spoke to her as soon as the doctors would permit. Doped up on painkillers, she stared hazily at him when he asked what had happened.

I don't know, she replied.

Was there a fight on the gallery?

Oh, yes. A mulatto wanted to buy some tobacco after the store opened. When I told him that we didn't sell tobacco, he attacked me.

The attack had taken place before the store opened. Mrs. Besumer had been found in her nightclothes, not dressed to wait on customers. Her story couldn't be true. But Capo dutifully wrote it all down.

Frank Mooney himself interviewed Louis Besumer. The grocer told him that he was sixty years old, from Poland, and had lived in New

Louis Besumer.

York before moving to Jacksonville, Florida, about two years ago. There he met and married Harriet Anna Lowe. They'd bought the grocery after moving to New Orleans three months ago.

Besumer said that he didn't have a clear memory of what had happened to them the night before. He had woken to find himself bleeding and the door leading into Laharpe Street open. When he'd discovered his injured wife, he said, he covered her with a sheet.

Later police interviews with neighbors told Mooney even more about Besumer. He was a strange man with pretensions to culture and sophistication unusual in a small-time grocer. Claiming to speak thirteen languages, he bragged about being rich. Rumors circulated that he'd traveled extensively in Europe and Mexico, that he'd owned a coffee plantation in South America and a sheep farm in Kentucky. Everyone said that he sold groceries cheaply, too cheaply some thought. How could he stay in business if he sold below cost? No one knew where he got his money.

The neighbors couldn't, however, tell investigators much about the early morning events at the grocery. And as Mooney thought about it, several oddities struck him about the attack. If, as the detectives calculated, the assault had occurred between 6 and 7 AM, the neighborhood would have been awake and moving. Yet a canvas of the surrounding area revealed that no one—mulatto or otherwise—had been seen leaving the People's Cash Store early that Wednesday morning. No one had heard any screams or sounds of a struggle, or spotted any strangers. Someone had seen a light on about midnight. But when questioned, Besumer denied knowing anything about that.

And almost right away, Mrs. Besumer had contradicted part of her husband's story. At some point in her pain- and drug-induced daze on the morning of the attack, she had babbled to a policeman, "My husband is a German. He claims he is not. I don't know where he got the money to buy his store." And that made him a possible suspect as well as a victim.

Mooney quickly sent men to search Besumer's private papers. The search revealed letters and documents written, according to which newspaper one read, in Russian (the *States*), Yiddish and English (the *Times-Picayune*), or German, Russian, and Yiddish (the *Item*). At any rate, it was a foreign correspondence that sent police into spasms of patriotic suspicion. Rumors of code books and international intrigue immediately ignited and led to accusations that the grocer was, at the very least, involved in propaganda for the Germans. HATCHET MYSTERY MAY LEAD TO SPY NEST trumpeted the *Times-Picayune*. Federal authorities were contacted and informed about the possible threat to national security, and Mooney barred reporters from talking to the Besumers.

Mooney took the possibility of espionage seriously. Charges of being a German agent were no joke in the summer of 1918. The United States had entered the war in Europe in April 1917, and fear of German saboteurs led to the Espionage Act of 1917, the Sedition Act of 1918, and a steady stream of propaganda encouraging citizens to be on the lookout for enemy agents.

Anti-German hysteria soaked the country during the war years. German Americans everywhere came under suspicion. Books in German were burned, and schools abolished German language instruction. Those suspected of disloyalty could be forced to kiss the flag, beaten, or literally tarred and feathered. In Illinois, persecution spilled over into murder when vigilantes lynched an innocent young German immigrant.

Louis Besumer could very well have been both a Pole and a German. That is, Poland had ceased to exist as a state in 1795 when it was divided among Prussia (which would later become Germany), Russia, and Austria. Besumer might well have been an ethnic Pole born into German-controlled territory and, as such, might have spoken German but have no great love for the German Empire. Most Americans in 1918, however, wouldn't have understood these finer details of Polish and German history.

Suspicion that Besumer was an enemy agent made his situation precarious indeed. Perhaps, the *Times-Picayune* suggested, Besumer himself had attacked his wife when they had quarreled over his secret work. The police were determined not to be outsmarted by any of the "spy's" clever tricks: when Besumer sent his wife a bathrobe for use in the hospital, officers ripped out its lining, fruitlessly looking for secret messages.

Still, Superintendent Mooney thought he should make an effort to find Mrs. Besumer's mulatto, and so, the day after the attack he ordered the arrest of Lewis Oubichon, a light-skinned, sometime employee of Besumer's. Oubichon couldn't satisfactorily account for his movements the night before the attacks, so the police held him for several days. But since no other evidence against him surfaced, he was soon released.

Among the newsmen who clamored for the latest information on the investigation was James G. Coulton of the *Times-Picayune*. Only twenty-three, Coulton was already a seasoned crime reporter with a reputation for fairness and accuracy. He also possessed a keen sense of justice, a commitment that went beyond mere platitudes uttered in the pressroom. His sense of right and wrong would lead him to become more involved with the Axeman case than he would have ever suspected. But in June 1918, all he wanted to do—along with every other reporter in New Orleans—was get details about the Besumers.

Louis Besumer was released from Charity six days after the attack and the next day found himself in Frank Mooney's office, answering the superintendent's questions. For Mooney, it was an infuriating interview. For much of the two-hour conversation, the eccentric grocer seemed more interested in showing off his erudition than in helping the police find the person who'd attacked him. While he answered some questions, he also wandered off on irrelevant tangents, and Mooney had difficulty keeping him on topic. When Mooney asked him a simple, direct question about one of the languages he claimed to speak, Besumer just smiled and "proceeded to tell about the people who speak it and sketched out their history."

Besumer also insisted that he wanted to take an active part in the investigation. One can only speculate what Mooney thought to himself when the grocer solemnly informed him that he was a student of chemistry and criminology, "a born investigator" qualified to help solve the crime. "I am a man who leaves nothing undone," he informed

Superintendent Mooney. "I will not rest until the case is cleared up. I want to know who attempted to kill [us]."

Louis Besumer was a pompous bore. But was he a criminal?

Mooney eventually dragged some relevant information out of the grocer. Before the war he'd been a wholesaler, buying goods in bulk and reselling at a profit. His health suffered from constant travel and endless fattening restaurant meals, and he opened his grocery, he said, to follow his doctor's advice: get into a lower-stress business. Because of his knowledge of the wholesale market, he could buy staples like coffee and sugar in bulk and, to attract customers, undersell his rivals. But, he pointed out, "The other articles in my store I sold no cheaper—some things I sold even higher—than other stores."

Besumer also elaborated on his relationship with the woman everyone thought was his wife. One of the first things he had done when he was released from the hospital the day before was announce (perhaps prompted by the rumor that his ex-wife was in town) that Mrs. Besumer was actually "Mrs. Lowe," a divorcee. She was not his wife. He was divorced, he said, and his former wife lived in Cincinnati. The twenty-nine-year-old Harriet Anna Lowe, he maintained, was only a friend with whom he had a brotherly relationship.

Still in the hospital, Mrs. Lowe was alarmed when she heard about his confession. By Wednesday, almost a week after the attack, physicians at Charity thought she'd probably survive. By this time Mooney had lifted the ban on press interviews, and she was well enough to talk to reporters. Mrs. Lowe insisted to Jim Coulton that she was indeed Besumer's wife, that they had been married two years ago in New York.

Harriet Anna Lowe was a naive, good-natured woman, devout and perhaps not overly intelligent. At one time she'd been attractive, but the blows to her head had permanently disfigured her. Her facial nerves had been so badly damaged that she couldn't move one side of her face; one eye stared out sightlessly, the other "twitche[d] uncontrollably." Her head was swathed in bandages; wounds on her arms and chest were also bandaged.

Harriet Anna Lowe.

Mrs. Lowe readily admitted that her mind and her memory hadn't been clear since the attack, but she told Jim Coulton, "I feel sure he and I are married," adding plaintively, "If we are not, then I don't know what I'll do."

Undoubtedly, Jim Coulton couldn't help but feel sorry for her.

As the opiates and shock wore off, the sort of incoherent rambling Captain Capo had encountered when he first interviewed Mrs. Lowe dissipated. Her answers to police and reporters' questions were perfectly lucid. She retracted her story about being attacked by a mulatto but also emphatically denied that Louis Besumer had been the one to take an axe to her.

As her mind cleared, Mrs. Lowe remembered more and more details from the night of the attack. After ten days in the hospital, she could remember closing up the store about 7:30 PM. Going from the grocery into the back rooms, she saw Besumer sitting in front of the safe, counting the day's takings. She turned into the tiny dining room, carved out of the hallway, and the last thing she could remember was the smell of prunes simmering on the stove.

Then everything went blank. A hazy memory of a black-haired man towering over her in the early dawn light had burned itself into her consciousness, followed by the recollection of waking up in a pool of blood on the porch. She got a glimpse of a man's shoes moving around her. The next thing she knew she was in the hospital.

Neither Mrs. Lowe nor Besumer could identify a possible suspect. Besumer could only suggest business rivals angry because he undersold them. At the same time, he tried to convince Mooney that the motive was robbery, arguing that a brass lock on a trunk in his room showed signs of an attempt to break it open.

The federal government was also interested in the immigrant grocer and suspected spy. Two days after his interview with Superintendent Mooney, he was picked up by agents from the Department of Justice, the forerunner of the FBI, and interrogated about the letters discovered by the police. Whatever they got out of him, whatever arcane erudition he inflicted on them, wasn't enough to hold him, and after several hours Besumer again went home to his grocery.

Mooney's investigation suffered a setback a week after the attacks when he had to reprimand two of his detectives working on the case. They'd been assigned to Besumer, ostensibly to help him with his own investigation but more likely to keep an eye on him. But one day during working hours, they'd skipped off to a dancing pavilion in Milneburg, a popular resort on Lake Pontchartrain, where they'd become embroiled in a brawl. Mooney not only gave them a dressing down, but also demoted both to uniformed patrolman, an almost unheard of action in the New Orleans Police Department but part of his campaign to impose stricter discipline on the police force.

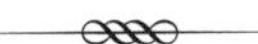

Many Orleanians speculated that the attack on Louis Besumer and Harriet Anna Lowe was connected to the Maggio murders, or even the whole previous series of axe and hatchet attacks. Newspapermen frequently mentioned the earlier attacks, even as mistakes in their articles showed that their memory of the details was a little foggy. Coming on the heels of the grisly slaying of Joseph and Catherine Maggio, the Besumer attack was naturally suspected of having some connection with the "fiend" who'd struck previously.

Initially, Superintendent Mooney had believed that the couple had been attacked by the Maggios' killer. As he mulled over the evidence, however, doubts began nagging at him. All the other victims were Italians. The victims in the Besumer attack were an Eastern European immigrant and an Irish American. Did it matter?

Aside from the question of ethnicity, however, this latest attack differed from earlier ones in important details. Most of the other attacks had occurred in sparsely populated parts of the city. But the Besumer grocery, only a few blocks from Esplanade Avenue, was in a heavily populated neighborhood. And the other attacks took place between 1 and 3 AM, the stillest time of the night, usually on moonless nights. The Besumer attack had come after sunup, between 6 and 7 AM (after a night during which the moon was out all night), just as the streets were beginning to stir and when the intruder ran a greater risk of being spotted. Yet no one had seen any strangers enter or leave the premises.

The Crutti, Rissetto, Davi, Andollina, and Maggio crimes all involved a break-in, and the victims were attacked while they slept. But Mooney had no evidence that anyone forced his way into the Besumer residence.

And Besumer and Mrs. Lowe had not been attacked in their beds. The blood evidence made clear that Mrs. Lowe had been attacked on the outside gallery: Not only did the quantities of blood pooled on the porch testify to this, but it was the only way to account for the blood spray pattern on the outside door. And the blood-smeared gallery door handle indicated that a bloody hand had grasped it and pulled it open after the attack. Later, Besumer would claim that the back doors and windows had been left open because it was so hot, but shortly after the crime, the *Times-Picayune* reported that he assured the police that the back door had been locked when he went to bed. Whoever had opened the door had done it from the inside.

Mooney wasn't sure where Besumer had been assaulted. Certainly not in his bed. It wasn't bloody enough. The only blood in the room were slight traces staining his pillow. Where was the blood spatter on the floor? The deep gash Besumer sustained would have bled profusely, and if he had been in his bed as he claimed, some of this blood should have ended up on the bedroom floor when he got up to answer John Zanca's knock. Moreover, Zanca had said that when Besumer had called to him, his voice had sounded as if it were coming from a distance, perhaps Mrs. Lowe's room, or from out on the porch, not his own bedroom as he had claimed.

And why was Besumer so slightly wounded compared to Mrs. Lowe? While he might have sustained a skull fracture, he'd only been hit once: he only had the one gash over his eye. But someone had made a real effort to smash her skull. In most previous attacks the full ire of the attacker had been aimed at the man rather than the woman.

Besides, Mooney found Besumer just plain shifty. The grocer had misled everyone about his relationship with Mrs. Lowe. Details of his story about living in Jacksonville hadn't checked out. He admitted to using aliases. No, Louis Besumer, or whatever his name was, could not be dismissed as a suspect.

Could Besumer have been the assailant?

Perhaps no one had seen a stranger in the vicinity that morning because no stranger had been in the house. Perhaps Mrs. Lowe struck

Besumer first, and he, wounded and enraged, grabbed the axe from her and chased her out onto the porch. If both were guilty, both had reason to keep silent about what had really happened. That would explain why Besumer didn't want the police or ambulance called. Mrs. Lowe told Mooney that Besumer had read about the Maggio case. Maybe he hoped that the attack in his home and grocery would be attributed to the same murderous fiend.

Mooney was convinced Mrs. Lowe wasn't telling him everything she knew, and the circumstantial evidence he had wasn't enough to make an arrest. The superintendent needed an eyewitness. If Besumer was to be charged, the woman's testimony would be crucial. Mrs. Lowe, however, refused to cooperate. So Mooney pursued other leads and bided his time.

On the fourteenth of July, as the city celebrated Bastille Day with a special fervor, given the American and French young men dying side by side in the war raging abroad, Louis Besumer arrived at Charity Hospital to take Mrs. Lowe home. After two weeks in the hospital, the doctors were ready to discharge her.

Besumer had reopened the People's Cash Store, and business, he boasted, was good. *Let us go back to the way things were,* he offered Mrs. Lowe. She had misgivings. By now she had conceded that they weren't married, either because her memory had cleared or because she'd decided it was useless to continue to pretend. But she had nowhere else to go. She had no family—other than an abusive ex-husband. Her mother was dead and her father and sister were in Ireland. Where else was she to go other than the little yellow grocery at Laharpe and North Dorgenois Streets?

The blows had left Mrs. Lowe mangled mentally as well as physically. In the days after returning home she showed classic signs of generalized anxiety and depression: she was shaky; she couldn't concentrate; she was indecisive. She'd give orders to Mrs. Sacriste, who'd been hired to nurse her and help with the cooking, and then countermand them. She spent hours each day on her knees obsessively praying, and having visions of Jesus Christ. Mrs. Sacriste worried about Mrs. Lowe's sanity.

Outwardly, relations between Besumer and Mrs. Lowe remained cordial, but something happened in the month after she left the hospital, something that made her fear Besumer. Maybe he threatened her. Perhaps as more and more of her memories fought their way to the surface and became clearer and clearer, she became more and more afraid of him.

Mooney didn't forget about Mrs. Lowe. He felt sure there was something she could tell him to help him close the case. He dropped by the People's Cash Store regularly to talk to her, taking Assistant DA Ben Daly with him. His efforts would eventually pay off. But not before another attack claimed the headlines.

Twenty-eight-year-old Mary Schneider was tired as she crawled into bed on the evening of August 4, 1918. Caring for three small children and expecting another any day was an exhausting business. Her husband Edward worked the night shift at the Southern Pacific wharf, so she was alone at their home at 1320 Elmira Street (now Gallier Street), in the Saint Claude neighborhood on the eastern edge of the city, with her children safely tucked into the other room, when she turned down the lamp and went to sleep.

Mary woke, days later, confused. This wasn't her bedroom. Where was she? How did she get here? Had the baby come yet? As she fought her way out of the opiate cloud that fogged her brain, Mary dimly remembered that her baby had been born, a girl, named Clara.

But why did her head hurt?

The Charity nurses summoned her husband Edward, who hurried to her bedside to explain. She'd been attacked in the night, he told her, and had been taken to Charity Hospital. She was in the maternity ward and the baby was safe. But now the police needed her to identify her assailant.

Did she see who had hit her? Did she know him? Shocked, Mary could only stammer, "Struck? Oh, no, I was not struck. Who said that anyone assaulted me?" She was even more surprised when Superintendent Mooney showed up at the maternity ward, detectives in tow, anxious to question her. But she could tell him nothing.

Gradually, as her mind cleared, she began to understand what had happened. Mary's sister Kate and her husband lived in one side of a double cottage; the Schneiders lived on the other. About two in the morning, Kate heard her sister scream. She shook her husband awake, and they rushed over to Mary's house to find her barely conscious, a nasty gash on her scalp and several of her teeth cracked and broken. Mary managed to say that she didn't know who had done this to her before she passed out.

Once the injured woman had been dispatched to Charity Hospital, Superintendent Mooney and Chief of Detectives Long took stock of the crime scene. They could find no evidence that the house had been broken into; none of the doors or windows had been smashed or pried open. But the wardrobe in the Schneiders' bedroom had been ransacked and its contents dumped on the floor. Questioning of Edward Schneider when he arrived home revealed that seven dollars was missing, but a tin box with a wad of cash—over a hundred dollars—hadn't been taken.

A broken lamp lying on the floor appeared to be the weapon used to batter Mrs. Schneider. The detectives spotted strands of hair caught in the prongs of the shattered lamp, and spots of oil that had been flung out as it smashed across her face stained the bedspread.

It looked like a straightforward burglary: an intruder rummaging through the wardrobe woke Mary Schneider, who might have been sleeping uneasily because of her pregnancy. When she screamed, he grabbed the nearest weapon—the lamp on the mantel—smashed her over the head with it, and fled.

But the citizens of New Orleans were primed to imagine more. After the recent Andollina, Maggio, and Besumer attacks, another mysterious attack in the dead of night wasn't going to be easily dismissed. No matter that the evidence indicated that the weapon used against Mrs. Schneider was a lamp, the *Times-Picayune* was first off the mark: POLICE BELIEVE AX-MAN MAY BE ACTIVE IN CITY.

Curious aspects of the case did make the more suspicious wonder if there wasn't a more sinister explanation than burglary gone wrong. An axe was missing, stolen from the Schneiders' shed, and a hatchet belonging to the couple had been dropped in the neighbor's yard. Most strangely of all, a couple of days after the attack, the Schneiders' eight-year-old daughter found one of her mother's skirts, stained with blood, stuffed under a doorstep a few houses away. But there was little evidence to connect this incident with the attacks on the Andollinas or the Maggios.

Young Jim Coulton, the *Times-Picayune*'s crime reporter, was most responsible for connecting the Schneider attack to the Axeman crimes in the public mind. Coulton became convinced early on of the existence of a single attacker, and his stories on Mary Schneider pushed that angle, even as he dutifully reported Superintendent Mooney's belief that the broken lamp had been the weapon. He cited police officers who opined "it probable that Mrs. Schneider was attacked by the hatchet-man who murdered Joseph Maggio and his wife and attempted to kill Louis Besemer and Mrs. Harriet Lowe." And the *Times-Picayune*'s headlines, POLICE BELIEVE AX-MAN MAY BE ACTIVE IN CITY and VICTIM OF AX-MAN NOW HAPPY MOTHER, contributed to the perception that the Axeman's taste extended to lonely mothers in addition to Italian grocers.

Over at the *States*, Andy Ojeda took a different tack, citing police who believed robbery more likely to have been the motive. Like Coulton, he'd entered journalism young—as a boy really, at seventeen—writing about cotton prices for the New Orleans *Daily News*, then working at the *Item* before joining the *New Orleans States* around 1907. Ojeda interviewed veteran detectives who scoffed at the notion that the attack on Mrs. Schneider was an "Axeman" crime. One—anonymously—told the *States*, "It is nothing more or less than a case of ordinary burglary, and the robber used some weapon upon Mrs. Schneider only when she either moved in her sleep or attempted to get up."

The *Item* steered a course between the two polarized viewpoints, reporting that some policemen believed the crime the work of a burglar, while others attributed it to "the axe man." But the paper was rather free with its headlines—AXE-MAN'S VICTIM CAN'T RECALL ATTACK, ARMED MEN GUARD SLEEPING FAMILIES FROM AXE-MAN, and AX-VICTIM TO

Be Taken to Her Home. No wonder many Orleanians assumed that Mary Schneider was, without question, another victim of the Axeman.

But Mary Schneider's nighttime visitor was unlikely to have been the Axeman. He targeted couples, usually injuring the man first and most severely. What's more, all his previous victims had been Italian grocers. Mary Schneider was neither male, nor Italian, nor a grocer. Her house was in the middle of the block, not at a corner, as were the other Axeman attacks. Her assailant hadn't used an axe or cleaver. The missing axe, misplaced hatchet, and bloodstained skirt were curious, but several detectives offered the explanation that they were a ruse to make the incident look like an Axeman attack.

But the headlines were enough to set off a minor wave of panic in the city, especially in neighborhoods near the crime scene, and most especially among Italians. Memories of the gruesome butchering of the Maggios were still fresh, and men too afraid to sleep stood guard at night over their sleeping families, loaded pistols or shotguns at the ready.

Superintendent Mooney hadn't made much headway in solving the Axeman crimes, but to calm fears, he sent regular police patrols through sparsely populated areas on the fringes of the city, the kind of neighborhoods the Axeman preferred.

The killer took note.

8

Axeman Hysteria

Experts argue that some serial killers carefully watch the news, enjoying the coverage of their crimes, relishing their notoriety, savoring the fear they inspire, and thrilling in the frisson of outwitting the police. How did the fiend react when he heard of another's attack attributed to him? Was he angry? Or flattered? Did he damn the stupidity of the police who could not catch him and the press who could not accurately identify him?

Such thoughts might have led the Axeman to slip up to 2336 Gravier Street during the night of August 10. In the empty lot next to the house, he looked around and picked up two boards, which he leaned against the fence. Then, he scrambled up and over into the backyard. In the shed behind the house, he found what he needed: the family's two axes. He selected the short-handled one and turned toward the house. A window at the back was open, and it was easy enough to crawl inside, axe in hand.

Fifteen-year-old Pauline Bruno lay in bed, unable to sleep, preoccupied with thoughts of the Axeman. From the papers, from the whispers of neighbors and customers and friends at work, she was painfully aware that the killer had a penchant for grocers. And Italians.

She turned over fitfully in bed, trying not to disturb her sleeping thirteen-year-old sister. What would keep the Axeman away from them?

She'd been born in Louisiana, but her mother and her thirty-one-year-old uncle Joe Romano had come from Italy. They all lived packed into the dingy double cottage at the corner of Tonti and Gravier. Pauline and her sister Mary were in one room, and Joe slept next door. Pauline's mother Lilly Bruno lived with her widowed daughter Rosie on the other side.

Together they managed to support themselves. Pauline worked in a candy factory. Rosie ran the little grocery in the front part of the house, trying to sell enough staples—beans, rice, and cigarettes—to bring in a little income. Uncle Joe was a barber, pulling in a much-needed fifteen dollars a week at the shop where he worked over on Canal Street. They were poor but not desperately so.

The Bruno home was in a crowded working-class neighborhood half a dozen blocks from Canal Street, not one of the less densely populated areas the Axeman seemed to prefer. But that thought gave Pauline little comfort. Her immigrant family was Italian, and they ran a grocery. No wonder she didn't sleep well.

Pauline finally nodded off into an uneasy slumber, but about 3 AM she awoke with a start. What was that? Some commotion in Uncle Joe's room? Then she heard a groan. Sitting up in bed, she looked up to see a man, a stranger, standing in the doorway. She screamed, waking Mary. Now both girls shrieked in utter terror. The figure in the door vanished.

As if in answer to their cries, Uncle Joe staggered out of his room, holding his bloodied head. In a stupor he sank into a chair in the small parlor next to their room. "Something has happened," he murmured to the girls. "My head hurts. Call for an ambulance." Then he slumped over in a faint.

The family was too poor to have a phone, and it was a neighboring grocer who rang Charity Hospital for an ambulance. By the time it arrived Joseph Romano had regained consciousness, and escorted by the Charity interns, the bloodstained barber made his own way out of the house to the waiting vehicle.

Superintendent Mooney and his men were on the scene within the hour, followed by the usual swarm of newspapermen. As grimly determined patrolmen spread out through the neighborhood searching for the attacker, and the Bertillon operator began fingerprinting the open window, Mooney and his detectives traced the intruder's path through the house. They noted the vacant lot next door and saw the open window in the rear of the house. In Joe Romano's bedroom, next to the kitchen, the bed and pillow were covered with blood. A bloodstained axe lay on the floor next to Romano's bed.

The assailant had fled through the kitchen, and on his way out he'd managed to rifle a pair of his victim's trousers before dropping it on the kitchen floor. Romano's pocketbook—the early twentieth-century version of a wallet—was missing.

Though shaken, Pauline was able to provide a description of the attacker: tall and heavily built, in a dark suit and black hat. She thought he was white, although she couldn't be positive. Even though he was

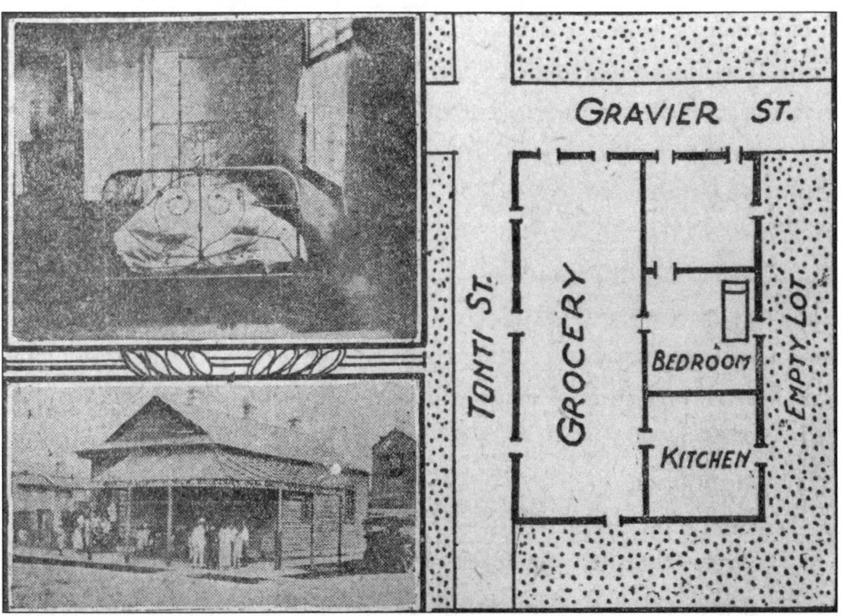

The grocery at the corner of Tonti and Gravier and the scene of Joseph Romano's murder.

a big man, when he fled, "He was awfully light on his feet," she said, adding, "I think he had rubber soles."

After an hour or so, word reached the family that Uncle Joe had died. At Charity Hospital, house surgeon Jerome Landry had immediately taken the badly injured man into the operating amphitheater, giving him just enough time to tell the doctor that he hadn't seen his assailant. Dr. Landry later told the police that Romano had been hit with a very sharp weapon: "The skull was not shattered but cut clean to the brain." Coroner O'Hara's report noted that he'd died of one blow to the head that had left a three-and-a-half-inch fracture in his skull. Joseph Romano survived less than two hours after being attacked.

This had the hallmarks of an Axeman murder. The Bruno-Romano household were the poorest victims yet, with a tiny little store. But the murderer's target remained the same. Romano was a barber, but he was the only male in a house with a grocery in the front room. Perhaps the Axeman had assumed that he ran the store. This attack differed from the Axeman's most recent exploits only in that he'd ventured into a more heavily populated neighborhood and that he'd found an open window and not needed to cut out a door panel. Perhaps Mooney's police patrols had driven him from his preferred hunting grounds into more dangerous territory.

Word of this most recent murder set off a full-scale panic among the population—and not only the Italians. Men who hadn't already done so rushed to arm themselves. Some began sleeping by day, guarding their families at night. Others banded together and shared the night watches, taking turns sleeping and standing sentinel. Husbands and fathers clutched buckshot-loaded shotguns, or nervously gripped Colt revolvers, jumping at every sound. A few fingered their triggers hopefully, longing for the murderer to choose their door that night.

In the meantime, Superintendent Mooney's investigations brought to light recent incidents no one had bothered to report earlier. Two weeks previously, Joseph Le Boeuf, a grocer only a block away from the Bruno-Romano residence, had chased away an intruder who tried

Cartoon in the Item *depicting Orleanians too terrified to sleep.*

to break in through his back door in the middle of the night. When he bolted, the intruder dropped an axe. A few blocks farther away, on Cleveland Avenue, Arthur Recknagle reported that he, too, had driven off a prowler who'd left behind an axe.

The police also identified three attempts to break into homes in the Gravier and Tonti neighborhoods just before Joseph Romano's murder that, in retrospect, they attributed to the Axeman. And Mooney's investigators discovered that the night after Joseph Romano's murder, a burglar had attempted to break into Al Durand's saloon at the corner of South Salcedo and Canal, not far away. He was in the process of chiseling a panel off a side door when something or someone scared him; he dropped his tools and ran. Durand woke the next morning to find an axe, a screwdriver, and a .38 caliber cartridge outside his door. The realization of what may have passed him by so unnerved the saloon-keeper that he refused to report it for fear the shock of it would kill his ill mother. A friend ultimately informed the police of the incident.

Frank Mooney was incensed. How could his detectives track down the murderer without all possible public cooperation? How many other incidents did he not know about? He immediately issued a statement demanding that the public alert the police to any potential clue that might lead to the murderer: any attempted or suspected break-in, any suspicious person skulking about the street late at night, anything that struck them as unusual or irregular. Mooney didn't temper his words: "I believe it is criminal for citizens to withhold such cases from the police," he declared. "To withhold information means to assist the axe man in his murderous work." The police needed the help of all New Orleans citizens, if they had any hope of catching "this blood-mad creature."

But nerves were so on edge that some people didn't need the chief's encouragement. Some went Axeman hunting on their own. The very day after Romano's murder, two overzealous public servants—a clerk in the criminal court and a deputy sheriff—crashed into the little shanty of Albert Alexander—a black man who, it was rumored, had been spotted chasing a young black girl with an axe. They dragged their quarry to the nearest police precinct station. Superintendent Mooney himself interviewed Alexander, concluded he was wholly innocent of Romano's murder, and turned him loose.

This wasn't the only "Axeman" spotting in the days immediately after Romano's death. The evening after the barber's murder, around midnight, a woman only four blocks from the Romano house spied a man meeting the description of the killer heading for her stable. Terrified, she raised the alarm, and within minutes armed, agitated neighbors poured out of their houses and commenced a manhunt. The posse gave chase, tracking the prowler over fences and through backyards before he melted into the warm August night air.

Other sightings followed. Early on August 16, six days after the Romano murder, three young men out on the town reported a man lurking near an Italian grocery. Before long, Chief of Detectives George Long had a dozen men on the scene searching the block, joined by armed residents of the neighborhood.

Other incidents followed, all carefully checked out by Mooney's men, all coming to nothing. Some wilder stories would have been amusing if they hadn't been fueled by desperate fear: the "Axeman" suspect reportedly disguised as a woman, only to turn out to be, in fact, a "badly frightened negro woman," or the police squad that responded to a hysterical caller who claimed to have seen the Axeman only to find a drunk chopping up his neighbor's porch steps for firewood.

A pattern targeting Italian shopkeepers did continue in the immediate aftermath of this latest killing, not a pattern of murder but of theft. Just over a week after Joseph Romano's funeral three Italian grocers were robbed in rapid succession by methods that echoed those of the Axeman. In the early morning of August 19, an intruder used an ice hatchet and pick to break into the living quarters of grocer Toney Caronna and his family at the corner of South Claiborne and General Taylor Streets. (He'd first picked up the family axe but decided against it, perhaps because it was too heavy.) He was in the process of stealing cash and a revolver from the bedroom, when Mrs. Caronna woke, saw him, and screamed. He ran. On the very next night, a burglar chiseled a panel out of the door of Frank Guarisco's grocery and saloon at the corner of Tchoupitoulas and Calliope and cleaned out the register, all without waking the family. The next evening—the third in a row—someone broke into Paul Lobella's drygoods store at the corner of Zimple and Cherokee using an iron bar, took eighty cents, and fled. The next morning an axe was discovered in the alley next to the house.

These break-ins were scattered all over the city, from Carrollton to downtown. Were any of these thieves the Axeman? Had he intended to attack the residents but was scared away in each instance? Or was murder for him just a sometime thing? Other criminals may have adopted the Axeman's—rather successful—methods for their own use.

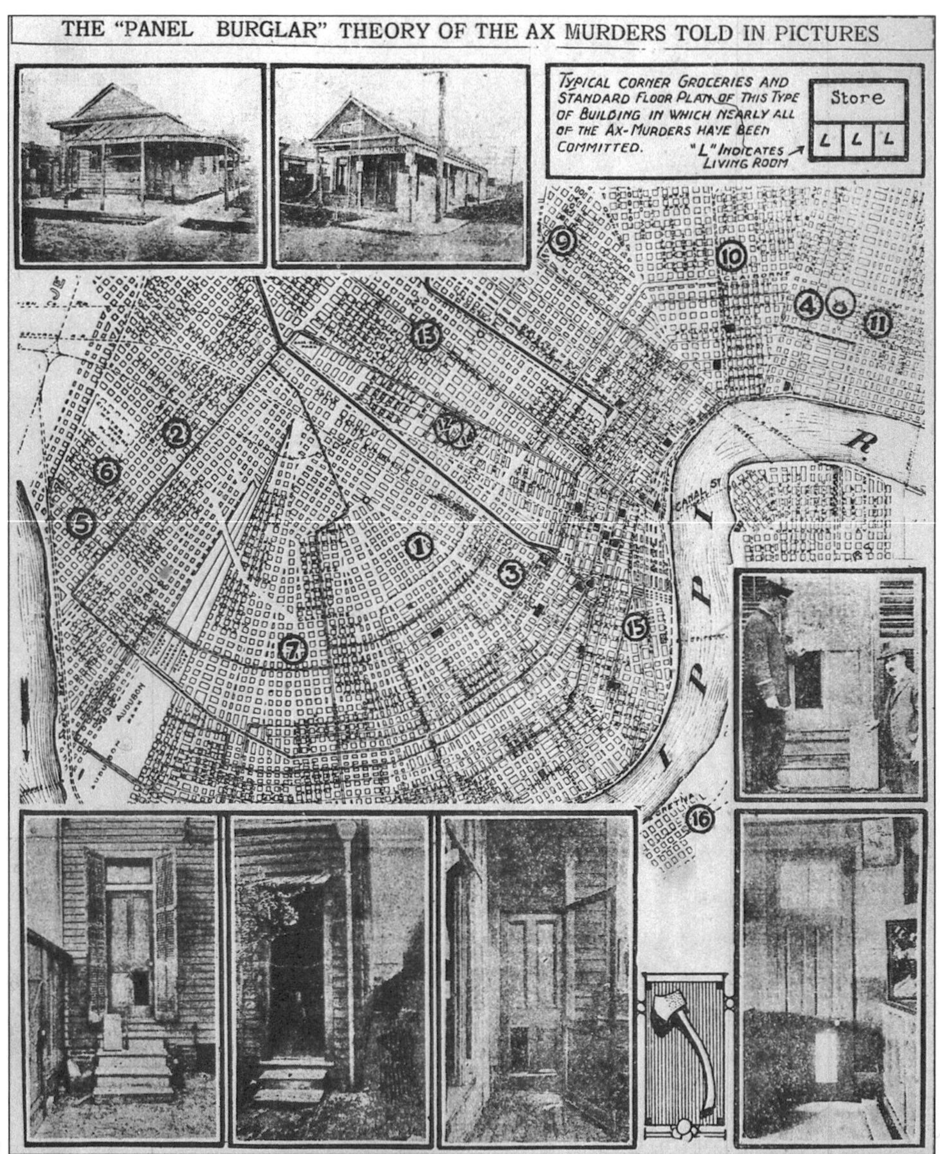

Times-Picayune *map showing Axeman attacks and panel burglaries.*

This was the beginning of a series of nighttime, Axeman-like burglaries that targeted Italians and non-Italians alike. For the next month at least, more than a dozen stores—not just saloons and groceries but furniture stores and stores that sold silverware, ladies' clothes, cologne, and furs—were robbed using what became known as the "Axeman method": the removal of a panel from a rear door. Frank Mooney, and probably much of the city, suspected that at least some of these incidents were Axeman jobs. They did nothing to calm the fears of the city.

Frank Mooney was getting desperate. He was facing, as the *Item* put it, "scathing criticism" from the public for his inability to catch the killer, and his "exhaustive investigation" of the Romano murder was getting exactly nowhere. He continued to reassure the public that it was only a matter of time until the Axeman was caught; he couldn't very well admit that the murderer had the run of the city. But how was he going to stop him?

Mooney sent patrols out to cover the city as well as he could with his small police force, the downtown neighborhoods where anxiety had been so high lately, and especially the "thinly settled sections" the Axeman seemed to prefer. The killer had shifted from the edge of town to downtown, and Mooney had a hunch that all the heat might drive him elsewhere. How right he would turn out to be.

Just days after Joseph Romano's murder, newspaperman Jim Coulton sought out former detective John Dantonio to ask his opinion on the recent attacks. He'd no doubt heard that Dantonio, the expert in Italian crime, had been involved with the Cleaver attacks years before. For his part, retired for over a year and now in poor health, Dantonio was probably delighted that his advice was sought.

Fifty years before the term *profiler* came into use, Dantonio provided a remarkably perceptive analysis of the killer. "This is very probably the man we tried to get ten years ago," he told the young reporter. "The murderer is likely a Jekyll and Hyde personality, like Jack the Ripper. A criminal of the dual personality type may be a respectable, law abiding citizen when his normal self. Then suddenly the impulse to kill comes upon him and he must obey it." Perhaps, the detective speculated, the

Axeman had been dormant for several years but now his dark side had reasserted itself.

No longer a public servant, Dantonio didn't feel an obligation to reassure the city. He warned that the police were unlikely to bring the murderer to justice, admitting that these killers, who planned their attacks very carefully, were hard to catch.

For Dantonio, the key to all the attacks was the victims' residences: "The homes of all the victims look alike. The Axeman apparently picks them out because of the resemblance which impresses him." Although Dantonio realized that most of those targeted were Italians, he doesn't appear to have considered this key to selecting the victims; he believed that the Axeman had attacked Mary Schneider, although he offered no opinion on the Besumer case.

Superintendent Mooney couldn't have been pleased by Dantonio's admission that the killer would be all but impossible to catch. In his efforts to catch the murderer, Mooney had immersed himself in the science of "fiends." He'd read up on current criminology and talked to local experts, hoping to find some nugget that would lead him to the killer. His own views came to mirror Dantonio's so closely that it's difficult not to believe that he also consulted the retired detective. Gradually the superintendent's views took shape: Robbery wasn't the Axeman's motive; he opportunistically grabbed small amounts of cash to throw off investigators. The crimes were the work of a madman, an insane killer in the grip of a depraved lust for blood, one who could nevertheless look and act normally until his obsession overcame him. He was a sadist, and likely a narcotics addict. Mooney sent two detectives to Joe Romano's wake in the event that the killer showed up to savor his kill.

But Mooney doesn't seem to have been persuaded by all of Dantonio's theory. The retired detective surmised—probably correctly—that the Cleaver of 1910–1911 was also the Axeman. Witnesses from that series of attacks—Harriet Crutti and Mary Davi—described the Cleaver as white. But for reasons unclear, a black man had become Mooney's favorite suspect: Charles Anderson, who'd served two prison terms for robbery. If Mooney was looking for a black man for the crimes of 1917–1918, he wasn't convinced his killer was the killer of earlier years.

The superintendent's efforts didn't end with consulting criminologists. Mooney also conferred with police in other cities and turned to private security agencies. Rumor said that he had even involved the famous Pinkerton detective agency. He wanted the public to be confident that the police were doing all they could to catch the killer, assuring the newspapermen in a steely tone: "Take this for the gospel: We're going to get him yet! I'm doing everything in human power to run down this murderous maniac. . . . We're going to get him."

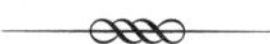

Not everyone was terrified of the Axeman. Those who didn't feel threatened by the killer could treat him as a joke. On August 23, a large ad appeared on page 5 of the *Times-Picayune*. "Attention Mr. Mooney and All Citizens of New Orleans," it read. "The Axeman Will Appear in This City on Saturday, August 24th. . . . He will ruthlessly use the 'Piggly Wiggly' axe in cutting off the heads of all High Priced Groceries. His weapon is wonderful and his system Unique. Don't miss seeing him."

The Piggly Wiggly grocery store chain had introduced self-service in 1916. No need for a nice Mr. Jordano to wait on customers. A housewife could now help herself to a can of tomato sauce or a jar of olive oil. The popularity of self-service grocery stores would eventually mean the growth of the supermarket and the end of the corner groceries. This would take some time, but for now Piggly Wiggly made a tasteless joke at the expense of the neighborhood grocers it would replace.

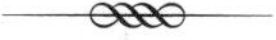

Superintendent Mooney's patience was rewarded. A month after she'd left the hospital, looking over her shoulder to make sure she wasn't seen, Mrs. Lowe stepped out of the store onto Laharpe Street and flagged down a passing policeman. She told him that she needed to see Superintendent Mooney at once. *But Mr. Besumer must not know*, she insisted.

This was what Mooney had been waiting for. Anxious not to spook his witness, he arranged for the grocer to be lured away for a couple of hours. Mooney, Assistant DA Ben Daly, two representatives of the Department of Justice, and a handful of policemen drove out to the grocery. *The cloud has lifted from my mind*, she told them when they arrived. *I now know that it was Besumer who attacked me.*

And she had something to show them. Mrs. Lowe led them to a trunk she said belonged to Besumer. Opening it, she showed them a cleverly concealed secret compartment in which, she claimed, he kept mysterious blueprints. Whatever documents the grocer had stashed there would later prove not to be incriminating, but a search of his clothes revealed a honeycomb of secret pouches.

Later that day, over the whir of an electric fan, Mrs. Lowe told her story to Mooney and the assembled throng of officials and newspapermen that crowded into his office. Shifting nervously in her chair like someone on the verge of a panic attack, her black hair plastered to her face with sweat, and glancing fearfully at the doorway from time to time, she said that she finally remembered what had happened that night.

"I met Mr. Besumer in Jacksonville, Florida," she began, with the inflection of the second-generation Irish, "through a newspaper advertisement. I had advertised for a position as housekeeper." She knew that Besumer was Jewish, but other than that, Mrs. Lowe didn't know much about him. He made frequent trips on mysterious business that he refused to discuss. She knew that he used a number of aliases and wasn't even sure "Besumer" was his real name. She had told them earlier that he didn't like to be questioned and he had such a nasty temper that she'd learned not to ask about his business. Mrs. Lowe wasn't really the curious type anyway. She had a roof over her head and food to eat, so even if Besumer was bad-tempered and peculiar, she didn't worry too much about it.

Then, three months before the attack, Besumer shaved off his beard and moved to New Orleans, taking Mrs. Lowe with him and telling her she'd now be going by the name "Besumer."

Around 7:30 PM, on the night of the assault, Besumer had just closed the store and was going over some blueprints when Mrs. Lowe entered the grocery and asked for money he owed her. She hadn't been paid for months. But he shot her such a nasty look that she, knowing his temper, backed away and turned to leave. She heard him say, "You'll get your money and more too" and then felt what she described as "a thousand bricks . . . hit[ting] her on the head." She passed out and when she came to, heard him say something strange: "Annie, you are going to make a fire in the ocean for me." She remembered being dragged through the house and undressed on the bed but then blacked out again until she woke up covered in blood.

When she got out of the hospital, Mrs. Lowe said, Besumer offered to marry her, at the same time that he warned her against talking to Superintendent Mooney. She remained in a fog, confused and unsure about the events that had put her in the hospital, but four nights ago the cloud lifted and it all suddenly began to come back to her: "As I lay in bed," she said, "the street light shown through my door and Mr. Besumer appeared in the doorway. Then my memory started to return by degrees. I felt the horror again and became frightened."

How did Besumer get hurt? Mooney wanted to know. She said she didn't know. Perhaps he hit himself, one of the other policemen suggested, in order to make his story more believable. Another suggested that Mrs. Lowe's wages had nothing to do with the attack; perhaps he'd tried to kill her because she'd caught him with the mysterious blueprints. Dr. Metz, the city chemist, had identified bloodstains on the hidden compartment in Besumer's trunk. Maybe she'd seen something he didn't want her to see.

Whatever the reason for the assault, Mrs. Lowe was visibly frightened of Louis Besumer. Although she was moved into a house where she'd be safe, her nerves became so frayed that she neared a breakdown. Two days later, she returned to Charity Hospital.

Mooney had Besumer arrested. Under interrogation, the grocer was as talkative and glib as ever. He laughed at the accusation that he was a secret agent. *That's ridiculous*, Besumer said. *I was born in Poland. I have no love for the Germans. I have two sons in the army!* He could explain everything. The secret compartment in his trunk and secret pockets in his clothes were for hiding important papers and cash. Likewise, he said, he sometimes found aliases useful in his business. Or sometimes in his pleasure, as he implied when he claimed to have switched to the name "Harrison" at one time to avoid a woman who, he added confidentially, "gave me some trouble."

About the night of the attack, his answers remained the same: He went to bed at the usual time and knew nothing until the bread man pounded on his door. He had nothing bad to say about Mrs. Lowe, only that she was of a "peculiar disposition." He repeatedly denied that he had struck her. No amount of questioning could dent his claim of innocence.

Besumer was charged with attempted murder and clapped into the parish prison. A few days later, he appeared for a bail hearing in the Second City Criminal Court. Superintendent Mooney and Agent W. C. Stillson of the Department of Justice wanted to make certain that Besumer remained in jail and within their reach. With his habit of aliases, there was too much risk he'd leave New Orleans, change his name again, and vanish. Attempted murder was a bondable offense, so after he made bail on the murder charge, Mooney had him immediately rearrested on a D&S charge—as a "dangerous and suspicious character."

Still on the edge of a nervous breakdown, wracked with anxiety, Mrs. Lowe was readmitted to the hospital five weeks after being released. And nerves were not her only problem: her head wound was not healing properly. After she'd been hospitalized for about two weeks, doctors decided that a piece of bone in her skull needed to be removed to relieve the pressure on her brain. The operation itself was successful, but she contracted pneumococcal meningitis, an infection of the lining of the brain and spinal column, most likely caused by bacteria introduced as a result of her fractured skull.

By the end of the first week of September, Mrs. Lowe was failing fast. A priest gave her the last rites. She asked to see Superintendent

Mooney one final time. As she lay in her hospital cot, knowing that she was dying, she again accused Louis Besumer:

> I feel that I am going to die. The statement that I make to you that Louis Besumer struck me with an axe is correct. I am not mistaken. I don't know what he struck me with in the grocery, but he struck me with an axe in the hall. He was in a nude form. He had no clothes on at all. I gave him no cause to strike me. I asked him for my money. I saw him with the axe in his hand before he struck me. I saw his arm coming down and felt the stunning blow. I can't be mistaken about this. I would not tell a story about him. I don't know why he struck me.

She rallied briefly, then died suddenly ten days later. Besumer, about to be released from his twenty-day sentence, was immediately charged with murder.

Louis Besumer—or whatever his real name was—almost certainly was Mrs. Lowe's murderer. The lack of evidence of an intruder doesn't leave much room for any other conclusion. His story of waking up dripping blood, with no evidence of blood on the bed or the floor, was transparently a lie.

Why, then, did Louis Besumer try to kill Harriet Anna Lowe?

In the weeks after his arrest the New Orleans papers reported that investigators believed Besumer attacked Lowe when she caught him with secret documents. The *New Orleans States* reported the discovery of spots of blood on his secret drawer and evidence that someone had tried to remove the blood by washing and then by scraping it off. Nothing ever came of the charge that Besumer was a German agent, so his secret drawer probably held sensitive business or personal papers, rather than anything related to national security. But investigators and newspapermen thought national security a more exciting reason for attempted murder than the usual squalid lovers' quarrel.

Whatever his motive, Louis Besumer, not some mysterious killer, took an axe to Harriet Anna Lowe. Her description of his highly inflated self-image and easily provoked, violent temper fit the profile of an abusive husband or partner. Writing over thirty years later, Robert Tallant, who probably relied on the accounts of reporters or policemen who'd been around at the time, reported that neighbors had heard Besumer and Lowe bicker—violently—about money and his jealousy.

It's easy to imagine that they got into a fight about who knows what—money, marriage, jealousy, his secret dealings, whatever. Perhaps he shoved her. Maybe he slapped her. Possibly, he did worse. To defend herself, Mrs. Lowe grabbed the first handy weapon, a knife or a meat cleaver, and struck Besumer in the head, a hard blow that sliced into his scalp above his right eye, a wound that could be mistaken for an axe wound. (Maybe she was even strong enough to wield the axe, although it's easier to believe she used a smaller and lighter weapon.) Besumer staggered under the blow, then recovered. He reached up to touch his forehead, then stared in disbelief at the blood on this hand. Realizing what she did, Mrs. Lowe froze in terror. She knew he would make her pay for this mistake. She turned to flee; she had to get away from him. Enraged, he chased her out onto the porch where he grabbed the axe and hit her, cracking her skull.

Perhaps afterward he cooled off quickly when he realized how badly she was wounded. What was he to do? He'd read about the Maggio attacks. He didn't have much time to formulate a plan, and he was still reeling from his own head wound, but he took a sheet (to protect himself from the blood), wrapped her in it, picked her up, and carried her to her bed.

When John Zanca, driver of the bread wagon, showed up on his doorstep, Besumer wasn't keen for him to call the police or an ambulance, but there was nothing he could do. The grocer didn't have many choices at this point, and the best he could do was keep his mouth shut, claim to have slept through the whole incident, and feign bewilderment that Mrs. Lowe was found half dead in her bed. And fervently hope everyone attributed this attack to the Axeman.

Mrs. Lowe's story wasn't exactly airtight either. When she first claimed that a mulatto had attacked her, she'd been pumped full of opiates. Later, because of shock or a genuine loss of memory, she was likely telling the truth when she said she couldn't remember who attacked her. However, she may well have suspected Besumer. But when questioned by police, she denied that such a thing could occur, like many abused women, then and now.

When she finally implicated Besumer, her story was, understandably because of her head injury, disjointed and incomplete, with scraps of memory interspersed with periods of blackness. She could recall being dragged into the hall, lying bloody on the porch, and being carried to her bed; a glimpse of a man's feet, clad in heavy black shoes, flickered off and on in her memory. But she couldn't fit all the fragments together into a coherent narrative.

Her recollections didn't always fit the physical evidence. Lowe said that Besumer attacked her with the axe in the hall, but the blood on the porch told a different story. She said that the attack occurred on the evening of June 25, but the fresh blood evidence indicated that it had taken place on the morning of June 26, shortly before they were discovered. These inconsistencies, strangely enough, make her story more believable. Surely deliberate lies would have been more coherent.

Mrs. Lowe also denied any knowledge about how Besumer came by his injury. One doesn't have to believe her denial to believe that the rest of her story was accurate—or at least as accurate as her fragile memory would allow. The detail that Besumer was nude raises some interesting possibilities. One might be tempted to dismiss it as the result of delirium brought on by meningitis in her final days, but the accusation was reported by the *New Orleans States* almost a month before her death, just after she defected from Besumer to Mooney, and before she entered the hospital for further treatment. Perhaps before Zanca's arrival, Besumer stripped himself of his bloody clothes and disposed of them. Since the police didn't always make thorough searches of crime scenes, they might not have found them. Why else would she include such an odd—and to an early twentieth-century audience—disturbing detail in a deliberate lie?

Readers also shouldn't dismiss the idea that Lowe's memories were the result of weeks of relentless badgering by Superintendent Mooney. Memories are not concrete realities that just need to be accessed. They are a *creation* of the mind and are influenced by a good deal more than what actually happened in the past. Memories can be manipulated and distorted, even created, by suggestive questioning. If Mooney had become convinced that Besumer was the attacker, his relentless questioning of Mrs. Lowe might well have shaped her recollection of events.

This possibility, however real, doesn't change the physical evidence, and the conclusions to be drawn from it: there was no intruder, and the attack differed in significant ways from the modus operandi of the Axeman. Then, as now, women were much more likely to be killed by an intimate than by a stranger.

Harriet Anna Lowe died on September 16, 1918, and Louis Besumer was charged with her murder the same day. Conveniently, he was still in jail, still serving a "dangerous and suspicious" sentence.

But Joseph Romano's death enormously complicated Mooney's case against Besumer. If there was an axe-wielding fiend in New Orleans, and if said fiend had killed both Lowe and Romano, Louis Besumer manifestly couldn't be guilty. But despite firmly believing that there was an Axeman at work in the city, Mooney was also convinced that he had a solid case against the Polish grocer.

Usually, Besumer would have gone to trial within months of being indicted, but his prosecution ground to a halt when the Spanish flu hit in the fall of 1918. Before it had run its course, Spanish influenza killed 30 million people worldwide in less than a year. The disease arrived in New Orleans on the oil tanker *Harold Walker* in the third week of September, just as Besumer was arrested for murder. Health authorities didn't know exactly how many cases New Orleans had because physicians, overwhelmed fighting the epidemic, reported the numbers only haphazardly. On October 9, the city health officer estimated that there were some 8,000 cases in the city. From October 8 to 20, at least 24,711 new flu cases were reported.

Hospitals were quickly swamped as beds filled and more came. The Moose lodge, the Knights of Columbus hall, and the Home for Destitute Boys all became temporary hospitals.

City officials fought to bring the epidemic under control. To limit transmission of the disease, city health authorities ordered public places closed—schools, churches, movie theaters, and dance halls. They even threatened to close saloons before new cases of the flu began to decline by the end of October.

Under such circumstances, investigation into the Axeman murders almost certainly slowed down. The police who weren't ill with the flu themselves would have been too busy enforcing health regulations to follow up on crime leads. Still, perhaps Mooney's efforts after Joseph Romano's murder had made New Orleans too hot for the killer.

The Axeman moved across the river.

9

The Mysterious Axeman's Jazz

Grocer Iorlando Guagliardo, of Convent, Louisiana, married in 1883, waiting until he was thirty-two years old and able to support a family. Lillie Billa, his bride, was nineteen. Two baby boys died at birth, both named Frank for Iorlando's father Francisco. But by 1894 the couple was blessed with the birth of Mary, and then in 1899, another girl christened Anna but known to everyone as Lena. Finally, in 1901, the boy named Frank whom Iorlando so badly wanted arrived; Louis followed in 1906.

After years in Saint James Parish, Iorlando decided to try his luck elsewhere. He briefly moved his family to Garyville, a small town in Saint John the Baptist Parish, before finally settling forty-five miles down the Mississippi in Gretna, a tiny community across the river from New Orleans. There, sometime between 1909 and 1911, he bought a grocery store—a modest little wooden structure—on the corner of Jefferson and Second Streets. At some point in his mercantile career, Guagliardo took the name Benedict Jordano when he bought a store and decided not only to keep the original owner's name on the business but to take it for himself. *Jordano* was easier on the American tongue than *Guagliardo*. That is how he was known in Gretna.

Years of constant labor and sixteen-hour days took their toll. By 1916, at age sixty-five, Iorlando was an old man. Gray and stooped, his eyesight was failing. His back was stiff with rheumatism and ached

Iorlando Jordano.

badly most days. He was "all crippled up," as his wife described him. Standing in the store all day was now out of the question. Responsibility for the business fell almost entirely on Lillie. Although she was only fifty in 1916, she, too, became unwell. Her doctor had to order her to stop working or, he said, "it would just kill her."

Their daughter Lena considered what to do. Her older sister Mary had married and started her own family. Frank and Louis were still in school. As the eldest daughter left at home, running the house fell mostly to her. Now, at seventeen, she was also running the grocery—and it was too much. She told her parents to lease the store; she would get a job. That's how she came to be at Penick & Ford, a mile and a half up the river in Amesville, labeling cans of Brer Rabbit Molasses.

The Jordanos leased the building and sold its contents to a young couple who only kept it for a few months before selling the business to Charlie and Rosie Cortimiglia.

Charlie Cortimiglia—his given name was Vincenzo, but *Charlie* was a common Americanization—was another Italian laborer whose goal had been to run his own place. He'd been born in Italy, and by the time he was twenty-five he'd saved enough to go into business for himself.

His wife Rosie was a native Louisianan, born in Plaquemine Parish in the extreme southeast of the state. Dark-haired and black-eyed, she was pretty in a young and robust and ruddy sort of way, what the newspapers called "a pronounced Italian type." A merry girl who laughed easily, she'd never been to school, but she could read Italian. Like many girls with few options, she'd wed young, marrying Charlie in 1913 when she was only fifteen. In 1917, she gave birth to a daughter, Mary, who became the particular pet of next-door neighbor Frank Jordano.

Frank Jordano had grown to be a hulking bear of a young man with a booming voice, black-haired and pink-cheeked and maybe a little cocky. One man described him as "of a manly bearing," which might have been another way of saying that he was big: at seventeen, he stood over six feet tall and weighed 275 pounds. Frank had the makings of a hard-headed businessman, but he was also a gentle, soft-hearted boy and loved to play with baby Mary every day after work. A photograph of the two of them shows the teenager lovingly cradling the toddler, an expression of delight lighting up his face.

Frank was an intelligent boy, but school hadn't interested him, and at fourteen he'd quit to enter the real estate business. Italians tended to prize work over education, and many sons of immigrants traded in school for a job when barely in their teens. Frank sold real estate for a while, and when the land market turned soft, he turned to selling insurance. He never showed much interest in the grocery business. He wouldn't be a small shopkeeper his whole life; Frank was fiercely ambitious and had a gift for salesmanship that would serve him well in the business world.

Frank's responsibilities and ambitions had matured him early, and he already had a serious girlfriend, Josie Spera. They'd gotten engaged on Christmas Day in 1918 and planned to marry when Josie's soldier brothers came home from the army. They set March 19, Saint Joseph's Day, as their wedding day.

Frank Jordano holding Mary Cortimiglia.

Meanwhile, the Jordanos decided that they needed their grocery business back. Why, exactly, is unclear. Lena later testified that she was about to lose her factory job, and so she decided to take over the store again. But perhaps she didn't want to furnish Frank with a motive for murder. Iorlando told a reporter that his wife wanted Frank to have the store so that he'd have enough money to get married.

At any rate, take it back they did in December 1918, to the annoyance of the Cortimiglias, who weren't at all gracious about it. Charlie and Rosie were doing a good business in this location and dragged their feet about relinquishing the property. When the Jordanos finally served them with an order to vacate, Charlie relocated his store just a few blocks away. But he wasn't willing to permanently give up his spot on Jefferson Street. He bought a vacant lot next to the Cortimiglias and built his own store at the corner of Jefferson and Second Streets, which opened in late February 1919. Some people said that the business, only open a couple of weeks before the attack, was already doing so well that Charlie was cutting into the Jordanos' trade. But if there had been a cooling of the friendship between the two families, there was no cooling in the affection between little Mary and big Frank.

After the Jordanos took over their grocery again, it was Lena and her mother—whose health had apparently improved—who ran it. Iorlando couldn't help much. Maybe he went into the store once a week when he felt up to it, but he had to lie down much of the time because of his back. The old man raised chickens, and he had a little garden he worked in when his rheumatism would let him. But mostly he took it easy.

On the evening of Saturday, March 8, 1919, Mrs. Jordano closed the store as usual at 10 PM. Shortly afterward, she sat at the kitchen table tallying the day's receipts when a hungry Frank came in the door.

"Mama, have you got anything to eat?" he asked.

"No," she replied, not looking up from her counting. "It was too busy in the store today for anyone to cook. We ate sandwiches. If you want something to eat, take the key and go to the store to get yourself something."

Frank was annoyed. It was hardly worth the bother. "Oh, hell!" he grunted. "If I have to go in the grocery now to get something to eat I won't go, I'm going to bed."

But he didn't go to bed immediately. When his parents got into their bed, he went to kiss them both good night. And he asked his mother about a frightening dream that his girlfriend Josie had had, a dream that she was standing in front of a door surrounded by writhing, squirming snakes. *Did it portend evil?* he wanted to know. Events later that night would suggest that it did.

The house was just settling down for the night when, about 11 PM, Iorlando heard his dogs barking furiously. Was someone trying to steal his chickens? He'd better look. His wife was tired after her long day, and they were his chickens anyway. He slowly and painfully got out of bed, fumbled with his spectacles, and hobbled out the kitchen door. He checked on the chickens and his little goat. Everything was in order. He looked around the yard. Nothing out of the ordinary. Reassured, he went back into the house and went to bed.

He slunk down the alleyway separating the two houses, board fences on either side of him. Behind one fence, the dogs sensed a newcomer, someone who didn't belong, and howled. The man wasn't worried. Once he was in the backyard, the wooden fence surrounding it would protect him from view. No one would pay any attention to the barking of a few dogs. He slipped over the fence into the yard. A half-grown puppy—a black and tan mixed breed—looked up from where he slept and glared menacingly at the newcomer. The man ignored the dog; it was too small to worry about. Pulling up a chair he discovered in the backyard, he checked through the bedroom window that his prey was indeed there. Then he looked around and found the axe he needed. Picking it up and pulling out a screwdriver, he crouched in front of the kitchen door. With the blunt side of the axe head, he began—as quietly as he could—hammering the screwdriver tip into the side of one of the lower panels.

Barking dogs woke City Councilman Manny Fink up at ten minutes to three. But once fully awake, he heard something else. Knocking. As if someone was rapping on a door. Then it stopped. A short pause. It started up again. Then it resumed—*tap, tap, tap, tap*. Careful not to wake his wife, Manny got out of bed, grabbed a lantern, and went out into his backyard. He held up the light, scanning the yard. Nothing. He went back inside and through to the front door, turning on the electric houselights as he did so. When he opened the front door and the light from the house spilled outside, the tapping abruptly stopped. Then a dog yelped. As if it had been kicked, Manny thought.

The fiend saw a light flicker on from somewhere across the street. He paused, holding the axe poised in the air over the screwdriver. The small dog took courage and edged menacingly toward the intruder, snarling. The man stood up and aimed a kick at the little fellow, who yelped in pain and fright before retreating, whimpering, toward the far side of the yard.

Manny walked out onto his front gallery and peered across Jefferson Street, first in one direction and then in the other. He could see the Cortimiglia place, about half a square down from him, the front of the property and the fence that surrounded it. Now he heard nothing except the normal nighttime summer sounds. Manny turned and went back into the house. After a few minutes, he heard it start up again—*tap, tap, tap*. What was it? Well, whatever it was, it wasn't on his property. Manny shrugged and went back to bed.

When the light switched off, the fiend waited a few minutes, until he felt it was safe to resume. Patiently, he chiseled at one side of the panel, and then the other, until he could pry it off and toss it to the side. Reaching through the small hole he had created in the door, he reached inside and up and unbolted the door. He paused and took off his boots. In his stocking feet, clutching the axe, he went inside.

Sheriff Louis H. Marrero had a firm grip on Jefferson Parish. He presided over a Regular Democratic machine that had kept him in power for over twenty years and given him a reputation as boss of the "Free State of Jefferson." Although he was a colonel only in the United Confederate Veterans, with his gray goatee and Panama hat, Marrero looked every inch the Confederate colonel, wealthy landowner, and powerful politician.

The end of the Civil War had found the eighteen-year-old Marrero a penniless veteran, but marriage to the daughter of a prominent Louisiana sugar and cotton planter improved his fortunes considerably. He entered politics in Jefferson Parish in 1883. First elected sheriff in 1896, Marrero was now in his sixth term and ruled the Free State of Jefferson with an iron fist.

He'd used his position to enrich himself considerably. His enemies accused him of corruption, extortion, embezzling tax money from the parish, and illegal gambling. That Marrero's own son Louis Jr. was district attorney of the Twenty-Eighth Judicial District from 1904 until his death in 1916 usually made it easier for him to maneuver around the law. The Good Government League, an antimachine reform movement, attempted to push back against the Marrero regime. In 1912, they tried, unsuccessfully, to impeach the Marreros, father and son, accusing the sheriff of "nonfeasance, malfeasance, extortion in office . . . grave crimes and misdemeanors . . . corruption, favoritism, and oppression in office." One day soon reformers would break the stranglehold the Marrero faction had on Jefferson Parish. Less than a year later, a wave of reform that swept over Louisiana would take Louis Marrero and other machine politicians with it. But in May 1919, that day had not yet come.

Sheriff Marrero was out of town on Sunday morning when Hazel Johnson roused Charlie and Rosie Cortimiglia's neighbors with her screams. By the time the Cortimiglias had been loaded into the wagon and sent off to the hospital, Gretna chief of police Peter Leson and Deputy Sheriff Charles Burgbacher had arrived to discover a house crowded with neighbors and curious onlookers.

The first thing Leson did was throw the gawkers out of the house and post a guard to make sure no one else got in. There wasn't much else he could do until the coroner arrived. No doubt meaning to be helpful, he and Manny Fink picked up the panel off the kitchen floor and nailed it back onto the door. The need to preserve the crime scene never occurred to them.

When Frank returned from notifying Charlie Cortimiglia's relatives in Amesville about midmorning, he put up his horse and buggy, went upstairs to put on the socks he'd abandoned in his hurry earlier that morning, went back outside, and stood on the banquette in front of the grocery looking over at the Cortimiglia place.

Dr. Charles Gelbke, the mayor of Gretna, and City Councilman Manny Fink had been standing together in front of the Cortimiglia store, discussing the morning's events. Seeing Frank standing on the street, they walked over. *Do you mind if we look around your house?* asked the mayor. Frank nodded. He understood that there had been a terrible crime and the authorities needed to investigate. Besides, he had nothing to hide. He took them in the house, led them through the kitchen and the little parlor in the front room, let them look into the bedrooms downstairs, and took them up the stairs to the room Frank shared with Louis. The mayor asked a few questions, which Frank answered as best he could. Then Dr. Gelbke asked to see the backyard. *Where is your axe?* he wanted to know. Frank retrieved it and handed it to the mayor, who peered at it closely. No blood, no hair. The mayor's investigation found nothing incriminating. But it would do little to allay mounting suspicions against Frank and his family.

All that afternoon people crowded in and out of the Jordano store. The only topic of conversation was the Cortimiglias—would they die? Who did it? Did it have anything to do with another middle-of-the-night break-in just up the river in the village of Amesville only two nights before? Someone had chiseled a lower panel off the door of a grocery belonging to Santo Vicari. The robber had entered the store and stolen some cash but not molested the sleeping family. Was the same night stalker responsible?

Iorlando was as curious as anyone, and as grieved. But he was also worried that people suspected him. He was convinced that everyone was staring at him, pointing him out as the killer. The old man insisted to anyone who would listen that his differences with the Cortimiglias had been patched up, and they were friends again. But all the neighbors knew about the quarrel between the Jordanos and Cortimiglias, and everyone noticed that the Jordanos had been among the first on the scene. Suspicion began to grow.

When Jefferson Parish acting coroner J. R. Fernandez arrived at the scene, the little girl's body had already been removed by the undertaker, but Dr. Fernandez got a good look at the site of the murder. Like the other Axeman crime scenes, the room had been ransacked, dressers emptied, and clothes and papers strewn all over the floor. Nothing had been taken. A search of the room revealed $129 in cash, a box of jewelry, and a loaded revolver. Clearly, Dr. Fernandez concluded, robbery had not been the motive.

The police had found two axes on the premises; only one had blood and hair sticking to it.

Fernandez managed that Sunday evening to swiftly impress five neighbors into service as a coroner's jury, including Manny Fink, who'd been one of the first on the crime scene. Dr. Fernandez and his jury crossed the river to view the body at the undertaker's about 7 PM, then returned to Gretna to examine the murder scene. They were shown two axes found on the Cortimiglias' property. The jurors stared somberly at the dark hairs plastered in blood to one of the axes.

Only a handful of witnesses were called to testify at the inquest. Lillie, Iorlando, and Frank were sworn in. They all said the same thing—they'd heard nothing untoward the night before, no hint of the horror taking place next door. They admitted that they'd had a falling out with Charlie Cortimiglia over possession of the property but insisted the quarrel had blown over. Frank testified that Mary's mother had continued to allow the child to frequently play over at their store.

Frank added one detail to his testimony, a detail that would come back to hurt him in an unexpected way. He was asked about the dream he'd mentioned to his mother. Frank was under oath, but he was also tired by the interrogation, drained from the distressing day, and harassed by probing questions. He didn't want to talk about Josie in front of all these men. What difference did it make who'd had the dream? So he told the inquest that he was the one who'd had an unsettling dream—of snakes all around him, a vision that many of the newspapermen reporting on the case interpreted as an evil omen. It was an impulse he'd come to regret.

Because the Cortimiglias couldn't be interviewed that night, the jury suspended its investigation without returning a verdict. But Dr. Fernandez offered the opinion that "the murder was the deed of a maniac, and that revenge was the only motive that could be advanced if the crime had been committed by a mentally normal person."

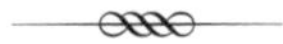

Frank Mooney couldn't have been shocked by the savage attack in Gretna. No doubt he'd been expecting something like it, and he was anxious to help the Jefferson Parish authorities. He didn't view the crime scene for himself—no need to give offense to the Gretna powers—but on Monday, he sent Bertillon Operator Maurice O'Neil across the river to process the scene. The results were disappointing. The crowds that had stampeded in and out of the house before the arrival of the police had trampled any footprints left by the murderer into oblivion. The axe had been handled by countless people in the last thirty-six hours. O'Neil couldn't find any fingerprints in the bedroom either.

To Bertillon Operator O'Neil it was readily apparent that the New Orleans Axeman had struck again, an opinion shared by Frank Mooney. The superintendent ordered his men to help the Gretna authorities in any way they could to find the murderer and to remain on alert against the killer in New Orleans. He expressed his predictable confidence that the murderer would be brought to justice. But the Italian community remained on edge. In New Orleans, Rocco Tramontana reported that someone had tried to break into his mother's grocery store at Peniston and Clara Streets during the night; the family's axe was found in front of the house.

While the investigation into the attacks began, Rosie's relatives, alerted to the tragedy, were pouring in from the surrounding towns and plantations. At first, the doctors allowed no one to see the wounded couple and told the family that Charlie had little chance of surviving.

Rosie regained a kind of hazy consciousness on Monday, and after Mary's funeral, her father and stepmother were allowed to sit by her bedside, taking turns holding her hand and talking softly to her in Italian. Occasionally, Rosie would feebly murmur something in response. When, every so often, she whispered, "Mary, Mary," her father would tell her to sleep, sleep and get better. No one was going to tell her Mary was dead until she was stronger.

By Monday night doctors began to feel more optimistic about Rosie's recovery. And by Tuesday morning even Charlie showed signs of improvement. He regained consciousness and appeared to recognize those clustered around his hospital cot. Perhaps, doctors Leidenheimer and Landry thought, he might survive after all.

Chief Leson and Sheriff Marrero—now back in town and taking the lead in the investigation—waited impatiently to speak to the Cortimiglias. On Tuesday Dr. Leidenheimer was sufficiently reassured by Rosie's and Charlie's recovery that he gave in to the importunate police officers and deputy sheriffs who had been cluttering the halls of Charity and agreed that the couple could be questioned about their assault. He warned that they might not be able to remember anything. And he was right. Speaking in Italian, all Rosie did was ask, again, after her daughter. Charlie said that his head hurt, and he needed to get back to his store. Neither had anything to say about the Axeman.

But Tuesday night, investigators were determined to question the victims again. For now they had a suspect.

Charles Anderson was a black man and career burglar who was well known to the police in New Orleans and Gretna. He was, at the moment, Superintendent Mooney's premier Axeman suspect. After the assault on the Cortimiglias, Mooney sent men looking for Anderson, and they caught up with him Tuesday morning, two days after the attack. Questioned about his recent whereabouts, the suspect was not entirely forthcoming, which, of course, made investigators even more suspicious. For several hours on Tuesday afternoon, Superintendent Mooney had Anderson in his office and subjected him to the full third degree. Mooney, Detective Marullo, and Chief Leson interrogated him nonstop, shooting question after question at him, not giving him time to think, trying to keep him off balance. They grilled him about all of the Axeman murders, accused him of being the killer, forced him to look at bloody photographs of Catherine and Joe Maggio, and demanded to know why he had targeted them. It was all designed to make a guilty man confess. Anderson, however, held his ground and continued to maintain his innocence, claiming that whenever something happened the police—unfairly, he insisted—picked him up. He had nothing to do with these murders. Some of the investigators began to believe he was telling the truth. To the eyes of trained detectives, the convicted burglar acted like an innocent man and didn't give himself away with the nervousness guilty men usually exhibited.

Finally, in desperation, Mooney loaded Anderson into a police car, drove to Charity Hospital, dragged him into Rosie Cortimiglia's ward, and handcuffed him to her hospital cot. *Was this the man who attacked you?* Marullo asked in Italian, as Mooney and Leson looked on. Rosie mumbled incoherently.

Doctors Leidenheimer and Landry were just walking out of Charlie's room, discussing his condition, when Mooney, Leson, and Marullo showed up with Anderson. The unfortunate suspect was again handcuffed to the foot of the bed, displayed in front of the patient. Charlie looked quizzically up at the gentlemen surrounding his hospital cot. Detective Marullo asked Charlie if this was the man who had attacked him. Charlie shook his head—no.

"Do you know who attacked you, Charlie?"

No, he again indicated with a shake of his head.

"Was it a white man?"

Yes, Charlie nodded.

Have you ever seen this man before? No response. Charlie stirred restlessly, clearly indicating that he'd had enough, and that was all they could get out of him.

Disappointed, Mooney realized he had nothing much to hold Anderson on. So he took him back to New Orleans and charged him with that policemen's consolation prize—being a dangerous and suspicious character.

For the next couple of days, it was much the same with the injured victims. Both seemed to be slowly getting better, to the point where each was asking about the other, but neither was able to give any clues about their attack. Dr. Landry showed particular attention to Rosie;

he checked on her frequently, three or four times a day. As a medical man, he was quite interested in her case; his own questioning of her indicated that her mind seemed to be a total blank from the time she went to bed on Saturday night until she woke up in the hospital. "Who hit you?" he asked repeatedly. Her reply was consistent: "I don't know."

Then suddenly on Friday, five days after the attack, Rosie identified her attackers and the killers of her baby daughter as seventeen-year-old Frank Jordano and sixty-eight-year-old Iorlando Jordano. Or so Leson and Marrero would later claim.

In the course of their inquiries, Gretna authorities had followed up on the rumors that the Jordanos had threatened the Cortimiglias and discovered a feed store operator named Rube Mayronne who claimed that two weeks before the attack, Frank said to him, "That son-of-a-bitch Cortimiglia won't be in his new store longer than two weeks." The Jordanos went from possible suspects to prime suspects. Still, all the police had was circumstantial evidence. But now, they said, they had eyewitnesses.

According to Sheriff Marrero and Chief Leson, when Leson went to see Rosie on Friday morning and asked for the hundredth time, "Who hit you?" Rosie finally had an answer: "Frank Jordano and the old man." Remarkably, they said that Charlie had confirmed this identification. Over the course of the day, the couple was questioned again and again, and each time, Marrero and Leson claimed, they implicated the elderly Italian and his teenaged son.

Sheriff Marrero, however, only made the identification of Frank public, and on Friday evening only Frank was arrested. Protesting his innocence, he was taken to the parish jail and held without bail.

Andy Ojeda thought all this was strange. As the *States* police reporter, Ojeda followed the course of the investigation carefully. He'd hung around Charity for days, talked to doctors, and kept tabs on the recovery of the Cortimiglias. He had been under the distinct impression that Rosie and Charlie had no idea who'd put them in the hospital. Hearing about Frank's arrest Friday night, he was at Charity first thing Saturday morning. If the Cortimiglias were implicating Frank Jordano, he wanted to hear about it firsthand.

When Andy Ojeda saw him, Charlie was not really up for an interview. He could barely speak and answered most of Ojeda's questions with a nod or shake of his head. "They've arrested Frank Jordano because you said he struck you with the axe," began the reporter. "Did Jordano hit you?" Charlie just shrugged his shoulders.

"Do you know who hit you?" asked Ojeda. He had to repeat his question several times. Again, Charlie only managed a shrug. Finally, slightly exasperated, Ojeda said, "You don't know who hit you, do you?" Charlie struggled to answer, and Ojeda leaned over him so he could hear the words: "I don't know."

"Did you see the face of the man who hit you?" pressed Ojeda. Charlie shook his head no. Asked if he saw the attacker's face, Charlie shook his head again.

"Was the man who hit you tall or short?"

"Big," mumbled Charlie.

This exchange exhausted Charlie, and Ojeda decided that would be all he could get out of him today. He left Charlie and headed across the hospital yard to the women's ward to see Rosie. Entering the ward, he found the charge nurse and asked if Mrs. Cortimiglia was up to answering questions. The nurse led him to Rosie's cot where she lay sleeping. Gently waking her, the nurse told her she had a visitor. Rosie opened her eyes and looked at the reporter.

"How are you feeling?" he asked her.

"I'm feeling all right," she answered.

"Mrs. Cortimiglia, who hit you?"

Rosie hesitated, and then said softly, "I don't know, but I believe my husband did."

Ojeda thought that was nonsense. He had just seen what condition Charlie was in. He hadn't beaten anyone with an axe.

"Who hit your baby?" he asked. She looked at him like she didn't know she had a baby.

"I don't know," she responded again.

Ojeda let Rosie go back to sleep. He had gotten what he came for.

On his way out of the hospital, Ojeda spoke with Dr. Landry, who told him that he thought it likely they would both recover. "I will not vouch for the condition of their minds, however," added Landry. "It may leave both permanently with faulty minds." He thought it was far too soon to have much confidence in anything either patient said.

Ojeda left Charity with the conviction that neither Cortimiglia could identify the attacker. What were the Gretna authorities up to?

The next Sunday, March 16, the *Times-Picayune* published an unusual letter. It had arrived at the paper two days before, handwritten in clear, distinct script. The letter purported to be from the Axeman himself:

> Hell, March 13, 1919
>
> Editor of the Times-Picayune, New Orleans:
>
> Esteemed mortal: They have never caught me and they never will. They have never seen me, for I am invisible, even as the ether which surrounds your earth. I am not a human being, but a spirit and a fell demon from hottest hell. I am what you Orleanians and your foolish police call the axman.
>
> When I see fit, I shall come again and claim other victims. I alone know whom [*sic*] they shall be. I shall leave no clue, except perhaps my bloody ax, besmeared with the blood and brains of he whom I have sent below to keep me company.
>
> If you wish you may tell the police to be careful not to rile me. Of course, I am a reasonable spirit. I take no offense at the way in which they have conducted their investigations in the past. In fact, they have been so utterly stupid so as to amuse not only me, but His Satanic Majesty, Francis Joseph [the Austro-Hungarian emperor who had died three years before], etc. But tell them to beware. Let them not try to discover what I am, for it were better that they never were born than for them to incur the wrath of the axman. I don't think that there is any need of such a warning, for

I feel sure that your police will always dodge me, as they have in the past. They are wise and know who to keep away from all harm.

Undoubtedly you Orleanians think of me as a most horrible murderer, which I am, but I could be much worse if I wanted to. If I wished to I could pay a visit to your city every night. At will I could slay thousands of your best citizens, for I am in close relationship with the Angel of Death.

Now, to be exact, at 12:25 o'clock (earthly time) on next Tuesday night, I am going to pass over New Orleans. In my infinite mercy, I am going to make a little proposition to the people. Here it is:

I am very fond of jazz music and I swear by all the devils in the nether regions, [*sic*] that every person shall be spared in whose house a jazz band is in full swing at the time I have just mentioned. If everyone has a jazz band going, well, then so much the better for the people. One thing is certain and that is some of those persons who do not jazz it on Tuesday night (if there be any) will get the ax.

Well, as I am cold and crave the warmth of my native Tartarus, and as it is about time that I have left your homely earth, I will cease my discourse. Hoping that thou wilt publish this, that it may go well with thee, I have been, am and will be the worst spirit that ever existed either in fact or the realm of fancy.

The Axman.

The real killer didn't send this letter. It was too well-written and too sophisticated to have been composed by the working-class Axeman. It also echoed several alleged Jack the Ripper letters sent in the fall of 1888 during his reign of terror in London. One was posted, like the Axeman's letter, "From Hell." Another, the so-called "Dear Boss" letter, ridiculed the efficacy of the police: "I keep on hearing the police have caught me but they won't fix me just yet. I have laughed when they look so clever and talk about being on the right track." The writer of the Axeman letter was well-educated and literate enough to have had some familiarity with details of the Jack the Ripper story, not to mention such elements of classical mythology as Tartarus. Maybe he didn't expect his joke to be taken seriously. Despite its macabre subject, the letter has a lofty, theatrical quality that doesn't sound like a genuine attempt to imitate a murderous maniac. The mocking tone of the letter made light of the genuine threat and very real fears created by an all-too-real killer. It was in the spirit of those who felt free to turn the murders into a joke, such as the creators of the Piggly Wiggly ad that used the Axeman to advertise self-service grocery shopping, and the party hosts (who sound like frat boys) who responded to the murderous threat by inviting the Axeman to a stag party. Surely the staff at the *Times-Picayune* realized this was a practical joke. That the letter wasn't printed until two days after it arrived suggests the possibility of a degree of hesitation. But like other Orleanians who had nothing to fear from a killer of immigrant grocers, the newspaper editors could afford to find the idea of an epistle-writing demon from hell amusing.

If not the real Axeman, who then wrote the letter?

Someone who stood to gain from the prank was local musician and businessman Joseph John Davilla. The thirty-five-year-old songwriter had his own music publishing company and had had success with hits such as "Why Do You Leave Me, Sweetheart" and "There's Something I Like About You." "Give Me Back My Husband, You've Had Him Long E-Nuff" had been his biggest hit, reaching a national audience. Written for vaudeville star Sophie "The Last of the Red-Hot Mamas" Tucker, it was what was known in that racist age as a "coon novelty song."

Now, he claimed, the Axeman's letter had inspired another novelty song, "The Mysterious Axman's Jazz (Don't Scare Me, Papa)." As much businessman as artist, Davilla recognized an opportunity when he saw it, even if it meant composing a theme song for a killer. The sheet music wasn't available on Tuesday, the "Axeman's" appointed night, but Davilla kept interest piqued by planting little advertisements in the *Times-Picayune*: WAIT—WATCH THE AXMAN'S JAZZ and COMING MYSTERIOUSLY, THE AXMAN'S JAZZ. And he hired a ragtime piano player to play the song continuously as he was pulled up and down Canal Street in a wagon.

Davilla turned everything to his advantage. He was clever enough to get the *Times-Picayune* to let him use a cartoon that ran in the paper on Saint Joseph's Day, the day after the Axeman's supposed advent. It showed a woman and her frightened family anxiously playing "The Mysterious Axman's Jazz" on various instruments in a desperate attempt to stave off the killer. Davilla made it the cover of his sheet music.

The Times-Picayune *cartoon that ran on Saint Joseph's Day, the day after the Axeman's supposed advent. J. J. Davilla quickly adopted it as the sheet music cover of his song "The Mysterious Axman's Jazz."*

Copies sold by the thousands at twenty-five cents apiece, and the tune could be heard from one end of the city to the other for months. If one man stood to profit from the "Axeman's" letter to the *Times-Picayune*, it was J. J. Davilla.

Nowhere did the so-called Axeman letter mention "Saint Joseph's Day," but the time he demanded that jazz bands be playing—"12:25 o'clock (earthly time) on next Tuesday night" (the evening of March 18)—was the first hour of March 19, Saint Joseph's Day. That timing would have had special significance for the Italian community, the target of the Axeman. It was a particularly nasty touch.

Given Saint Joseph's special significance for Sicilians, Saint Joseph's Day was an important holy day for New Orleans's Italian population, a feast day of thanksgiving and charity, and a welcome respite from the fasting and penance of Lent. The devout built altars decorated with candles and flowers and around a statue of the saint heaped foods of every description—fish, vegetables, bread, cakes, pastries—everything except meat. Dried fava beans were included for luck.

On the morning of Saint Joseph's Day, Saint Mary's Italian Church was packed for a solemn high mass. After the congregation returned to their homes, a little ritual was enacted. Three children representing the Holy Family entered the home and sampled the food on the altar. Then the feasting could begin. Saint Joseph's Night was a time for parties—galas, receptions, dances, and fancy dress balls for all of New Orleans. The sound of jazz bands could be heard all over the city.

The night designated for jazz by the "Axeman," the night of March 18, Italians would be busy preparing for the next day's feast. To try to frighten the Italian population on that particular night was a cruel twist on an already tasteless joke.

Not a few in New Orleans used the letter to the *Times-Picayune* as an excuse for jollification. From dozens of house parties and late-night cafés jazzy sounds floated out as merrymakers laughingly congratulated each other for avoiding the "fell demon from hottest hell." No doubt there were some who didn't want to admit a fear of the Axeman but for whom the syncopated beat of a jazz band was a welcome comfort.

Most of the city ignored it, despite later legends to the contrary. The idea of an axe murderer demanding to be appeased with jazz bands was too silly to be taken seriously.

Some people were genuinely frightened, the poor and superstitious, who might not even have been able to read the letter in the newspaper but who might have heard the city humming with the news—"The Axeman is coming!" With four dead in less than a year—five if they believed Mrs. Lowe had been an Axeman victim—it's no wonder that some panicked. Families banded together for the night, hoping for safety in numbers; fathers loaded shotguns and kept them within easy reach until dawn. Italian immigrants, including grocers who had cause to feel especially vulnerable, likely dominated their number. Pity the poor schoolboy piano or banjo players forced to jazz it up in improvised bands through the night to protect their families from the music-loving demon.

Not everyone sophisticated enough to realize the Axeman letter was a hoax found it funny. An editorial in the *Herald* roundly castigated the *Times-Picayune* for not "think[ing] of the great amount of harm it has done to the ignorant classes who are superstitiously inclined and believed to a certain extent that this ax-man would visit certain families who did not have a jazz band." The editorial also thought tasteless the cartoon the paper ran the next day, the cartoon Davilla used to such effect as the cover of his sheet music: "We fail to see the joke."

Frank Jordano probably didn't see the joke either. Saint Joseph's Day, the day he'd planned to get married, found him locked in the Gretna city jail.

Three days after her brother's arrest, Lena Jordano watched through tears as her father was taken from his grocery by the police. Like Frank, Iorlando Jordano was charged with murder and pleaded not guilty. Sheriff Marrero and Chief Leson now announced that the Cortimiglias had identified not only Frank but Iorlando as one of their attackers.

It is difficult to understand how Sheriff Marrero and Chief Leson could have convinced themselves that the mild-mannered, elderly, arthritic grocer would kill a toddler who called him Grandpa. Their fixation on the Jordanos can be attributed, in part at least, to their ignorance about serial killers. Since the term has existed for over fifty years, it's easy to forget how counterintuitive is the idea of killing with no discernible motive. Such depravity was something completely beyond the experience of the small-town police chief and the machine-politician sheriff. While Superintendent Mooney was confident that the Axeman attacks were the work of a deranged fiend, he couldn't convince everyone, even in his own department. Some New Orleans police officers continued to believe that the Axeman attacks could be blamed on Italian vendettas.

Marrero and Leson didn't know anything about serial killers, but they understood—or thought they understood—the vendetta. It was an all-purpose way of explaining violence among Italian immigrants. Barely a year before, an Italian farmworker had been found bleeding to death on the levee, shot and stabbed as the result of a quarrel with another Italian over a girl. This was the vendetta. For Sheriff Marrero and Chief Leson, one Italian killing another over a business dispute was easy to fathom. The Jordanos had quarreled with the Cortimiglias. Neighbors whispered that Frank had been overheard boasting that their competitors wouldn't last long. Convinced by circumstantial evidence, sure of their guilt, the sheriff and police chief were determined to convict the killers even if they had to manufacture the evidence to do so.

Even so, why insist that the old man was involved? If the police had evidence that Frank threatened the family, why did that implicate his father?

Perhaps a clue can be gleaned from reports about the crime scene. Because the bolt on the kitchen door seems to have been located high above the open panel, and not in easy reach, several police officers speculated that the killer hadn't simply extended his arm through the door after removing the panel but had actually squeezed through the hole to open the door from the inside. Later events would demonstrate that even someone as big as Frank could wedge his head and shoulders through the hole, so for a smaller accomplice such a feat might have been possible. It was pretty obvious that 275-pound Frank hadn't stuffed himself through the opening into the kitchen, but his father had a much smaller build.

Whatever their reasoning, the authorities of the city of Gretna and Jefferson Parish had made up their minds: Frank and Iorlando Jordano were guilty. Now, how were they going to prove it?

The Cortimiglias' claims implicating the Jordanos were made only in front of police, not in the presence of reporters or physicians. To Dr. Landry, Rosie always denied that she knew who hit her. Medical personnel at the hospital, in fact, continued to insist that nothing the couple said could be relied upon yet. Not only was their mental condition affected by their head injuries, but the opiates they were given for pain also made their mental state unreliable. Reporters who went to see him discovered that Charlie would answer "yes" to anything he was asked.

"Did Frank Jordano attack you with an axe?" one inquired.

"Yes," responded Charlie.

"Are you a Frenchman?" asked another.

"Yes," came the reply.

A few days after authorities claimed that Rosie had identified Frank as her attacker, she told her doctors that she didn't know if the man was white or black.

In fact, the so-called statements given by the Cortimiglias consisted of agreeing to highly leading questions when they probably had little idea of what they were saying:

Q: "Did Frank Jordano hit you with the axe?"

A: "Yes."

Q: "Was Iorlando Jordano with Frank Jordano at the time he made the axe attack on you?"

A: "Yes."

Even Sheriff Marrero admitted that Charlie "was unable to give details" but admitted to no doubts about the arrests. "I am confident we have the right men and that the Cortimiglias will recover to tell the complete story of the attack made upon them," Sheriff Marrero assured reporters.

Frank and Iorlando's arrest was greeted with general approval in Gretna. Popular sentiment was not on their side. Charlie Cortimiglia was an agreeable, energetic young man who was well liked in the community. Everybody knew about the quarrel over the store—if they hadn't before, they did now—and that the deadly assault occurred shortly after the Cortimiglias had moved into their new place. The murder had badly shaken the people of Jefferson Parish, and, like the sheriff and police chief, many people found it easier to believe in revenge as a motive than they did a homicidal maniac.

Feelings against the Jordanos were so strong that some began clamoring for a special session of the grand jury to consider the case immediately. But since the chief witnesses were still in the hospital and likely to remain there for some weeks, District Attorney Rivarde vetoed the idea. It would have to wait for the regular session of the grand jury, he said, which would convene in early May.

L. Robert Rivarde was district attorney of the Twenty-Eighth Judicial District, made up of Saint Charles, Saint John, and Jefferson Parishes. He'd been a state senator and a district judge, and when Sheriff Marrero's son Louis Jr. died in 1916, Rivarde had been selected to replace him as DA. An active member of the Marrero political machine, Rivarde could be counted on to cooperate with Sheriff Marrero in prosecuting the Jordanos.

Sheriff Marrero still had a problem. He was confident that the Jordanos were responsible for the attack on the Cortimiglias and little Mary's death. But his witnesses were problematic. So far neither one of them had identified the Jordanos in the presence of anyone but police officers, and Andy Ojeda's coverage in the *States* had undermined his claim that they had clearly singled out the accused. Marrero needed to be certain of his witnesses.

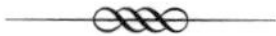

On March 28, almost three weeks after the attack, Rosie was at last well enough to leave the hospital. Sheriff Marrero saw a way to solve his problem. The third degree could be used on witnesses as well as suspects. He arrested her.

Sheriff Marrero obtained a warrant for Rosie's arrest as a material witness, an unusual move for someone who was the victim of a crime. When she left the hospital with Chief Leson, one of Marrero's deputy sheriffs, and two of her brothers-in-law, Rosie had no hint that anything was wrong. She was in a good mood, lightly bantering with the men as they rode the ferry across the river, assuming they were taking her home. Instead Leson delivered her to the Jefferson Parish jail.

Rosie was taken completely by surprise. Not allowed to see a lawyer and separated from her family, she was thoroughly frightened and confused by the time Marrero and Rivarde began questioning her again.

Was it the Jordanos who attacked you, Rosie?

I can't remember.

You must remember.

I don't remember seeing anyone.

Who else would have done it? Didn't Frank say he was going to run you off?

Did you see Frank and the old man that night? You'd better remember if you want to go home.

As she was being put in a cell to sleep that night, one of her jailers said to her, "You must make up your mind who did it, Rosie. Go to bed tonight and get a good rest, and make up your mind who did it."

The next morning she signed an affidavit swearing that Frank and Iorlando Jordano were the assailants. In twenty-four hours, Rosie went from claiming no memory of who killed her baby to a detailed recollection of the attack.

Because Rosie couldn't read or write English, Clay Gaudet, a notary and lawyer hired by the Cortimiglias to assist the prosecution, wrote it out for her. Rosie signed. Satisfied, Marrero let her go stay with one of her sisters.

Now that Rosie was out of the hospital and well enough to testify, the coroner's jury could finish its job. On April 13, Dr. Fernandez reconvened his five-man jury, and after hearing Rosie's testimony, they returned a verdict of murder at the hands of Frank and Iorlando Jordano.

In the meantime, the Jordanos had retained an attorney, William H. Byrnes Jr., a thirty-eight-year-old graduate of Tulane University Law School. The first thing Byrnes did was demand a preliminary hearing, charging that Rosie had been jailed illegally in order to coerce her into accusing the Jordanos. He also wanted her mental competence evaluated.

Judge John Fleury granted his request and set the preliminary hearing for May 7. But on the afternoon of May 5, a Jefferson Parish grand jury indicted Frank and Iorlando Jordano for the murder of Mary Cortimiglia. Judge Fleury set a trial date of May 19 and canceled the preliminary hearing, ruling that the indictment had made it "useless and unnecessary."

In two weeks, the Jordanos would go on trial for their lives.

10

"Hung by the Neck Until Dead, Dead, Dead"

New cases of Spanish influenza were declining by the end of October, and by February 1919 the *States* could declare the Flu Is Almost Wiped Out Here. Meanwhile, Louis Besumer had been brooding in the parish prison since his arrest in August.

The long months waiting for trial had worn down some of the eccentric grocer's natural cockiness. He'd been sued by his landlady for not paying his rent, proving that his claims of wealth were a lie. Imprisonment and illness had aged him, and he began to despair that he'd die in jail. In February, he wrote to an Orleans Parish grand jury complaining that he was being held without trial. The attack on the Cortimiglia family a few weeks later gave him another opportunity to draw attention to his plight. He wrote to the *Times-Picayune*, appealing for help in getting a trial so he could be cleared of blame in Mrs. Lowe's death.

The *Times-Picayune* was a good target for Besumer's plea, which resulted in a sympathetic interview on the front page of the newspaper a week after Mary Cortimiglia's death. Reporter Jim Coulton, believing that one man was responsible for all the axe attacks, was inclined to accept Besumer's claims of innocence, and he liked to remind readers that the evidence against Besumer was "largely circumstantial."

The article prompted a speedy reply from District Attorney Chandler Luzenberg, who blamed the delay on a combination of judicial vacations and the Spanish flu. He promised to bring the case to trial as soon as he could. Louis Besumer's day in court finally came at noon, April 30. Prosecutors were asking for the death penalty. The trial lasted all of two days.

The most important witness called by the state on the first day was Superintendent of Police Frank Mooney, and defense lawyer Henry Rhodes quickly cornered him into a damaging admission. Had Mooney declared after Besumer's arrest, and again after Mary Cortimiglia's murder, demanded Rhodes, that he believed a single crazed killer responsible for all the axe attacks of the last two years? Mooney conceded that he had. Henry Rhodes left it up to the jury to draw the obvious conclusion: If all the axe attacks were the work of one man, Besumer couldn't be guilty. He'd been locked up in the parish prison when Joseph Romano and Mary Cortimiglia were killed.

The next morning Dr. Hiram W. Kostmayer, the surgeon who'd treated Mrs. Lowe at Charity, was sworn in as a witness. The outcome of the trial would revolve around two issues for which the doctor's testimony would prove critical: First, what had been Mrs. Lowe's state of mind when she exonerated and then when she accused Besumer?

Immediately after the attack, Rhodes reminded the jury, Mrs. Lowe accused a mulatto, then recanted her identification, all the while emphatically denying Louis Besumer's involvement. It was only weeks later that she recalled Besumer hitting her. Dr. Kostmayer testified that despite her horrific head injuries, Mrs. Lowe's brain function had not been affected, and she had been of perfectly sound mind in the aftermath of the attack when she'd denied that Besumer had been her assailant.

On the stand later that morning, Jim Coulton corroborated this statement. He testified that Mrs. Lowe seemed confused her first day in the hospital, but afterward she appeared completely lucid.

It was later, when she turned on Besumer, that she seemed mentally unbalanced. Mrs. Sacriste, the housekeeper, would tell the court that Lowe seemed unhinged, with her obsessive praying and visions of Christ.

The second issue on which Dr. Kostmayer's testimony was critical was the question of how Besumer came by his head wound. Police theorized that he'd inflicted it himself so that he could claim to be another Axeman victim. The defense was at great pains to discredit the idea that Besumer would have been able to deliver a blow with enough force.

How hard would it be, Rhodes asked Dr. Kostmayer, to give oneself the kind of injury Besumer sustained? Kostmayer refused to answer directly.

I'm not testifying as an expert on such a question, he replied. *But,* he continued, *it could have been self-inflicted only by a man of powerful physique.*

The members of the jury looked over at the old grocer. Was this a man of "powerful physique" who had brought down an axe on his own head?

When it came the turn of the defense to present its case, Rhodes called no witness except Louis Besumer. He testified for four hours, telling his story once again, accusing Assistant District Attorney Ben Daly of coaching Mrs. Lowe on her accusation.

In his closing statement, Rhodes argued that Harriet Anna Lowe and Louis Besumer had been "victims of the murderous Axeman who had terrorized the people of this city for the last two years."

Testimony wrapped up after 10 PM Thursday night. The jurymen retired to consider their verdict. They were back by 10:30 PM. Only one ballot had been necessary to find Louis Besumer not guilty.

The newspapermen covering the trial weren't at all surprised by the verdict. They didn't think the prosecution had a very strong case. The testimony that Mrs. Lowe had been perfectly rational when she exonerated Besumer of the attack, coupled with the evidence that she wasn't altogether in her right mind when she did blame him, made a guilty verdict unlikely.

Nobody considered that perhaps she'd been in her right mind but was too afraid of Besumer to accuse him. Little was understood at the time of the dynamics of domestic violence, certainly not by the legal system. Still, while it may not have been a correct verdict, it was a fair verdict. The defense had introduced more than enough reasonable doubt.

The strongest argument in Besumer's favor was the Axeman himself. Newspaper articles for the last ten months had repeatedly linked the Besumer case with the Axeman crimes. Since the Axeman had continued to strike while Besumer was in jail, it wasn't a stretch for the jury to believe that Louis Besumer and Harriet Anna Lowe had been the Axeman's victims.

After tearfully thanking the jury, Besumer announced that he would stay in New Orleans, yet no record shows him living in the city after his trial. The man who called himself Louis Besumer but was known by other names may well have vanished under one of his many aliases.

The State of Louisiana v. Frank Guagliardo, alias Frank Jordano, and Iorlando Guagliardo, alias Iorlando Jordano went to trial in the Twenty-Eighth District Court on Monday, May 19, 1919, almost a year after the brutal murders of Catherine and Joe Maggio. Crowds began to pack the Gretna courthouse early. The gray brick building stood at the corner of Second Street and Copernicus Avenue (now Huey P. Long Avenue), fronting Second Street and facing the nearby riverfront. Built in the classically inspired Renaissance style, the three-storied courthouse boasted a front portico, ornate Corinthian columns, rounded arches, a copper cornice, and grand colonnades. For the proud residents of Gretna, it was a veritable "temple of justice," as the *Item* boasted when the building was dedicated in 1907.

The opulence of the high ceilings, tiled corridors, and marble decoration of the inside matched the classical elegance of the outside. But the small third-floor chamber, where the Jordano-Cortimiglia drama would play out, belied the grandeur of the court building. It was a cramped little courtroom. The clerk of court's desk, positioned directly in front of the judge, was only a couple of feet from the defense table. Prosecutor Rivarde sat just outside the jury box. The prosecution and defense teams sat right next to each other.

The throng that pressed into the courtroom made it seem even smaller. Italians from all over Jefferson Parish, many of them relatives of either defendants or victims, streamed into Gretna to join the crush of onlookers willing to squeeze themselves into the little courtroom to satisfy their curiosity. Hours before the court was called to order at 10 AM, every available space had been taken. Family and reporters had reserved seats; the merely inquisitive—most of them women, many with children—jammed together, anxious for a glimpse of the proceedings. Observers not lucky enough to get a seat stood at the back of the room or in the hallway or jostled each other for a few inches of standing room on the balcony. Many had packed lunches in anticipation of a long day in court.

Most residents of Gretna had already reached a conclusion about the guilt or innocence of the Jordanos based on what they'd read in the newspapers or heard from their neighbors. Opinion was running strongly against the father and son; their guilt was widely assumed. Only a few cautious individuals expressed reservations about convicting them based solely upon Rosie Cortimiglia's say-so.

District Judge John E. Fleury presided over the trial. Only thirty-four, he'd been a state representative before being elected judge. In fact, in 1914, he'd been the legislator who'd introduced the bill creating an additional judgeship for the Saint Charles–Saint John–Jefferson district, the same judgeship he then ran for. Fleury was a very capable politician, if, perhaps, not a great judge.

At forty-one, District Attorney L. Robert "Bob" Rivarde was a slim, boyish-looking figure. He'd left school at eleven and worked a variety of jobs before completing night school and graduating from Tulane University Law School. He'd become associated with the Marrero faction early in his career when he'd taken a job working for Sheriff Marrero's son Louis Jr. The Marrero connection made John Fleury and Bob Rivarde political allies. They'd also served together as the two judges of the Twenty-Eighth Judicial District before Rivarde became DA on the death of the junior Marrero.

Assisting the prosecution was the attorney hired by the Cortimiglia family, Clay Gaudet.

Defense attorney William Byrnes had as associate counsel two up-and-coming young lawyers: Andrew H. Thalheim, who would go on to serve as Gretna's city attorney for thirty-five years, and Archie Higgins, a future state supreme court justice. Byrnes himself came to the case straight off a win; at the beginning of May, he'd gotten a charge of arson against one of his clients dismissed. Frank and Iorlando had an excellent legal team.

Reporters expected the trial to be over in a few days. But proceedings got off to a slow start. After spending an entire morning dealing with a defense objection to the panel from which the petit—or trial—jury was to be chosen, the actual empanelment of a jury took an unusually long time. Due to the extensive newspaper coverage of the murders, many potential jurors had already made up their minds about the guilt of the defendants, and they admitted as much. Juror after juror was dismissed "for cause."

The Twenty-Eighth District Court of Gretna during the testimony of Frank Jordano. Iorlando Jordano and his attorney William Byrnes are seated at a table near the bottom of the picture and are looking up at the photographer. Andrew Thalheim and Archie Higgins are seated next to Byrnes.

Murder was a capital crime, so Bob Rivarde closely questioned each potential juror about his—they were all men—willingness to sentence a man to death. None had any misgivings. An attorney watching the proceedings commented that before the war (which had concluded only the previous November), many prospective jurors would have expressed reservations about capital punishment. The United States had had an active anti–death penalty movement in the late nineteenth and early twentieth centuries, and it had had its effect. But the Great War, the observer said, with its long lists of dead, had "obliterated their awe of death." To a man, each juror was prepared to send the Jordanos to the gallows.

By 5 PM Monday, the court had exhausted the regular panel of jurors but seated only five trial jurors. Judge Fleury ordered the sheriff to summon seventy-five more potential jurors to appear in court the next morning. Fleury also ordered the five selected jurymen sequestered, and sheriff's deputies escorted them to the jurors' dormitory on the third floor of the courthouse.

Over the next two days, Judge Fleury had to order that additional men be summoned for jury duty twice more because of the difficulty of finding suitable jurors. Finally, the all-male jury was complete late Wednesday night. It had taken three days to seat, longer than most murder trials.

At 10:30 PM, the trial started in earnest when, despite the lateness of the hour, Judge Fleury ordered potential witnesses removed from the courtroom, and the state began its case by calling Dr. J. R. Fernandez. His evidence wasn't expected to take long.

Dr. Fernandez testified about viewing the body of the murdered child and holding the inquest; he described for the court the injuries Mary Cortimiglia had suffered: two traumatic head wounds, one on her right temple, the other just above her ear. While Mary's skull had been fractured, he couldn't determine what had caused the blows, he said. The coroner, quite mistakenly as it turned out, explained that "there was no evidence of an axe there; the injury might have been caused by numerous things." His testimony lasted until 11:30 PM.

The next morning, Thursday, May 22, the state called its chief witness, Rosie Cortimiglia. This was the centerpiece of the trial. Without her, the prosecution had no case. Frank and Iorlando's fate depended on how believable the jury found the young woman.

All eyes in the crowded courtroom followed Rosie, straining for a glimpse of her as she made her way to the front of the courtroom. She made a good impression: an attractive, modest young woman, wearing pince-nez eyeglasses and a boudoir cap hiding her still-visible injuries.

Rosie was sworn in and took her seat in the witness chair.

Clay Gaudet began for the prosecution. After introductory inquiries about how long she and her husband had been in their new building, Gaudet turned to the events on the night of March 8 and the early morning of March 9. Rosie stated that she went to bed at 11:30 PM and that Charlie followed around forty-five minutes later. Sometime later, she'd woken up when she'd heard knocking. She turned to her husband.

"Charlie," she said, giving him a nudge, "you had better get up, maybe somebody wants some groceries."

But he just grunted, "It's too late. I closed the grocery and I'm not going to get up," and went back to sleep. Rosie said she started nursing the baby while lightly dozing; she continued to hear the noise but dismissed it as the new puppy they'd left in the yard.

Suddenly, she opened her eyes to see Frank Jordano and his father in her bedroom, clearly visible in the glow of the electric bulb.

Puzzled, she sat up and asked, "Frank, what are you doing here?"

He didn't answer. He just looked at her.

"Frank, what kind of trick is this?"

Frank continued to stare at her without saying a word.

Now sure that something was wrong, Rosie reached for the pistol under her pillow, but Frank grabbed her wrists and restrained her. Frightened, Rosie looked up at Frank and pleaded, "Do what you please with me and Charlie, but don't touch the baby!"

Frank replied tersely, "I have got to kill the baby because it is crying," even though, Rosie testified, Mary wasn't crying.

The courtroom was deadly silent as Rosie described how "he"—and she pointed to old Mr. Jordano—"went to get the axe." Then, she continued, Frank hit Mary three times with the axe—"three licks" is how she phrased it—and when he finished with the baby, he struck her twice.

Gaudet then turned to what the prosecution believed was the motive for this brutal attack. He quizzed Rosie about the dispute she and Charlie had had with the Jordanos over the grocery store, and she narrated the story of how they'd rented the building before the Jordanos demanded it back.

When William Byrnes stood up to cross-examine the young woman, he had a delicate task. Frank and Iorlando vehemently denied assaulting their neighbors and killing their daughter, and neither had any idea why Rosie would claim they'd done such a thing. So Byrnes had to persuade the jury that her story wasn't credible. Which meant he needed to discredit the story of a very sympathetic defendant. He began gingerly.

"Miss Rosie," he said, "you don't mind me calling you by the same name that Mr. Gaudet called you?"

"No sir," she replied.

Byrnes requested to see the scar on her right arm. Rosie held up her arm for the jury. He asked her how she came to have the scar. She said she didn't know. Byrnes pressed her, and Rosie insisted again that she didn't know. This would be a point the defense would return to.

Byrnes questioned Rosie about how old she was, how long she'd known Frank, where she went to school. He asked who had brought her to the Gretna jail and how long she was there. Then he turned to more important matters.

"Now, Miss Rosie," Byrnes began, "we have to come to a very unpleasant thing, but we have to ask you these questions." He needed her to revisit the night of the attack, and he grilled her closely, but as gently as he could, about the events that had culminated in her daughter's murder.

Rosie repeated the story she'd told before. She'd heard a noise that she thought was the puppy and then napped while the baby nursed.

About forty-five minutes later, Frank and Iorlando Jordano had appeared in her bedroom. She sat up, pulling the baby away from her breast. Frank told her he had to kill the baby; Iorlando left the room to get the axe, and when he returned, Frank hit Mary and then swung at Rosie.

"I know he hit me two licks," she said. "I could hear them two licks hit." As she fainted from the blows, Rosie continued, she'd dropped Mary, and Frank had snatched her up.

"Was the baby crying?" Byrnes asked, referring to the moment when Frank took the axe from Iorlando.

No, Rosie replied. The baby was asking to nurse, saying, "I want ninny, mama, I want ninny." So she said, "All right honey, I am going to give you ninny."

Byrnes asked, ever so slightly disbelievingly, "You did not have time to scream?"

Rosie flatly repeated herself: "I had no time to scream."

"But you had to tell the baby those words, 'I'm going to give you the breast'?"

"Yes, sir."

Byrnes had to hope the contradiction made an impact on the jury. He also had another point that showed her story didn't make sense. "Miss Rosie, you said when Frank hit you with the axe that the baby fell and he grabbed the baby?"

"Yes, sir," Rosie agreed. "He grabbed the baby."

"Now, how could he grab the baby, *and* have the axe in his hand *and* hit you a second time?"

Rosie looked unhappy. "I don't know how he was doing it; but I seen him grab the baby."

Byrnes inquired as to why she didn't holler when the old man left the room to get the axe.

"Because," she retorted, "it didn't take"—she snapped her fingers—"that long!"

Disbelief in his voice, the attorney responded: "You had no chance to holler while he held your hands, and his father went in to the other room and got the axe, and brought the axe back into that room, and handed it to Frank, and Frank hit the baby three times and then hit you? You mean to tell this jury that you did not have time to holler?"

"I was worrying about my baby," Rosie protested.

"You did not jump out of bed?"

"No."

"You did not wake Charlie up?"

"No."

"You did not scream?"

"No."

"You did not fight?"

"No."

"You didn't run?"

"No."

"You didn't kick Charlie?"

Rosie laughed. "No, I didn't kick Charlie."

Byrnes was startled. "This is no laughing matter," he said. "But go ahead and laugh as much as you please."

He continued probing: "All Charlie would have had to do was to reach his hand out and take the revolver to have protected you and that baby. Isn't that correct?"

At this, District Attorney Rivarde objected. "Your honor, this elicits an opinion from the witness as to what Charlie could or could not have done."

Byrnes was happy to be reasonable. He offered to ask the witness only how wide the couple's bed was. He turned to Rosie. "It's a double iron bed, is it not?"

Rosie hesitated and looked unsure of herself. "How do you mean 'double'?"

The attorney clarified: "I mean for two people to sleep in."

"Yes, sir."

"Why didn't you wake Charlie up when you saw Frank and his father there?"

"I never thought Frank was going to kill my baby."

"You didn't think it necessary to wake your husband up when you saw two men enter your room in the dead of night?"

Well, Rosie replied, it had all happened so quickly.

"Now, if you had time to talk to Frank, then why didn't you scream?"

"I never had any idea to scream."

"You said a moment ago you didn't have a chance to scream."

"No, I hadn't a chance; and I hadn't the idea either."

"But you had the chance to tell Frank, 'Do what you please with me and Charlie, but spare my baby'?"

"Yes, sir."

Then Byrnes turned to the length of time Iorlando Jordano had been out of the bedroom to get the axe. "And all that time, you say, you didn't have a chance to scream, or to awaken your husband?"

"It was done so quick I didn't know what to do. I was studying about my baby."

"It was done so quick, that the father had a chance to go into the other room, and maybe as far as into the yard, and then came back, and you call that quick?"

"Yes, sir."

Now the defense attorney's cross-examination was catching fire. "Miss Rosie, how were Frank's hands that night; were they warm or cold when he took hold of you?"

Rosie looked offended. "I don't know how they were; I was so scared after he done that. Do you think I had cheek enough to know how his hands were, whether cold or warm?"

The defense lawyer was sharp: "Yes, I think you should have had cheek enough; I think you had; and there were a whole lot of things you should not have done."

Byrnes picked up the axe police had found at the crime scene and approached Rosie. "Now, how did Frank take the axe?"

"In both hands," she said. "Right here," pointing to the center of the handle.

"Then he turned you loose completely?"

"Yes."

"He didn't hold you and the baby?"

"No."

"He took the axe in both hands?"

"Yes."

"How high did he raise it?"

"I don't know how high he raised it. I was looking at my baby."

"Why weren't you looking at him?"

"I didn't think he was going to hit my baby."

Byrnes was incredulous: "He picked up the axe, and you told him do what he wanted to do to you and to your husband, but to spare your baby; and after he told you, according to what you say, he was going to kill your baby, you didn't think he was going to do anything?"

"I didn't think he had such a heart as that."

"You never thought he had such a heart as that after he told you he was going to do it?"

"No, sir."

"You say he hit the baby three times?"

"Yes, sir; three times."

The attorney lifted the axe above his head to illustrate. "He hit the baby like this?" Byrnes asked, bringing the axe down in a hacking motion. "And again? And then again?" He brought the axe down three times, simulating three strikes.

"Yes, sir; just that way."

"Why didn't you throw your baby out of the bed?"

"I never had that idea."

"It is natural to scream when a person gets frightened. What do you usually do when you get frightened?"

Rosie didn't answer.

The witness had been on the stand all morning. Judge Fleury ordered a midday recess for dinner.

In the afternoon session, Byrnes's goal was to lay the foundation—in a technical legal sense—for impeaching Rosie's testimony. For this, he needed her to make statements that later witnesses would contradict.

Byrnes returned to the subject of the scar on Rosie's arm. He asked her if she knew a real estate agent named Paul Dupas. She knew him, she said, because he had sold them several lots of land.

"Now," Byrnes continued, "do you recall making a statement to him about how you received that cut on your arm?"

She thought for a second. "I told him I was cut, but I didn't know who done it."

"Miss Rosie," Byrnes cautioned, "I want to warn you that I intend to contradict you on that matter and have summoned Mr. Dupas for that purpose. So I want to ask you now, again, if you did not make the following statement to Mr. Dupas: That Frank Jordano had hit you on the arm with the axe and had made that scar on your arm?"

Rosie could only stutter. "U-n-g—h-un."

"Did you make that statement to him?"

"I did not tell him that Frank done that with the axe; I did not know who cut that."

Byrnes questioned Rosie for several more minutes, hammering her on what she had told Paul Dupas. He asked about a second encounter she'd had with Dupas, when she'd told him that the cut had been done in the hospital "by the doctors putting something in your arm." Rosie repeated that she didn't know how she'd received the cut; she'd never known. Byrnes had accomplished his task; he'd laid the groundwork to show that Rosie was lying—or at least unreliable—when he would later call Dupas to the stand.

But he wasn't finished. He had another witness to impeach Rosie's narrative. Byrnes asked Rosie if she knew a woman named Margaret Williams, a detective hired by the defense to pose as a door-to-door seller of women's toilet articles in an effort to talk to Rosie. Rosie didn't know the name, so Miss Williams was brought into the courtroom. Yes, Rosie, acknowledged, when she got a look at the young woman, she'd met her twice. The lady had told her "she was selling cologne, powder and face soap."

Byrnes asked Rosie what she'd told Margaret Williams about the case. At first, she denied telling her anything. Then she contradicted herself, saying that she'd told Miss Williams that Frank Jordano had attacked her and Charlie.

"Now Miss Rosie, didn't you tell her that you didn't know whether it was Frank Jordano, or his father that had hold of your hands?"

Rosie emphatically denied telling her that.

Again, Byrnes warned Rosie that he was planning to contradict her with Margret Williams's testimony later.

"Did you tell her that you were awakened suddenly?"

"What do you mean 'suddenly'?"

"Quickly. That you were awakened; seeing two men by your bed, you recognized them as Frank Jordano and his father, but did not have time to scream; that one of the men caught you by the arm; that you don't remember which man struck the baby. Do you remember making that statement?"

Rosie did not: "I never told her that."

Suddenly, Byrnes changed direction. "Now Miss Rosie, who was the first one to tell you that Frank Jordano had been arrested for this crime?"

Rosie: "I don't remember who told me, but I remember he was in jail, and I knew he done it, and I said he done it."

"You don't remember anybody telling you?"

"No, sir."

"Well, how did you learn of it?"

"Didn't I know who done it? What do you think he was going to be put in jail for?"

Not unkindly, Byrnes replied, "No, I am not asking you that, Miss Rosie. I am asking you this question, and I am going to go over it very carefully because I do not desire to confuse you, or be funny, or smart, or anything else. Who was the first person that told you that Frank Jordano had been arrested and put in jail and accused of this crime?"

Rosie insisted that she couldn't remember who told her Frank was in jail; all she knew was that he was.

"You had left the hospital when they told you that Frank Jordano was in jail?"

"Yes, sir."

"Do you remember making a statement while in the hospital that it was your husband that struck you?"

"No, sir."

"Do you believe you might have made it?"

"When I was unconscious I don't remember what I was saying; I might say anything."

"What was told you when they took you on the ferryboat on the day they brought you over here? What did they tell you when they brought you to the jail?"

Rosie misunderstood the question. She replied that being taken to jail left her so shaken that she couldn't say anything.

"Now during that time [in jail] did you make any statement?"

"Yes, sir; I made two statements."

"Now, did you write those statements down?"

"No. I cannot write in American."

"Were those statements written down?"

"One was; the second one."

"Did you sign it?"

"Yes, I signed it."

Byrnes turned to Judge Fleury. "Now, if your Honor please . . . I now call upon the District Attorney to produce that statement."

Bob Rivarde denied that he possessed any such statement. He added, however, that if he did, he would have no obligation to turn it over to the defense. Judge Fleury sided with the DA, ruling that the defense had no right to the state's evidence.

Byrnes turned back to the witness. "Before whom did you make the statement?"

Rosie again was puzzled by the language. "Before whom? How do you mean?"

Byrnes clarified: "Who was present, and who took it down in writing?"

Rosie named Charlie Burgbacher (the deputy sheriff in charge of the jail), Clay Gaudet, and another man who came with Mr. Gaudet whose name she didn't know.

"It was this gentleman—Clay Gaudet—who is now assisting the District Attorney who took down your statement?" Byrnes asked.

Rosie: "How you mean 'assisting'?"

"He is helping the District Attorney. The same man that took that statement down in writing, and had you swear to it, is the same gentleman that is now here with Mr. Rivarde, Mr. Clay Gaudet?"

"Yes, sir."

Again, Byrnes turned to the prosecution. "I call upon Mr. Gaudet, an associate counsel for the prosecution, for the production of that statement." He argued that he was entitled to it because he believed it would contradict Rosie's testimony.

Once again, Rivarde demurred. "We refuse to produce it because it is not a public record."

The judge ruled against the defense again, another short-term defeat. Byrnes turned to other matters. After quizzing her about her statement to the coroner's jury, Byrnes asked Rosie about the relationship between the Jordanos and Mary.

"Now Miss Rosie, where did you get your baby from the night before this crime happened—on Friday night."

"Mrs. Jordano's house. She was playing, and I told her to come on home, and Frank said, 'Let her stay,' and I said, 'No, it's time to put her to bed,' and I picked her up and went home with her."

"Now, is it not a fact, that Frank Jordano was very fond of your baby?"

"Yes, he loved the baby; but I don't know if he meant it in his heart. He always loved the baby, and kissed it."

Byrnes asked Rosie about her relationship with Frank. "Had you and Frank ever had any words or fuss?"

"No, sir."

"Were you friendly?"

"I was friendly."

"Whenever Frank was there he played with the baby, didn't he?"

"Yes, sir."

"What did the baby call Mr. Jordano, the old gentleman?"

"Grandpa."

"One time when the baby was very sick didn't Mrs. Jordano nurse the baby?"

"Yes, sir; many time when the baby was sick. I always got her to do something for the baby, and she always done it."

"She was very fond of the baby?"

"Yes, sir."

"And Mr. Jordano, the old gentleman, was very fond of the baby, too?"

"Yes, sir."

"And the baby was very fond of him?"

"Yes, sir."

Byrnes hoped he'd made his point.

At this point Byrnes passed the cross-examination over to his co-counsel, Archie Higgins. Higgins's task was to question Rosie again about how she and Charlie had been ejected from their grocery. It was a risky strategy, dangerously emphasizing the conflict between the two families. But perhaps it would suggest to the jury a reason that Rosie might invent testimony against the father and son.

He asked her a few questions about the legal notice that was served forcing them to give up the store, how long it took them to actually move, and how hard Iorlando had pressed them to leave.

Then, abruptly, Higgins switched back to the night of the attack. "I want you to tell us why you didn't arouse your husband when you saw two men coming into your house."

Rivarde was quick with his objection. "This witness has been on the stand the whole of the afternoon, and that question has been asked and answered." Judge Fleury agreed. Higgins asked Rosie a few more questions before ending his interrogation of the witness.

But before he sat down, he gave her one final opportunity to reconsider her testimony. Rosie was an unsophisticated, uneducated, and not especially bright twenty-one-year-old. Was it possible that she didn't understand the consequences of accusing two men of murder? How much thought did she give to what would happen to her two former neighbors, especially the young man who'd been so fond of her daughter?

"Now Mrs. Cortimiglia, you realize that two men are being tried for murder, and that your testimony in this case is going to be heard as evidence for the State to convict them of murder, and if these men are convicted of murder, Frank Jordano and [Iorlando] Jordano sitting here, they will be hung by the State of Louisiana by the neck until they are dead, dead, dead. You realize that fact?"

Rosie looked confused. "How do you mean? I don't understand."

Higgins responded gravely: "I want you to realize the seriousness of this, because I don't want you to make a statement [without] . . . realiz[ing] the seriousness of it. I ask you now if you know that the testimony that you are giving here . . . [is] made under oath . . . and that evidence is being taken here in court in an effort by the State to convict two men of murder when the penalty is death?"

Rosie didn't seem to understand that either. Higgins patiently explained it to her again—she was testifying under oath, she had to tell the truth and nothing but the truth, and the crime for which the Jordanos had been charged was punishable by hanging.

Finally, Rosie nodded, "Yes, sir," she understood. The defense could only hope that the jury had understood that she did not, in fact, understand and that the jurymen believed that her account was so hopelessly muddled that they dare not send a man to the gallows on it.

When Rosie got off the stand at 5:30 PM, she had testified for over five hours, much of it under intense cross-examination. Those who'd listened to her so intently had been favorably impressed, and a murmur of sympathy swept through the crowd as she was escorted out of the courtroom.

Later that night, the jurymen settled back into their chairs to hear from half a dozen more witnesses. First, Dr. Fernandez, at his own request, again took the stand because he wanted to correct some of his earlier testimony. The previous evening, he had testified that he didn't know how the injuries on Mary Cortimiglia had been inflicted. But, he told the court, he'd forgotten that "there was an axe produced at the inquest which was bloody and had hair on the end of it . . . which made me think that probably the instrument had some connection with it."

Byrnes asked the doctor about Rosie's testimony in front of the coroner's jury. Then he asked Dr. Fernandez why he hadn't put her testimony in writing. "Didn't you know this was a murder trial?" he asked.

The coroner replied that Sheriff Marrero told him that she'd already signed a notarized statement.

"The Sheriff told you not to take her statement down in writing?"

Rivarde interrupted. "I object, if your Honor please, to what the Sheriff told him, upon the ground that it is a conversation of third parties."

Byrnes argued that it was a legitimate question since Sheriff Marrero was a law enforcement officer. Judge Fleury, however, dismissed the exchange between Dr. Fernandez and Sheriff Marrero as irrelevant hearsay.

Dr. Fernandez stepped down from the stand, and other witnesses took his place. Drs. G. W. Rossner and Marvin Odom testified about being called to the scene early that Sunday morning. Hazel Johnson and her nephew George Bolden (who had accompanied his aunt that morning) testified about finding the injured Cortimiglias.

The last witness Thursday evening was City Councilman Emmanuel Fink, who recounted being woken up about three o'clock on the morning of March 9 by barking dogs and a distant knocking or tapping sound. Fink described the discovery of the Cortimiglias later that morning and told of telephoning for an ambulance and the police. At some point during the ensuing chaos, someone handed him an axe they had discovered under the house, and he, noticing a swatch of dark hair on the blade, gave it to Chief Leson. At the prosecution's request, the witness identified one of the two axes found on the Cortimiglia premises as the axe he meant, pointing out that a piece of hair was still visible on the blade.

Court adjourned at 11:30 PM.

The final witness for the state was sworn in at 10:25 the following morning. Charlie Cortimiglia, who had only been out of Charity Hospital for a few weeks, wasn't on the stand for long. He said that he'd gone to bed on the night of March 8 with a pistol and cash under his pillow and woken up in the hospital weeks later. He remembered nothing of the attack or his daughter's death.

When Charlie was through, DA Robert Rivarde rested his case.

11

Verdict

THE FIRST WITNESS CALLED for the defense was Frank's sister Lena. The twenty-year-old young woman narrated in chilling detail the morning Hazel Johnson shot out of the Cortimiglias' house shrieking, "Jesus! Oh, Jesus! Oh, Jesus!" Byrnes used Lena to make several points. He wanted to demonstrate that Frank had no interest in the grocery business—and thus no motive for killing the Cortimiglias—so he quizzed Lena about her brother's work history in real estate and life insurance. Byrnes also elicited from Lena the fact that on Sunday morning Frank was wearing the same clothes he'd worn the night before, presumably indicating he'd not splattered them with blood during the night. She provided alibis for her father and brother, testifying that she hadn't heard her father in the next room getting up during the night and that Frank had gone upstairs sometime after 10 PM and hadn't come down until she'd started screaming about the Cortimiglias. Under cross-examination, however, the prosecution got her to concede that it was possible for either Frank or Iorlando to have sneaked out of the house without her knowledge.

Byrnes's next witness was Paul Dupas, a thirty-five-year-old New Orleans real estate agent for whom Frank Jordano had once worked. Dupas had been aghast at the charges against Frank. He liked the boy and had trouble believing that he could do something so appalling. But a lot of people in Gretna thought Frank was guilty. And why would

Rosie Cortimiglia—whom he also knew slightly—make up such a thing? Her little girl, after all, was dead. Dupas had felt an acute need to know what had really happened.

Quite by accident, he had his opportunity when he was out on business over the river and realized that he was near where the Cortimiglias were living with Rosie's sister in Amesville. On impulse, he decided to call in on them.

Both Charlie and Rosie were home. Charlie had little to say, still recovering as he was from his ordeal. Rosie, however, was talkative and quite happy to tell Dupas what had happened. Animatedly, she recounted the attack, saying that when Frank had tried to kill Mary, she had fought him, attempting to protect her little girl. *Here,* she said eagerly to Dupas, pulling up the sleeve of her dress. *He cut me here,* she said, pointing to a scar on her arm, on the inside of her elbow.

Dupas returned home profoundly grieved by what he had learned. Frank must have done it. The cut on Rosie's arm was proof that she'd tried to fight off her attacker and proof, in Dupas's mind, that she was telling the truth. He'd told everyone in his office what Rosie had said, and word had spread. One day, Dupas received a telephone call from William Byrnes. When he'd heard the story, far from believing that this information indicted Frank, the lawyer knew that it might help exonerate him because it contradicted what Rosie had told the police. And since Rosie was the only eyewitness against Frank and his father, any evidence that demonstrated her unreliability as a witness could help win his clients' freedom.

Byrnes asked Dupas if he'd be willing to see if Rosie would repeat the same story. So the week before the trial started, Paul Dupas headed back out to Amesville, determined to see Rosie again.

Under questioning from both the state and the defense, Dupas narrated his story for the jury. Finally, Rivarde addressed the witness: "Now, Mr. Dupas, what was the sum and substance of the conversation between you and Mrs. Cortimiglia on your second visit?"

The sum and substance, he replied, was that she flatly denied telling him that she'd struggled with Frank or that Frank had slashed her on the arm. She completely repudiated her previous account. No doubt Byrnes hoped that Dupas's testimony would help convince the jurors that they would be foolish to convict men of murder based solely on Rosies's testimony.

After the midday dinner break, the defense called on a witness who added not so much an understanding of events as human pathos. Mrs. Jordano was on the stand for some time but mostly covered ground that had already been gone over. She described the events of the night of March 8 and morning of March 9, and her account matched that of Frank and Lena. She testified that her husband Iorlando—"my old man"—had been in bed with her the entire night; he had trouble getting up now, with his rheumatic back. She ended by turning to the jury and tearfully declaring, "My old man and my child are innocent!"

Next, the defense called the *New Orleans States* police reporter Andrew Ojeda. Ojeda told of seeing the Cortimiglias in Charity on the day after Frank had been arrested. He testified that when Rosie had told him that her husband had been the attacker, he hadn't believed her because Charlie was himself so badly injured.

In his cross, the DA tried to suggest that Ojeda's account of Rosie's statement had been exaggerated or even fabricated by the newspaper. But the newspaperman swore that the *States* accurately reported what she told him.

Iorlando Jordano was the next witness. He slowly made his way to the witness chair, his back trouble painfully evident. Two months in jail had not improved his health. In heavily accented, broken English, he testified as to his movements on Saturday afternoon and evening and about being called to the murder scene Sunday morning.

He added that he had loved the baby who called him, in her childish lisp, "Ganpa."

Rivarde rose to question him and asked Iorlando if he knew a man named Ed Hanson. When Iorlando hesitated, Rivarde directed that Hanson be brought into the courtroom. "Yes," Iorlando nodded, "I know this man." Rivarde warned the old grocer that the next question he was going to ask was "for the purpose of impeaching and contradicting your testimony."

Rivarde walked up to Iorlando: "Do you remember meeting Hanson at the Sportsmens Café?" Iorlando didn't even remember the saloon until Rivarde prompted his memory.

Rivarde repeated his question: "Mr. Jordano, did you or did you not meet Ed Hanson on Sunday, February 16 at the Sportsmens Café in Gretna? Did you, or did you not, have a conversation in which Hanson said to you: 'I see you have gone back in the grocery business and you are going to have opposition, the Cortimiglias are going to open a store. I hope you do well.' Then you said to Hanson, 'The opposition don't worry me, I will get rid of them, I will kill them all.' Did you, or did you not have that conversation, and tell Mr. Ed Hanson that?"

"I never said that!" The old man's voice shook. "If he told you that he told you a God damn lie; I never said that."

Judge Fleury broke in to gently reprimand the witness. "Listen, Mr. Jordano. I don't want to be harsh with you, but that language is not permissible in the Courthouse. I appreciate your situation as a witness, but the Court is not going to permit that kind of language."

Rivarde continued: "Then you deny having said that?"

"I never said that," Iorlando repeated. "I never told nothing to that man."

When it was again Byrnes's turn to question the witness, he approached Iorlando. "Mr. Jordano, did you at any time say to Mr. Hanson, or to any other person, that you were going to kill Charlie Cortimiglia, and his wife, and the child or any words like that, or any words that could be taken like that?"

"No," Iorlando replied. "I didn't say that."

"Mr. Jordano, did you at any time tell anyone, white or black, that you were going to kill Charlie Cortimiglia, or his wife, or his child?"

"I never opened my mouth [like that]," insisted Iorlando. "I don't belong to the Black Hand!"

With this firm denial Iorlando's testimony ended.

After the supper break, Byrnes requested that the sheriff bring the Cortimiglias' kitchen door, taken off by the hinges, into the courtroom. A couple of deputy sheriffs carried the heavy door in and set it down before the jury. Byrnes then called Superintendent of Police Frank Mooney to the stand.

Byrnes's defense strategy became apparent. He wanted the jury to see Mary Cortimiglia's murder and the attack on her parents as part of a larger pattern—the Axeman's crimes. So he wanted witnesses who could testify to the pattern of the attacks and show how the Cortimiglia assault and murder fit it. The Jordanos hadn't killed Mary Cortimiglia, he wanted to show the jury. The murder was the degenerate killer who had been terrorizing New Orleans for months.

Byrnes attempted to ask Mooney about the axe attacks and robberies connected to the "Ax-man" in New Orleans, but each time the prosecution objected on the grounds that the witness's testimony wasn't directly connected to the Cortimiglia case.

Judge Fleury agreed, saying, "We are only concerned with the investigation of the particular case under consideration. The mere fact that they may have had several other cases of a similar character, has no bearing on this particular case."

Byrnes argued that it was relevant to show that someone other than his clients had a motive for the crime and was responsible for a series of similar crimes. His clients had an alibi, he said. They were at home in their own beds when Mary Cortimiglia was killed. When defendants claim an alibi, he continued, they have a legal right to show that someone else had committed the crime—in this case, a "degenerate . . . a pervert . . . a sadist . . . [a] Jack the Ripper type."

Byrnes reserved a bill of exception, a written statement of his objection to the judge's ruling, which would put into the legal record his argument for an appeal. He would do this repeatedly throughout the trial.

Realizing that Fleury would continue to rule the same way, Byrnes nevertheless persisted in asking questions that showed that the Cortimiglia murder was similar in critical details to the Axeman attacks.

He continued asking questions he knew the judge wouldn't allow so he could keep filing bills of exception.

Byrnes asked Mooney for crime scene photographs that showed similarities among all the Axeman crimes. He asked the police superintendent if the Axeman cut out a door panel. He asked if the Axeman targeted corner houses, like that of the Cortimiglias. He asked about what kind of weapon the Axeman used. And how was the weapon usually disposed of? Were fingerprints ever found? Were sums of money often left, indicating robbery was not the motive? Didn't evidence indicate the Axeman wanted "a deluge of blood"?

In each case, the prosecution objected, the judge agreed, and Byrnes reserved a bill of exception. If he wasn't making much headway in getting evidence in front of the jury about the Axeman's crimes, he was laying the groundwork for an appeal if his clients were convicted.

Finally, Judge Fleury had listened to enough: "The court has ruled that testimony is inadmissible," he told Byrnes, "and that's an end of it."

But Mr. Byrnes wasn't finished. He called Maurice O'Neil, the New Orleans Police Department's Bertillon operator, as a witness. He tried to ask O'Neil whether the Cortimiglia case resembled the Axeman crimes in New Orleans, but again, the prosecutor—and the judge—shut him down.

Then he called to the witness chair Santo Vicari, the Amesville grocer who had been a victim of an Axeman-like burglary of his home and grocery only a few days before the attack on the Cortimiglias. And Louis Besumer, whose acquittal earlier in the month had confirmed his status as an Axeman victim in the public's eyes. And Jim Coulton, the *Times-Picayune* reporter who'd done so much work on the Axeman case. In no instance did the judge allow him to question the witnesses about similarities between earlier crimes and that of the crimes against the Cortimiglias. Judge Fleury was not permitting an Axeman defense.

Byrnes's next witnesses had seen Frank the morning of the attack or the evening before. Their testimony helped fill in for the jury Frank's actions in that time period but added nothing controversial.

Margaret Williams, however, had some surprises. She was a detective hired by Byrnes to get Rosie to talk. This was the kind of stratagem employed by defense lawyers before pretrial discovery gave them access to the prosecution's case. She testified that on May 1, posing as a door-to-door seller of toilet articles, she had called on the Cortimiglias and found Rosie eager to talk. Rosie told her that she'd woken to find Frank Jordano and his father in her room. She didn't have time to scream, she said, before one of the men hit the baby, and then her, with an axe. At first, she wasn't sure whether the men had had to leave the room to find the axe, then she decided that yes, they did. Neither of the men said anything to her, and it all happened too quickly for her to say anything to them.

Miss Williams's testimony continued. She thought Rosie seemed embarrassed by her shorn hair, the result of her head injuries, so the next day she returned with the present of a boudoir cap. On that visit, Rosie's story changed. This time she claimed she had spoken to Frank, and she said that "one of the men held her hands, but she didn't know which one." About the axe, Miss Williams said that Rosie told her that "she didn't remember whether they had [the axe] when they came in, or whether they went out to get it."

By the time the court adjourned Friday evening, it was almost midnight.

At ten o'clock the next morning, Frank Jordano took the stand in his own defense. The big, hulking youth was pale from two months' imprisonment, and he had lost weight. He hadn't been allowed to see his father, brother, sisters, or fiancée since he'd been imprisoned in the Gretna jail. He had only been allowed to see his mother a couple of times in the presence of Detective Marullo. He had a hard time understanding why he was here, why he and his father were standing trial. Now was his opportunity to set things right.

At Byrnes's request, Frank told the jury how he'd dressed up that Saturday night, dropped off his suit to be cleaned and pressed, gotten a haircut and shave, briefly visited with an aunt, then walked to Lee Hall—a dance hall—where he watched the dancing for several minutes before going home. When he got home, his mother told him that if he wanted anything to eat, he'd have to get it from the store. He decided to skip supper and finished up some paperwork before saying good night to his parents. He recounted his girlfriend Josie's dream to his mother, then went to bed.

The next morning he was startled awake by his sister's screams, and he flung himself half dressed down the stairs to find out what was wrong. He joined the crowd of people rushing into the Cortimiglias' home and found the baby dead and Charlie and Rosie gravely wounded. He asked Charlie, "Charlie, for Christ sake, who done this?" But all Charlie could do was ask Frank to tell his brother-in-law. So Frank hitched up his horse and buggy and rode out to Amesville, calling on Dr. Gelbke and Dr. Rossner on the way.

Byrnes asked him if he'd been in the Cortimiglia house at any time that night. Frank emphatically denied it: "No, sir. I was not in there."

Byrnes asked him about Rosie Cortimiglia's testimony that she had seen him hit baby Mary with the axe.

Frank must have thought of little else in the last two months. Now, all he could do was deny it in the strongest of terms: "I didn't strike that baby with any axe; it is one of the biggest false stories that ever came from a living human being's mouth in the State of Louisiana, if she said I struck the baby with an axe."

Byrnes: "Were you in the house that night, and did you strike that baby with anything?"

Frank: "No, sir, I did not."

Byrnes: "Is her statement true?"

Frank: "It is untrue." He turned to look directly at the jury. "It is false."

Now Byrnes turned to the kitchen door taken from the crime scene. Someone had pried off the door panel that Manny Fink and Chief Leson had nailed back into place. Byrnes pointed to the missing panel and asked Frank to climb through the opening. Would he fit?

Frank dutifully took off his coat and rolled up his sleeves. Bracing himself against the wooden platform on which the clerk of court's desk sat, he stretched one arm and then the other through the hole as he tried to pull himself through it. He paused when he heard a slight rip as one of the jagged edges of the door tore his shirt. Frank took a deep breath and, steadying himself, managed to force himself a surprising distance through the opening before he got stuck and could move no farther.

That was one theory of the crime debunked; whoever had attacked the Cortimiglias and however they got into the house, Frank Jordano couldn't have climbed through the hole in the door. At the request of one of the jurors, however, Frank easily reached over to slide the latch.

Frank extracted himself from the door, tugged his coat back on, and sat down in the witness chair.

His lawyer proceeded to ask him about his feelings toward baby Mary. "I loved the child with all my heart," he said. "Every time I came home in the evening the little child was over [at my] home and I grabbed her up and played with her until I . . . went out again."

On cross-examination, the district attorney asked him about the dream he'd told his mother about. Josie had dreamed about snakes, and he'd asked his mother if it was a good or bad dream. Rivarde asked Frank what he had told the coroner's jury. Frank admitted he'd lied. He'd said that he'd had a bad dream. "I didn't want to mention my sweetheart's name," he explained. But Frank pointed out that he'd come forward with that information himself. He had recently admitted the truth to Chief Leson in the Gretna jail.

Rivarde still hammered on Frank because of his falsehood.

"Now, you do admit, that when you swore before the coroner's jury, you absolutely swore to a falsehood?"

"I told Chief Leson I did wrong."

"That is not an answer to my question. Did you know when you made that statement to the coroner's jury, after you had been sworn, that you were swearing to an absolute falsehood?"

"I did know."

"You did know that you were swearing to an absolute falsehood?"

With some desperation, Frank said, "I did. . . . I did tell them that I had the dream, because I didn't want to mention my girl's name amongst men. I know I did wrong. I told Chief Leson I done wrong. . . . But that night they questioned me so."

Rivarde let the matter drop and moved on to other questions. He asked Frank if he'd gotten into a fight Sunday morning or Saturday night. Puzzled, Frank said, no, he hadn't. Rivarde then asked if he knew a streetcar conductor on the Algiers line named Fandel. Still puzzled, Frank admitted that he did. Wasn't he on Fandel's streetcar on Sunday morning after the attack on the Cortimiglias, and didn't he tell the conductor when asked how he'd hurt his hand that he'd gotten into a fight? Frank said no, he didn't go to Algiers that morning, he hadn't seen Fandel, and he hadn't been in a fight.

Suddenly, Rivarde switched to a different line of questioning: "Do you know a man named Rube Mayronne?" he demanded.

Frank admitted that he did. Rivarde asked if he recalled talking to Mayronne at his feed store about two weeks before the assault on the Cortimiglias. "Did you go and ask him if he had made a loan to the Cortimiglias, which would enable them to build their store?"

"No, sir," Frank replied, "I did not."

"And did you," the DA continued, "tell him, 'That *son of a b* will not be there longer than two weeks'?"

Frank vehemently denied saying any such thing. But he said he had been in Mayronne's store about the time that they had gone to court with Charlie Cortimiglia, and Mayronne didn't seem to like it. Mayronne cursed him and called him "a dirty little low down dago" for evicting Cortimiglia.

Frank testified that he'd told Mayronne that he didn't know what business it was of his, and continued: "So then he says to me, 'That dago says he is going to kill you if you fool with him.' I looked at him and burst out laughing, and said, 'It takes more than one man to do that job.' That is all I said to Rube Mayronne."

When he had the opportunity to question Frank again, William Byrnes tried to undo some of the damage done by the prosecution by exposing Frank as, technically, a perjurer. "Now Frank, about that dream, why did you tell that story about the dream, saying you had it when your girl had it? Did you tell it to mislead the coroner's jury about the Cortimiglia murder; did you tell it to hide anything that you knew?"

Frank was adamant that he had not.

"Did you know at that time that you would have to answer for every word that you said—every statement?"

"No, sir; I did not."

"Were you preparing a defense at that time?"

"No, sir."

"But did you make that statement for the purpose of throwing the coroner's jury off the trail of the murderer, or did you connect it in any way with the murder?"

"No, sir."

"What did you do it for?"

"I did not want to mention my sweetheart's name before the coroner's jury."

"When you told your attorneys that it was you who had the dream, what were you advised to do?"

The DA objected to this, so the question went unanswered, although it suggests that when Frank had his attack of conscience he'd gone to his lawyers, who'd advised him to confess to the truth. And, probably, a male jury of that era might have understood his hesitation at mentioning a young woman's name in a public proceeding, "notoriety" being something that no well-brought-up young woman aspired to.

When Frank rose from the witness stand after three hours of testimony, he and his lawyers had reason to worry. He'd admitted under oath that he'd lied under oath. Arguably, his lie had been trivial, and arguably, it had been justifiable in defense of a young lady's reputation. But there was no way to know if the men on the jury would see it that way. No doubt, his lawyers hoped that other witnesses scheduled that day would repair some of the damage.

The star in this lineup of witnesses was Dr. Jerome Landry, the house surgeon who had cared for Rosie while she was in Charity. Under direct questioning by Byrnes, Landry testified that he kept a close eye on Rosie while she was in the hospital, checking on her up to five or six times a day. For the first few days, she'd been unconscious but had "gradually regained consciousness." She had no memory of anything from the time she went to bed on Saturday night until she woke up in Charity weeks later. She didn't know what had happened, how she got there, or who had struck her. Landry said that he had asked her numerous times who had attacked her, and her consistent reply was "I don't know."

Byrnes asked him if Rosie had been in any condition to identify her attackers on March 14 when Frank had been arrested. Landry's response was brief and to the point: "No." Byrnes asked him what he thought of the fact that the day after she'd been discharged from the hospital, Rosie signed a statement identifying her assailants. Dr. Landry was suspicious: "It does seem strange to me that here to-day is a woman who has a perfectly blank mind, does not know anything, and the next say she remembers everything. She leaves the hospital this evening and knows nothing about it, and the next day she knows everything [that] happened at the time of the murder."

Landry also testified that although he couldn't be absolutely certain, he thought he'd heard the investigators ask Rosie if Frank had done it.

Nothing Rivarde asked could shake the doctor's testimony, so when Landry left the stand, Byrnes must have been relieved; the doctor had done the defense a lot of good. The physician who had taken the greatest care of Rosie was the one who discredited her the most.

Dr. Henry Leidenheimer, who had also worked at Charity when Rosie and Charlie had been patients, followed Dr. Landry. He was the physician who attended Charlie when the Cortimiglias first arrived at the hospital, while Landry operated on Rosie. It was clear that Byrnes called him as a witness not because he had observed either of the wounded as closely as Landry had observed Rosie, but because of his views on Rosie's injuries. Leidenheimer testified that he didn't believe that Rosie's head wounds had been caused by an axe. An axe, he said, would have torn the soft tissues of the head to a greater degree than he had found. Rosie, he believed, had been hit with something lighter. Charlie's injuries, however, were consistent with those caused by an axe; a heavy, sharp implement had sliced cleanly through the soft tissues of the scalp, through the skull, and into the brain.

Dr. Leidenheimer may well have been wrong in his assessment of the cause of Rosie's head wounds. He was a surgeon, not a forensic pathologist, and spent his time saving lives, not studying wound patterns the way a coroner or, today, a medical examiner does. Or perhaps he was correct and the attacker had hit her with something other than an axe, as he had done to Mary Davi. Either way, for the defense his testimony was a godsend because it directly contradicted Rosie's assertion that Frank had hit her with an axe.

Leidenheimer also testified that the cut Rosie had sustained on her arm could have come from an infusion injected into her at the hospital. He didn't recall if she'd had such a cut while in the hospital, but it was plausible, he thought, that a spot on her inner arm, at the bend of the elbow, just where she had a scar, had been "cut [to] expose the vein" for a medical procedure. This suggested that Rosie's story that she'd been cut on the arm by Frank might also be inaccurate.

From the questions jurors asked, it was clear they didn't want to give up on Rosie's story about being struck with an axe. One asked if her wounds could have been caused by a corner of the axe; another if they could have been caused by the inability to "swing the axe properly in close quarters." The DA chimed in and asked if the injuries could have been caused with the axe handle. To all, Dr. Leidenheimer replied, "No."

After Landry and Leidenheimer's testimony, reporters thought that the defense was in the best shape it had been in since the trial began. Then Chief of Police Peter Leson took the stand. He was the person for whom Rosie had first identified the Jordanos as culprits. Leson testified that he had visited the Cortimiglias in the hospital twice a day after they had been admitted. Finally, one day—he couldn't remember which one—Rosie told him that it was "Frank Jordano and the old man." He denied asking her if the Jordanos had done it and denied later warning her to "stick" to her story about the Jordanos. Initially, Leson testified that there were no other witnesses to Rosie's accusation, but later he amended his statement, saying that when he brought Dr. Gelbke to the hospital, Rosie told him that Frank and his father had hit her.

When asked by Byrnes why he took Rosie to the parish jail after she was discharged from the hospital, Leson explained that it was done out of concern for her safety. They feared "someone might harm her," he claimed, although he never explained who that someone might be. They needed someplace safe to keep her "until we could find a place for her to be taken care of. . . . She had no place at that time to stay." Moreover, he added, when Byrnes pressed him, she was a material witness in a murder case.

He denied realizing at the time that she had relatives in Amesville, despite the fact that two of her brothers-in-law—at least one of whom lived in Amesville—accompanied her from the hospital to the jail. When Byrnes asked him if he had questioned Frank Jordano about visiting these same relatives on the morning the crime was discovered, Leson said he didn't remember. When Byrnes asked why, if he was so concerned about Rosie's safety, he thought it safe to release her the next day, Leson disavowed responsibility; he lost control over her when he turned her over to Sheriff Marrero and Charles Burgbacher, the deputy in charge of the jail.

The final witness of the day was the coroner of Orleans Parish, Dr. Joseph O'Hara. O'Hara had not examined either of the Cortimiglias, but he was a specialist in brain and nerve diseases, head of neurology at Touro Infirmary, and a consulting neurologist at both Charity Hospital and the New Orleans City Hospital of Mental Diseases. Perhaps as one who had worked with both Inspector of Police James Reynolds and Superintendent of Police Frank Mooney on Axeman cases, he, too, believed that a mad killer was loose and the Jordanos were guiltless. He certainly didn't think they should be convicted on Rosie Cortimiglia's evidence.

O'Hara was on the stand for several hours, from the late afternoon until after the dinner break. Most of the defense's questions were about Rosie's injuries, but they were always couched as hypotheticals about someone who'd been injured in precisely the way Rosie had been. The gist of O'Hara's response to defense questioning was that someone who had sustained the head injuries that Rosie Cortimiglia had sustained, and had made the claims that she had made, was likely "suffering from a paranoiacal [*sic*] state, . . . [which] is a firm, fixed, systematized, forced delusion or hallucination, the result of trauma, from an emotional shock, or from external forces of the head." O'Hara's expert view was that (underneath all the hypotheticals) Rosie's mental condition made her an untrustworthy witness. In particular, he believed it unlikely that she would be able to recall her attack with such precision since people who had received this type of brain injury were usually unable to recall the events leading to the injury in so much detail.

Byrnes asked if such a person was more likely to be suggestible. O'Hara replied yes, "Those people are very prone to suggestions, and easy to be led."

Byrnes then asked if such a person would be more open to suggestion if arrested and thrown in jail. O'Hara thought so: "Yes, she would be if she was put in jail. If she came out of the hospital suffering from an emotional shock and was put in jail, certainly she would be more depressed. If she was more depressed she would be more susceptible to suggestion."

The prosecution, playing the same hypothetical game, tried to get O'Hara to say that because some circumstantial evidence supported Rosie's accusation, it should be believed, but failed. Dr. O'Hara continued to maintain that Rosie's testimony shouldn't be trusted.

After Dr. O'Hara completed his testimony and rose from the witness chair, at 10:30 Saturday night the defense rested its case.

Rivarde and his team must have thought O'Hara's testimony seriously damaged their case because they immediately scrambled to find an additional expert medical witness. Rivarde had had Dr. C. V. Unsworth, a specialist in mental and nervous diseases, examine Rosie earlier but hadn't known if the state would need him. He decided it did. Late Saturday night, Judge Fleury issued a subpoena for Dr. Unsworth, and the case was adjourned until Monday.

On Monday morning, the prosecution's rebuttal began. Everyone hoped that today the case would finally go to the jury. The trial had already been the longest for a murder that anyone in Jefferson Parish could remember. The jurors had been living in the courthouse for almost a week, eating and sleeping in the building and attending court thirteen or more hours a day, breaking only for meals. They were ready for it to end. Everyone was ready for it to end. The defense even dispensed with the usual character witnesses—friends, neighbors, and business associates who would testify to the men's kind natures and excellent reputations.

The state's first witnesses Monday morning were Robert J. Langridge, a young railroad security officer, followed by John Fourcade, a Gretna patrolman. In his earlier testimony, Frank Jordano had denied seeing either Langridge or Fourcade the Saturday night before the murder. The prosecution wanted to show that Frank had been out and about in Gretna later than he'd said he'd been and that he'd lied about not seeing the two men.

Langridge and Fourcade both testified that on the night of March 8, they were chatting across from the dance hall when they'd seen Frank walk by sometime between 11:30 and midnight. That put Frank in the area later than the 10:30 or 11 PM that he'd testified he'd gone home. Langridge also stated that he'd seen Frank Jordano "walking fast" past the dance hall, not stopping to watch as he had claimed; they both testified that he'd said hello.

Under cross-examination by Byrnes and Higgins, however, the two men didn't recall much else about the night. Neither could name anyone else he'd spoken to in that neighborhood, nor name anyone else he'd seen in or around the dance hall that night. Officer Fourcade couldn't say how big the crowd at the dance hall was, and he couldn't recall whether it was a dark night or who his partner had been. His sighting of Frank Jordano seemed to be the only thing Fourcade remembered. Jim Coulton at the *Times-Picayune* thought that Byrnes did a pretty thorough job of tripping him up.

Byrnes also elicited the information that Langridge was a deputy sheriff who'd received his commission from Sheriff Marrero. Langridge explained that he needed it for his work for the railroad and didn't work for Marrero, although, he conceded, he had worked for the sheriff at one time.

Next, the state brought out its own medical experts, beginning with Dr. R. M. Van Wart, a specialist in nervous and mental diseases. After getting the facts of the case from Dr. Unsworth and spending an hour with Rosie that morning, he pronounced her "sane and . . . perfectly responsible [with] . . . no evidence of any mental disorder." He testified that he thought it possible for Rosie's memory of the attack to appear suddenly in such crystal clear detail.

The jurors found some of the doctor's answers confusing, and at the end of his testimony one of them put a question to him. "Doctor, we bunch of boys understand some of it, but we don't understand it all," he said. "Do we understand that this woman now has her good sense and her reasoning power?"

"She has, in my opinion," answered Van Wart.

That's all the jury needed to hear.

The dinner break had been taken during Van Wart's testimony, and he stayed on the stand into the early afternoon. It was midafternoon by the time Dr. Unsworth was sworn in. He had interviewed Rosie several times in the last three weeks, and his professional opinion was that "she is now sane and responsible for her acts, and qualified to make a competent statement."

About 5 PM, the state rested its case, and the court broke for supper. The trial entered the final stretch when the court reconvened at 6 PM. The crowd of interested spectators had not diminished during the last week. It had, if anything, grown. Hundreds of people packed into the small courtroom, squeezing into every last inch of standing room and spilling out into the hallway where dozens—maybe even hundreds—tried to listen to the proceedings. Rosie, who had been banished to the witness room for much of the trial, now sat with Charlie at the front of the courtroom, behind the team of prosecutors, and right in front of the jury. Mrs. Jordano, Lena, and Josie sat anxiously behind the defense team.

The time for summing up had come. Judge Fleury firmly admonished spectators against any disruption in the courtroom; anyone who interrupted the proceedings in any way would be in contempt of court. The prosecution would make its summation first, followed by the defense; the prosecution would then be allowed a rebuttal. For almost six hours, the attorneys summarized their case, marshalled their evidence, and employed rhetorical flourishes as they used both reason and emotion in an attempt to sway the twelve men who sat before them.

No record of the summations in their entirety exists, but it's not hard to guess what points each side emphasized. The state's strongest evidence, both legally and emotionally, was the eyewitness Rivarde and Gaudet presented as the grieving mother who had watched helplessly as her only child was murdered and now waited for justice. Frank and Iorlando Jordano were the wicked business competitors driven to murder by jealousy. And Frank, the prosecution argued, had already proved himself to be "a perjurer! A self-confessed perjurer!"

At one point, Clay Gaudet, swept up in his own eloquence, demanded, "Is there any doubt in your mind how Mary Cortimiglia met her death? There is no doubt where the responsibility lies for the murder of this child. The finger of justice"—and here he turned and pointed dramatically at Frank and Iorlando sitting only a few feet away—"by various witnesses and the mother of the child whom you have heard, points at the murderers who sit at the bar of justice."

Of course, Byrnes, Higgins, and Thalheim were simultaneously on their feet, objecting to the remarks as highly prejudicial. They leaped up again a little later when Gaudet, in another rhetorical flourish, asked, "Who killed Mary Cortimiglia?" then, again pointing to the defendants, answered his own question: "These are the villains!" Both times the defense asked for a mistrial, and both times the judge refused, only cautioning the jury to disregard the remarks.

The defense, for its part, pointed out weaknesses in the state's case. Rivarde had introduced Ed Hanson, who, he said, claimed that Iorlando had threatened to kill the Cortimiglias. Yet Rivarde had never backed up his claim by calling Hanson to testify.

Likewise, the DA had argued that feed store owner Rube Mayronne heard Frank threaten the Cortimiglia family. And that a streetcar conductor named John Fandel had seen Frank in Algiers later on the morning of the murder with a scratch on his hand that Frank said he'd gotten in a fight. But the state produced neither as a witness.

And Bob Langridge and John Fourcade—what did they prove? Both men said they had seen Frank on Saturday night at almost midnight, over an hour past the time he'd sworn he'd gone home. Neither, however, could tell the jury anything more about the evening—who else they saw, whether the moon was shining. Perhaps they did see Frank. Perhaps, though, they got the time wrong. Or maybe they had seen him some other Saturday night. Both officers had connections to the police, who were convinced that the Jordanos were guilty, so both had a possible motivation to misremember.

What about the state's medical witnesses? Neither had seen Rosie in Charity Hospital, and both had spent limited time examining her since her discharge. Wasn't the testimony of her Charity physicians more persuasive?

Most of all, they hammered on the unreliability of Rosie Cortimiglia as a witness. Her own attending physicians didn't think she could be believed. While in the hospital she had maintained that she could remember nothing, and hadn't even been told of her daughter's death. Yet after only a few hours in the sheriff's custody, she not only knew that Mary was dead, she finally recalled—in exact detail—how she had died. How had this happened? How had she even learned that Mary had died? How could she have known her baby was dead unless someone told her? Yet no one—certainly not Chief Leson or the deputy sheriffs—admitted telling her. What else were they not admitting?

What about the inconsistencies in Rosie's story of the attack? She said she had no time to scream, but Iorlando had time to leave the room and come back with an axe. Rosie also had time to talk to Frank. She said that the killer had hit the baby with the heavy axe that many members of the jury had handled. If husky Frank had hit little Mary three blows with such a weapon, he would have smashed her skull. But

Dr. Fernandez, the coroner, testified that he found only two round wounds slightly larger than a half-dollar coin.

Wasn't it likelier that someone had fed Rosie the story of the assault? Someone who'd convinced her that the Jordanos must have done it? What if she had been told over and over that the Jordanos must have done it, and she, in her weakened state, had simply accepted their guilt? The Jordanos, after all, were the competition. They had thrown the Cortimiglias out of a successful business. If everyone else thought they did it, then they must be guilty, right? In her vulnerable state, if Rosie had been asked over and over again, "Did the Jordanos do it?" she could easily have become convinced that they did.

And if Rosie's testimony was disregarded, all the state had was very thin circumstantial evidence, not enough to hang two good men.

For Rosie, sitting behind the DA's chair, listening to her mental state denigrated at such length proved too much. About halfway through the summations, as Andrew Thalheim pointed out inconsistencies in her account of the attack, she leapt from her chair, shook her fist at him, and shrieked, "You can say what you please but before God he did it!"

The tense silence of the packed courtroom immediately dissolved into chaos, the audience buzzing with exclamations of surprise and sympathy for the mother of the murdered child and of outrage against the murderers. The bailiffs quickly reestablished order, and, angrily, Fleury ordered the deputy sheriffs to escort Rosie and Charlie from the courtroom.

Once again, Byrnes and his team demanded a mistrial. Such an outburst on the part of the main prosecution witness was so prejudicial, they argued, that "the effect on the jury could not be remedied." Once again, Judge Fleury denied their request but directed the jury to disregard the outburst.

Bob Rivarde finished his summation for the state around midnight. By the time Judge Fleury delivered his charge to the jury, it was around 12:30 AM when the jury filed out to their deliberation room on the third floor. The courtroom settled in for what was expected to be a long night.

But at 1:45 AM, the jury was back. Why so soon? Frank had reason for a surge of hope. Surely they couldn't have convicted so quickly. A guilty verdict would have taken longer.

Frank and Iorlando rose. The foreman handed the clerk of court the verdict: Frank Guagliardo, alias Frank Jordano—guilty as charged.

Iorlando Guagliardo, alias Iorlando Jordano—guilty without capital punishment.

By finding him guilty, the jurors had sentenced Frank to hang. Death was the automatic penalty for murder.

Shocked, unbelieving, Frank swayed a little on his feet as the judge thanked and dismissed the jurors. Reporters surrounded the Jordanos, pounding them with questions. All Frank could say was, *It wasn't a fair trial. She lied. Miss Rosie lied.* Bailiffs pushed the reporters out of the way, handcuffed the condemned men, and escorted them out of the courtroom.

Months later, when the two prisoners again stood in front of Judge Fleury for formal sentencing, seventeen-year-old Frank spoke to the court with dignity and courage. Fighting back tears, he said, "It is true, judge, that I may hang, but I would rather go to the gallows than tell a lie in order to have an innocent man executed. If Mrs. Cortimiglia is possessed of her faculties, she knows that she is lying and I would not swap places with her today."

He then made mention of some of the inconsistences in her testimony and continued, "If you think, judge, that I should hang on testimony of that character, then I am ready to die, but there is no excuse for sentencing my old father, who is all crippled up with rheumatism and is almost blind. I pray to God that Mrs. Charles Cortimiglia will come forward and tell the truth before my father dies in prison."

Judge Fleury then did as he was required by the law and sentenced sixty-eight-year-old Iorlando Jordano to life in the state penitentiary and seventeen-year-old Frank Jordano to the gallows.

12

False Lead

As the authorities in Gretna convicted the wrong men for the killing of Mary Cortimiglia, so subsequent Axeman authorities have wrongly convicted Joseph Mumfre of being the Axeman. Or at least suggested that he's the most plausible suspect for one or more of the murders. In *Ready to Hang* (1952), Robert Tallant planted the seeds of this legend by telling the story of Mumfre's murder in Los Angeles by the widow of one of his alleged victims. And his version of events had its roots in sloppy newspaper reporting that probably grew out of the psychological need to provide a comforting solution to the Axeman crimes and resulted in conflating a Black Hand thug with a serial killer. But Mumfre's story is in fact the story of blackmail and retribution.

In 1909, Joseph "Doc" Mumfre began a twenty-year sentence at the Louisiana State Penitentiary for bombing an Italian grocery in a failed extortion plan. He was sent to Angola, one of the prison farms that made up the Louisiana penitentiary system, a place so brutal that prisoners had been known to deliberately cross the "deadline" to be shotgunned by a guard. Not Doc Mumfre. He survived to be paroled in June 1915—only to become a suspect in a murder investigation five months later.

Vincent Moreci, a foreman for the United Fruit Company, was gunned down on November 19, 1915, as he walked home from work.

Moreci had survived an attempt on his life five years before and then gotten off after being charged with the murder of one of the suspected gunmen, George Di Martini. Paul Di Christina, suspected along with Di Martini of attempting to kill Moreci, was shot by grocer Peter Pepitone, who was then convicted of manslaughter and sentenced to twenty years in the penitentiary. The police saw it as a typical Italian vendetta.

So when Moreci was killed in 1915, John Dantonio, the detective in charge of the investigation, saw it as a continuation of the vendetta. Dantonio had several suspects but not enough evidence to arrest them.

So it was that Joseph Mumfre, well-known Black Hander on whom the police had been keeping an eye since his release from prison, was picked up, charged with being dangerous and suspicious, and grilled about the killing. Mumfre denied any involvement. And the witness who'd gotten a look at one of the shooters couldn't identify him, giving Dantonio no choice but to let him go.

Black Hander and alleged Axeman Joseph Mumfre.

But Mumfre couldn't stay out of trouble. In the January 1916 Democratic primary election (which in Democratic-controlled Louisiana was the only election that mattered), Sheriff Marrero was fighting off a challenge from Reform candidate Peter Leson. On the day of the election, January 25, one of Marrero's deputies picked Mumfre up in the town of Kenner, across the river, not far from Lake Pontchartrain. Armed with marked ballots, he was canvassing—some said intimidating—the Italian population on behalf of the Reform candidates against the Regular, or Ring, Democrats in general, and against Sheriff Marrero in particular.

As an example par excellence of a machine Democrat, Marrero wasn't very happy about this. And, since Mumfre was also arrested for carrying a concealed revolver (a violation of the law) and was suspected of drinking in saloons (a violation of his parole), Sheriff Marrero jailed him and immediately notified the penitentiary's Board of Control.

The president of the penitentiary Board of Control instructed the sheriff to hold Mumfre until he could get orders from the governor to ship him back to prison. So Marrero did everything he could to make sure Mumfre didn't get out of the parish prison.

Two other men who'd been arrested with Mumfre—Angelo Albano and his cousin—posted bond and were released. Although Mumfre, too, posted bond, Sheriff Marrero refused to free him. The penitentiary's Board of Control, he said, had instructed him to hold Joseph Mumfre, and hold him he would. So it was a considerable shock when Marrero received his next instructions from the Board of Control: he was to release Joseph Mumfre immediately. But the sheriff again refused. Mumfre had violated his parole, and as far as Marrero was concerned he was going to stay in jail until he went back to the penitentiary.

In the meantime, Marrero's son, District Attorney L. H. Marrero Jr., conveniently charged Mumfre with an additional offense—possessing obscene pictures. It's hard to avoid the conclusion that this was a maneuver cooked up between Marrero Jr. and Sr. to make sure that Mumfre stayed where he was. The convict was ordered held on $500 bond, but, as the *New Orleans States* observed, "no bondsman [was] forthcoming." Perhaps the sheriff had something to do with that.

Joseph Mumfre came to trial in Gretna on February 16 on the charge of carrying a concealed weapon. His attorney, Louis Gosserand, was ill with the flu, so Mumfre, not unreasonably, asked for a continuance. DA Marrero refused. The trial went on as scheduled, without the defendant's lawyer.

With no attorney to advise him, Mumfre took the stand in his own defense. He admitted that he had been campaigning for Chief Leson and other Reform Democrats with marked ballots at the behest of Gosserand, who had been defending him free of charge. Moreover, he took the courtroom by surprise by admitting that he'd received his parole with the assistance of George Wesley Smith, private secretary to Governor Luther Hall; Mumfre had paid Smith for his help. Apparently, Governor Hall had granted Mumfre parole because of paid intervention by his private secretary.

All the pieces fell into place, and Mumfre's connection with the Reform Democrats became clear. A member of a Reform administration had used his influence to get Mumfre paroled. At the next election, Mumfre solicited votes for the reformers, and when he was arrested, a Reform lawyer defended him. This also made sense of the apparent change of heart of the penitentiary Board of Control. The administration had obviously pressured the board not to send Mumfre back to prison. And this was the "Reform" party!

Unsurprisingly, in a trial that lasted a day, Mumfre was convicted and served four months in the Jefferson parish prison for the unlawful possession of a weapon. After completing his sentence, he was shipped back to the penitentiary. But with the time off earned for good behavior, he was released again on April 21, 1918.

And, less than a month later, he was under arrest again. Accused of trying to extort money from a woman, Mumfre served three months in jail—only to be arrested again in January 1919 when Detective Marullo picked him up as a "dangerous and suspicious" character suspected of sending Black Hand letters.

So by the time Joseph Mumfre appeared before Judge J. J. Fogarty, the authorities of the city of New Orleans were heartily sick of him. He was an "undesirable" Italian, the kind associated with the vendetta and the Mafia. As the *States* reported:

> For years Monfre [*sic*] has been looked upon by the police as a member of an undesirable band of Italians in the city and on several occasions when vendetta activities gave the police trouble, Monfre [*sic*] was taken into custody and questioned. He was believed to have had knowledge of these activities. But Monfre [*sic*] always—except in the Graffignino [*sic*] case—wriggled out of it.

It was time to run him out of town.

When Mumfre was brought up before Judge Fogarty, the judge looked at him and said, "It would do the city no good to send you to the parish prison for thirty days. I am going to give you twenty-four hours to leave the city. Be sure that you do so." If he stayed in the city, the judge warned, he would be arrested again.

Doc Mumfre left New Orleans. If he couldn't be a Black Hander in New Orleans, there were other cities with Italian populations. He had a daughter, Lena, in California, who had been taken there by her maternal grandparents. He would try his luck there. California turned out to be not at all lucky for Joseph Mumfre.

By the time murder found another Italian grocer in New Orleans, Mumfre was long gone.

Nineteen-year-old Sarah Laumann woke at 3:30 on the morning of August 3—a Sunday morning—to see a man leaning over her. Instinctively, she shrieked. The intruder fled from her room. She screamed again. Her alarmed parents, woken by her cries, raced from their room to see what was wrong.

They found her terrified but apparently unhurt. Only after she complained about a pain in her head several hours later did her mother realize that Sarah had been wounded. The Laumanns immediately summoned their family doctor, who found a small laceration behind Sarah's right ear, the result, it seemed, of some sort of blunt instrument. The doctor assured the worried parents that it was only a slight injury; the girl would be fine.

The Laumanns didn't alert the police until midmorning. One of the first questions the responding officer asked was *Where is your axe?*

Mrs. Laumann took the policemen out to the woodshed in the back where the axe was kept. It was gone. Mr. Laumann said he'd used it only the day before and had left it on a stack of firewood in the shed.

Patrolmen blanketed the neighborhood. One of the officers found the blunt axe on the grounds of the next-door Saint Francis de Sales School. Looking closely, the policeman could see no bloodstains on the blade.

The Laumanns lived at 2123 Second Street, a modest house in the middle of the block between South Saratoga Street and Loyola Avenue, in the Central City neighborhood. Both of Sarah's parents had been born in Louisiana, although her grandparents were from Bavaria. Mr. Laumann was a carpenter. Sarah was the youngest of four children and the only one still living with her parents. She worked in a cigar factory.

When he heard that there had been another axe attack, Superintendent Mooney went out to see for himself. The intruder had climbed onto a gallery on the side of the house and then through an open window into the dining room. Although the shutters had been locked shut, it had been a simple matter to force them open.

"I felt a stinging of the left ear," she told the officers. "That is what probably awakened me. I saw a man bending over me under the mosquito bar." The young woman was considerably shaken by her encounter, but she could describe her attacker: "About 26 years old, of rather dark complexion, 5 feet 8 inches in height, about 165 pounds in weight and wearing a dark coat and pants; his shirt was white with dark stripes and he had a dark cap pulled down over his eyes."

The next day the girl's parents took her in to see Dr. Landry at Charity Hospital. The doctor reassured them; Sarah had sustained a mild concussion, but her skull hadn't been fractured. He didn't, however, believe her injury had been caused by the axe, as everyone seemed to have assumed. It was a circular wound, the result, he thought, of "a thick, blunt instrument."

How her assailant would have fled carrying a heavy axe was a mystery anyway. Sarah said that she hadn't seen anything in his hands when he'd been leaning over her. "So," Mrs. Laumann pointed out to a reporter, "if he had hit her with the axe, he would have had to pick it up and jump out the window with it. But when she screamed, he didn't stop for anything, but just scrambled out of the window and over the fence."

Opinion was divided. Although the Laumanns and their neighbors shrugged off the Axeman theory, some investigators were convinced that the girl had been his latest victim. Others, probably those who'd never believed in the Axeman anyway, thought that this was merely a bungled burglary. On the other side of town, on Frenchman Street, the following night, a thief had broken into a house and snatched a chain and pendant from around the neck of a sixteen-year-old girl before running off.

It was all speculation because there were few clues. But the lack of evidence didn't stop the newspapers from lumping the attack in with the other unsolved axe attacks. Jim Coulton was still pushing the Axeman angle hard: A *Times-Picayune* headline declared that the attacker had been the MYSTERIOUS "AXMAN," and the article listed Sarah Laumann among the Axeman's victims: the Cortimiglias, Joseph Romano, Louis Besumer and Harriet Anna Lowe, the Maggios, Epifanio Andollina, the Sciambras, and Joseph Davi.

But this was probably not the Axeman's work. The girl was barely injured, not beaten half to death. The assault had more in common with the attack on Mary Schneider a year earlier than the serial killer's other victims. And the description given by Sarah Laumann didn't match that of Joe Romano's niece. Pauline Bruno described her uncle's attacker as tall—"probably six feet"—and heavily built, while Sarah Laumann's assailant, described as about twenty-six years old, was only five foot eight and 160 or 165 pounds.

There was a lull of three months before the next "Axeman" attack, but the literary history of the Axeman story has it otherwise. In *Ready to Hang*, New Orleans writer Robert Tallant claimed that on August 10, the Axeman pried off a door panel on Elysian Fields Avenue and attacked grocer Steve Boca, slashing his head open. In pain and dripping blood, Boca managed to make his way next door to the home of his friend Frank Genusa, who summoned help. Boca had little memory of the attack and couldn't describe his attacker, but the Axeman left his calling card on the kitchen floor: the blood-stained axe.

Tallant also recounts the case of druggist William Carlson, who sat up late reading on the night of September 2. Hearing a noise at his back door, he hastily picked up his revolver and nervously called out, *Who is it? What do you want?* When he got no answer, he fired in the direction of the noise. The next morning, the police found the unmistakable sign of chisel marks on one of the door panels.

Other authors have repeated these incidents in accounts of the Axeman's crimes. But they seem to have no basis in fact. No New Orleans paper carried an account of an Axeman attack on Steve Boca or of an averted attack on William Carlson. No Steve, Steven or Stephen Boca, William Carlson, or Frank or Francis Genusa are even listed in the 1919 New Orleans city directory (although in 1920, a Frank Genusa was living on Saint Philip Street, over two miles from where Tallant said Boca lived). It's inconceivable that with the city on high alert for the axe murderer, the newspapers would ignore an Axeman attack or even a near miss. The more likely explanation is that Tallant got it wrong, and the attempts on Boca and Carlson are just myths.

The attack on Mike Pepitone, however, was real enough.

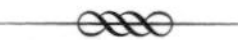

Esther Pepitone was a heavy sleeper. And this night she especially deserved her sound slumber. She and her husband Mike had worked all day and long into the night on both Saturday and Sunday when the Sells-Floto Circus was in town. There was a small fortune to be made selling soft drinks to the crowds of delighted children and adults who walked past the Pepitones' grocery at the corner of Ulloa and Scott in midcity to the circus a block away. Sunday night it wasn't until midnight that the exhausted Mrs. Pepitone was able to fall asleep next to her husband Mike in their bedroom behind the store.

When she first heard the voice, she thought she was dreaming. From a distance, she heard someone calling for help. The voice got closer and closer. Then she woke abruptly to the sound of her husband's exclamation: "Oh, Lord!" Sitting up in bed, she saw the shapes of two men slipping out of the bedroom into her children's room next door. She looked over to see her husband lying next to her covered in blood, moaning. Panicking, she shook him: "Mike! Mike, what happened?" Mike groaned in reply.

On the verge of hysteria, she leapt out of bed and rushed out of the bedroom shouting for help. Her oldest child, eleven-year-old Rosie, ran outside to summon a neighbor.

Around 1:20 AM on October 27, Deputy Sheriff Ben Corcoran was walking down Scott Street on his way home when Rosie ran into the street hollering for help. *My father is full of blood!* she cried. Corcoran followed Rosie back into the house, where he met Mike's terrified and bewildered wife.

"Mr. Corcoran," she said, "it looks like the Axeman was here and murdered Mike." She pointed toward the bedroom. Corcoran entered to see Mike lying unconscious on the bed, awash in his own blood. The bedroom wall was speckled crimson, blood splashed eight or ten feet high. Mike had been viciously pummeled. His skull was fractured in several places and his face beaten into an unrecognizable mess. On a chair near the bed lay the bloody weapon: a fourteen-inch iron bar with a heavy three-inch iron nut on the end.

Deputy Corcoran immediately called for the Charity Hospital ambulance and reported the attack to the New Orleans police. Chief of Detectives George Long and a squad of detectives quickly arrived, with Superintendent Mooney, Captain Thomas Capo, and other detectives and senior officers not far behind.

Another dead grocer, must have been Mooney's first thought. *The Axeman is back.*

Mrs. Pepitone told her story to the investigating officers and gave a description of the attackers: a tall, thin man and a shorter, stockier one. She had only gotten a glimpse of them as they escaped through the children's room into the backyard.

Broken glass littering the dining room floor testified to the manner of entrance. The intruders had gotten in by smashing two glass panes, unlatching the window, and raising the sash.

The intruders were not intent on robbery. Nothing had been stolen: receipts from the sale of drinks to the circus crowds remained safely tucked in a cupboard. There were no signs that the house had been searched for jewelry or other valuables.

Mike had been discovered wearing trousers. But Mrs. Pepitone said that he'd gone to bed in only his underwear. Detectives theorized that he'd heard the sound of the break-in and was preparing to investigate when he was attacked.

While policemen in the midcity neighborhood combed over the Pepitone residence and grocery, doctors at Charity tried to save Mike's life, but the thirty-five-year-old grocer was dead by 3:15 AM. He bled to death from multiple wounds on both sides of his head. In addition to multiple lacerations, his skull had been fractured twice on the left side and once on the right. Any one of those blows would probably have been deadly. Whoever beat Mike Pepitone meant to kill him.

If Mooney arrived thinking the Axeman had struck again, it didn't take long to change his mind. He quickly decided that the killing was another act in the vendetta between Paul Di Christina and Peter Pepitone.

Although Peter Pepitone had sworn that his son Mike had nothing to do with Di Christina's murder in 1910, the police at the time had believed he was involved. Apparently, so did Di Christina's friends. After Di Christina's murder, Mike Pepitone had taken his family and business to the south, to Plaquemine Parish, perhaps to escape retribution for the killing. He'd only moved back to New Orleans about a year earlier because his business had failed. Peter Pepitone served five years in the penitentiary before being paroled in 1915. He had been terrified of retaliation, and now, it seemed, the Di Christina faction had struck back against the Pepitones.

The little evidence Mooney's detectives uncovered pointed in that direction. Several Italians who'd been in the store in the week before Mike's murder raised suspicions that they had been plotting the vendetta. Investigators didn't find much else. No one was very optimistic about solving the case. The *States* warned that the murder would probably remain "another vendetta mystery."

Nevertheless, Jim Coulton at the *Times-Picayune* fed the Axeman narrative. All three of the major papers were quick to report that Mooney was treating the case as a vendetta murder (and the *States* was explicit that "Mooney does not connect the Pepitone murder with the recent ax butcheries"), but unlike the other two papers, the *Times-Picayune* repeatedly emphasized the similarity of Pepitone's murder to the Axeman crimes. The subheading of the first report of the attack on Pepitone read CASE OF MIKE PEPITONE HAS POINTS OF SIMILARITY TO AX MURDERS. Coulton reported that the attack "bore some of the characteristics of an ax-man case." He pointed out that like the Axeman attacks, Pepitone owned a corner grocery, and, he noted, "The assailant escaped as in some of the ax cases that terrorized New Orleans during the last four years." In a later story, Coulton observed that "the Pepitone case is not unlike the long string of mysterious murders committed in New Orleans during the last few years. . . . During the last three years there have been nearly fifteen people murdered with an ax or other instruments."

Coulton certainly could overstate the case: it was more accurate to say that there were nearly fifteen mysterious *attacks* in the last few years. One gets the distinct impression that whatever the police said, Coulton couldn't quite give up the possibility that Mike Pepitone was a victim not of Mafia vengeance but of the Axeman.

Widowed and with six children under the age of twelve, Esther Pepitone's situation was precarious. Desperate, she farmed at least some of them out to family or orphanages. Then she had a fortuitous encounter with an old friend. In January of 1921, Esther took the train out to Los Angeles to attend the wedding of her niece, Rosa. Esther's sister Jenny had been married to Angelo Albano, but Jenny had died in the 1918 flu epidemic, leaving her husband with daughter Rosa and son Dominick. Within a few years of his wife's death, Angelo had left New Orleans and moved out to Los Angeles, where he became the owner of a successful grocery.

After Esther had been in L.A. for several months, Angelo proposed to his former sister-in-law. She was an attractive, good-natured young widow—only thirty-one or thirty-two—with children to support. He was a well-to-do widower with children of his own. It made sense. Romantic sensibilities didn't need to enter into consideration; if she was put off by the thirty-year age difference, it was probably outweighed by the reality that he was a successful businessman who could reunite her with her children. They married on September 2, 1921.

But Joseph Mumfre would destroy any chance they had for happiness. When Albano had first arrived in California, he was in business with Mumfre, who in California went under the alias Leone J. Manfre, or sometimes M. G. Leone. Regardless of what he called himself, Mumfre and Albano had known each other for at least thirteen years. After his parole from Angola, Mumfre hung out in Albano's barroom in New Orleans, and the two men were arrested together in Kenner in January 1916.

They moved out to California about the same time in 1919 and went into the real estate business together. Although their business ventures prospered, Mumfre was too unscrupulous a character to be trusted by anyone for long, and they eventually had a falling out. Albano bought out Mumfre, who then opened a drugstore in San Bernardino, about sixty miles from L.A.

Angelo and Esther had been married only eight weeks when, on the morning of October 27, Angelo told his wife that he was going to the produce market three miles away. He kissed her good-bye and walked out the door of the home they shared with his elderly father and their children humming happily to himself. That was the last Esther Albano ever saw of her husband.

When Angelo didn't come home, Esther reported him missing to the police. Investigators located witnesses who saw him at the market, and a bank teller at the Bank of Italy remembered him withdrawing money from his account. Then his trail disappeared. Angelo Albano had just vanished.

Esther tried to carry on as best she could, sending the children to school and taking care of the home they shared at 554 East Thirty-Sixth Street. Around noon on December 5, five and a half weeks after Angelo's disappearance, the house was quiet. The younger children were at school and the eldest daughter was in the kitchen preparing dinner; Angelo's elderly father Jerome was napping in his room. Esther was busy with housework when Joseph Mumfre climbed the stairs that led into the family's rooms on the second floor and walked boldly into the house.

Esther remembered Mumfre from New Orleans, she knew about the disagreements he had had with Angelo, and she knew his reputation. Looking into his unsmiling dark eyes and scarred face, before he even spoke, she felt a tremor of fear. Did he have anything to do with Angelo's disappearance? Had Mumfre tried to blackmail him and, failing, killed him?

Mumfre came straight to the point. *I want money,* he said to her in Italian. *I want $500.*

I don't have any money, she answered.

He wasn't to be put off. *I want $500 in cash and all your jewelry.*

When she hesitated, he sneered, *If you don't give me the money and your jewelry, I'll kill you like I did your husband.* Esther would later tell police that as he issued the threat, his hand went to his hip pocket where deputies later found an automatic pistol.

So Angelo was dead. At least now she knew. And she knew what she had to do.

Wait here, she said to him. She went into her bedroom as if she were going to retrieve her valuables. But when she returned to the dining room, she carried not her jewels but a revolver. She raised it and fired. The first shot went wide. But she steadied her aim, and the second hit Mumfre. As did the next and the next.

Stunned, Mumfre reeled from the shots, then stumbled out of the house, trying at the same time to draw his own pistol. Esther followed him, relentlessly firing. When she emptied the first revolver, she dropped it, ran to get another, and again pulled the trigger until the hammer clicked. Mumfre tumbled down the stairs until he lay still at the bottom, eleven bullets riddling his body. When she'd emptied the second revolver into the blackmailer, Esther let the smoking weapon drop to her side. She stood at the top of the stairway, staring down at the crumpled body while her niece Rosa ran down the street to call the police.

When the L.A. police questioned Mrs. Albano about the killing, they were intrigued to hear the story of her first husband's death. Could the dead man have had something to do with that? Tipped off by an Italian informant to "Leone Manfre's" real identity, investigators contacted the New Orleans Police Department asking about his criminal record. The informant also told them that Mumfre may well have killed Esther Albano's first husband, Mike Pepitone. With an axe. Already, the story was being garbled.

Because she'd shot Mumfre three times in the back, Esther's lawyers weren't able to get the charges dismissed as they'd hoped. Four months later, she stood trial for first-degree murder. Fortunately for her, she made a sympathetic defendant.

The trial began in the Los Angeles Superior Court on April 7. The basic facts of the case weren't in dispute, so it was a quick trial. The prosecutor took less than three hours to lay his case in front of the jury. His witnesses included Lena Manfre, who testified that the dead man was her father, the county surgeon who performed the autopsy, several police officers who attended the scene, and Rosa Albano Casimano, who had overheard the entire incident.

When its turn came, the defense called A. R. Kallmeyer of the Los Angeles Police Department Investigation Bureau, who had received Joseph Mumfre's criminal records from New Orleans and could testify to his long criminal history. A neighbor of the Albanos asserted that after Angelo Albano vanished, Mumfre told her, "Albano has a big house and plenty of money. He is being held for some of that money. His wife will be asked for it after things quiet down."

But the crucial witness for the defense was Esther Pepitone Albano herself. Her lawyer had her tell the whole story in her soft Italian accent, beginning with the killing of Paul Di Christina by Peter Pepitone and including the murder of Mike Pepitone. She testified that she didn't know why Mike was killed or who the killer was, and she didn't know whether Mumfre had been involved. She didn't add that the New Orleans police suspected that she knew much more about Mike's death than she was willing to admit.

She detailed Angelo Albano's business partnership with Joseph Mumfre and its dissolution, Albano's disappearance, and her suspicion that Mumfre was involved. She recounted the day Mumfre turned up at her front door, demanding money and threatening to do to her what he'd done to her husband. She had assumed, she said, that he meant Albano, not Pepitone.

After two days of testimony, the jury retired to consider their verdict. They were gone for forty minutes. They found Esther Albano not guilty. Clearly, members of the jury thought that Joseph Mumfre/Leone Manfre was a man who needed killing.

Robert Tallant's version of the Axeman story had its roots in the reporting of Mumfre's death at the hands of Esther Albano by the New Orleans press. The New Orleans police learned of his death when Los Angeles authorities contacted them for information about Mumfre. And the city's press immediately misreported the news.

Although it was clear at the time of his death that Mike Pepitone's death was no axe murder, that fact quickly faded from public memory.

The *Times-Picayune* reported that "motive and probable solution of the killing of Mike Pepitone . . . one of the series of ax murders that stirred New Orleans two years ago, is seen by the police in the killing of Joseph Mumfre." That the New Orleans police jumped to the conclusion that Mumfre killed Pepitone makes it likely they suspected him all along, even though Mumfre had been run out of town nine months before—and even though there is no evidence Esther Albano ever claimed that Mumfre was Pepitone's killer.

The assumption that Mike Pepitone was hacked to death with an axe fit together very nicely with the assumption that Mumfre murdered him, to "solve" the mystery of the Axeman. It was the *New Orleans States*, where Andy Ojeda was the crime reporter, that sketched out what would become Tallant's Axeman tale. The story that appeared on December 15, 1921, was unambiguous: AX MURDERS SOLVED; MUMFRE IS KILLED. The article claimed that in 1919 and 1920, New Orleans was terrorized by a killer who especially targeted Italian grocers. The first axe murders—victims Crutti (misidentified as a butcher), Joseph Davi, and Tony Sciambra—took place before Mumfre was first sent to the penitentiary but stopped when Mumfre was in prison. He was paroled only for a short time in 1917 before being sent back to prison. Then Mumfre got out again in 1919. And the axe murders began again—Andollina, the Maggios, the Cortimiglia child, and Mike Pepitone. The killings stopped again, the article claimed, when Mumfre left for California. Now Mumfre was dead by the hand of Pepitone's widow, whom police had always suspected of knowing more about her husband's killer than she would admit. "Perhaps it was just a coincidence," the *States* hedged. "Perhaps Mumfre knew nothing of these murders." But the clear implication of the story was that the Axeman had killed Pepitone, and Mrs. Albano had known that Mumfre had killed her first husband and had exacted her revenge. And Mumfre was the Axeman.

This version of the Axeman murders is wrong on many counts. The first axe attacks (neither of them fatal) began with the assaults on the Cruttis and Rissettos in the fall of 1910. Joseph Davi was the first actual murder, his skull smashed in June 1911. Mumfre couldn't have assaulted any of these men because he was in Angola the entire time. The Axeman failed to strike from the time Mumfre was paroled in 1915 until he was returned to prison in 1916. Released again in April 1918—*after* the attack on the Andollinas—he was rearrested by May 18—before the killing of Joseph and Catherine Maggio on the morning of May 23—and served three months. He probably wasn't yet out of jail when Joseph Romano was killed on August 11. And finally, Mumfre was arrested again in January 1919 and ordered out of town. If he had been in New Orleans or the surrounding areas when Mary Cortimiglia or Mike Pepitone was killed, he would have faced immediate rearrest. While it's not physically impossible for Joseph Mumfre to have killed Mike Pepitone, it's more likely that by this time he'd joined his daughter in California.

The *New Orleans Item* jumped in to try to correct the record, pointing out that Joseph Mumfre had been in the penitentiary when the Andollinas were attacked and in the parish prison when the Maggios were slaughtered. But it wasn't enough.

Robert Tallant was a New Orleans native and lifelong resident who published novels and nonfiction in the 1940s and 1950s. In the later '50s, he wrote for the *New Orleans Item*. He was ten years old at the height of the Axeman scare in 1919 and may well have remembered the city's terror. He'd also no doubt heard the story told by newspapermen and policemen who'd been around thirty-five years before; Tallant thought he was the first to write it down. Almost certainly, he knew the reporters who'd most closely followed the Axeman's career and who still lived in New Orleans. Andy Ojeda worked for the *New Orleans States* until he retired in 1949, and Jim Coulton became a lawyer and then a district attorney in the city. They died within fourteen months of each other in 1949–1950. Most likely, the scrambled version of the truth that Tallant heard from them and read in some old newspapers found its way into his *Ready to Hang*.

Tallant undoubtedly relied on oral tradition for the end of his story, and he'd clearly heard it from someone who didn't remember the story very well. In "The Axman Wore Wings," Tallant writes that Mumfre was shot as he was walking down a busy street. No mention is made of Angelo Albano or any blackmail attempt. And, according to Tallant, Esther claimed that she had seen him when he murdered Mike Pepitone: "He was the Axeman. . . . He killed all those people."

In this way, the Black Hand blackmailer and bomber Joseph Mumfre was forever linked with the tale of the Axeman of New Orleans. Certainly Mumfre was deeply unsavory. After all, the jury that tried Esther Albano quickly decided that he'd had it coming. But if any part of the mystery has been solved, it is that Joseph Mumfre was certainly not the Axeman.

13

Rosie and Saint Joseph

IORLANDO JORDANO HAD TAKEN the verdict better than his son. At sixty-eight, Iorlando was an old man who in his modest way had made a success of his life. But Frank's life was still ahead of him, or it had been. Now that life was taken away. By the mother of the toddler he adored. By a friendly neighbor lady who lied, swearing that he was a murderer, that she had seen him murder little Mary with her own eyes. Frank could scarcely believe it. Perhaps he had naively thought that since he was innocent he had nothing to fear. He'd remained optimistic throughout his trial, even to the point of what some called "nonchalance." But now he faced a hangman's rope. *It wasn't a fair trial,* he told reporters who asked for a comment as he was handcuffed to be led back to the parish prison. *We didn't get "reasonable doubt."*

How had Frank and Iorlando been convicted? The jurors were serious men, diligent about their task. They'd listened carefully to the evidence and paid close attention as the experts contradicted each other about Rosie's reliability as a witness. The testimony of the physicians who treated her was consistent—Rosie wasn't mentally competent because of her head injuries. But the jury had to weigh that against the doctors who had examined her recently, who pronounced her "sane and responsible." The emotional testimony of the young mother weighed heavily on the twelve jurymen. In 1919, research had not yet raised doubts about the reliability of eyewitness testimony. Yes, elements of her story were unlikely and hard to believe, but there was no doubt that her daughter was dead and no doubt about her grief. Rosie might be a young and ignorant girl, but she was a mother who'd lost a daughter; what motive, the jurors might have reasonably wondered, did she have for lying?

Many in Gretna thought the boy and old man were guilty, and public pressure on the jury shouldn't be underestimated. A change of venue might well have dramatically lowered the Jordanos' chances of conviction. But the case had been tried in Gretna and the jurors' names printed in the newspaper. If they acquitted men widely believed guilty of hacking a toddler to death, all their neighbors would know it. Not that members of the jury consciously convicted men they believed innocent, but knowledge of the community's verdict couldn't help but have influenced them in reaching their own.

Frank had one comfort. After the verdict was announced and the stunned Jordanos were led from the courtroom, Jim Coulton of the *Times-Picayune* followed them out and caught up to them. He put his hand on Frank's shoulder and looking straight into his eyes told him, "I believe you, Frank, and I'm going to work to help you out." Gratitude welled up in the boy. But what could the reporter do now?

Coulton was outraged at the verdict. He had no doubt that all of the recent axe murders were the work of one crazed fiend. Couldn't the jury see that the Cortimiglias had been the latest victims of the Axeman? But Judge Fleury hadn't allowed jurors to hear evidence that the Cortimiglia attack resembled other Axeman crimes.

Despite his generally good relationship with the New Orleans Police Department, Coulton knew that not all policemen—and by extension officers of the court—were completely trustworthy. He himself had recently been tossed into jail by corrupt police officers during his investigation of a shakedown scheme. And, as a crime reporter who'd often sat in court, surely he knew that witnesses could lie and juries could be wrong. He was convinced of it in this case and was determined to do something about it.

Two days after the verdict, defense attorney William Byrnes announced he would file a motion for a new trial, swearing that he'd go all the way to the Supreme Court if he had to. By the time he filed his appeal, the judicial summer vacation was imminent and Judge Fleury refused to rule on the motion until the fall.

Frank and Iorlando had to spend an oppressively humid Louisiana summer in the confines of the Jefferson parish prison waiting for the Twenty-Eighth District Court to come back into session. Since grounds for appealing the verdict were based mostly on mistakes the defense alleged that Fleury had made, it came as no surprise when, at the end of the summer, the judge denied the motion for a new trial.

No doubt Byrnes expected that. He had prepared his appeal to the state supreme court, amassing over thirty bills of exception to Judge Fleury's rulings. When he filed his appeal in mid-November (just before Frank's eighteenth birthday on the twenty-third), the defense attorney was confident that he had grounds for the conviction to be overturned.

The appeals process, even in a capital case, wouldn't drag out for decades. The Jordanos' case would be resolved within a year or two of the trial, two or three years even if there were grounds for an appeal to the U.S. Supreme Court. If the convictions were upheld, Iorlando would be sent to the state penitentiary; Frank's execution would be carried out promptly, in a matter of months at most.

Everyone who read the newspapers would have been familiar with the mechanics of an execution. In 1910, all hangings had been moved to the state penitentiary in Baton Rouge, but eight years later, executions were shifted back to the parishes. Hanging a man locally made a better example of him, reasoned state legislators. At the same time, a ritual intended to give dignity and solemnity to the event was scrupulously observed. The night before, the condemned man was given his last meal. His jailers ordered it special from a restaurant, and he'd sit down to what would in other circumstances be a comforting meal of steak and potatoes and biscuits with butter, washed down with a bottle of wine or a pot of strong coffee.

The prisoner spent his last night in his cell or sometimes, if he couldn't sleep, outside in the corridor talking to the deputies on the deathwatch. In the morning, he took a cold bath in the prison bathroom, after which he dressed in a somber suit of clothes provided by the sheriff: black trousers, black coat, black tie, white vest, white shirt, turn-down collar, and soft black slippers.

Once dressed, if the condemned man was a Catholic like Frank, he'd be taken to the chapel to celebrate mass and see his family one last time. After his family was escorted out of the prison, the prison matron brought him the breakfast he had ordered the night before, probably ham and eggs, biscuits, and coffee. If he decided at the last minute that he had a taste for something else, like fried or raw oysters, jail personnel scrambled to get it for him.

The prisoner spent the remainder of the morning with his priest receiving spiritual solace. He was even given a bracer of whiskey if he needed it to keep up his courage. At noon, the sheriff came for him accompanied by the fifteen men sworn as official witnesses. The sheriff read the death warrant and asked the prisoner if he had anything to say. Then with the priest at his side, the prisoner began his last walk, the death march down from the condemned gallery, out into the prison yard and up the steps of the wooden-framed gallows to stand at the trapdoor. Quickly, the black-hooded hangman bound the prisoner's hands and feet and whipped a black hood over his head. He positioned him just right over the trapdoor and adjusted the noose under his jaw. If the condemned man was lucky, he had an experienced executioner; one who knew what he was doing made the difference between a quick, painless death and an agonizingly slow one.

When he had the prisoner properly positioned, the hangman called out: "Gentlemen of the Jury, I call upon you to witness that this execution is being conducted according to the high formalities of the law." Then he threw the lever that sprung the trap, sending the prisoner plunging into eternity. When the rope jerked suddenly, the body convulsed for a few seconds, then went still, swaying gently at the end of the rope. Under the circumstances, the best possible scenario was that his neck would snap instantly and the spinal cord would be severed, making death more or less instantaneous. The hangman gauged the drop by the height and weight of the condemned; if he botched it, the prisoner could dangle at the end of the rope for more than fifteen minutes, slowly strangling. For this reason, the law required that the body hang for at least twenty minutes before being cut down.

The priest pronounced the last rites, standing on a box to reach up and anoint the motionless body with holy oil. After an examination, the coroner pronounced death. The body was taken down and placed in a simple wooden casket that was loaded into a horse-drawn hearse. The gates of the prison swung open, and the horse plodded forward to return the prisoner to his family.

This is what Frank had to look forward to if his appeal failed, and it's hard to imagine that the scenario did not run through his head as the long, muggy summer of 1919 turned into the mild Louisiana winter. But he could do nothing except comfort his father and pray for deliverance. Had Saint Joseph, protector of Sicilians, deserted him?

As the months passed, Iorlando's health deteriorated in the cold, damp jail cell. His rheumatism flared up, and he ached all the time; Frank's hands were sore from rubbing liniment on his father's back every night. Iorlando's eyesight grew dimmer, and Frank noticed that he had to speak more loudly for his father to hear him.

But they clung to their faith that their innocence would free them. Frank decorated his cell with pictures of the saints and the Virgin Mary and prayed every night for vindication.

They started off the new year hopefully in January 1920, when their drab prison existence was brightened by a wedding.

For two years Lena had been engaged to Anthony Spera, the twenty-two-year-old brother of Frank's girlfriend Josie. Tony had joined the army when the United States entered the First World War, and he'd seen active service with the 151st Field Artillery. He'd returned home a war hero, expecting to marry his girl only to find that her father and brother were in the parish prison and might never return home.

What should they do? Frank and Iorlando's appeals could take several years. And what if the appeals failed? Did they want to risk Frank being hanged before he could see them as a married couple?

Lena and Tony decided not to wait. The future would take care of itself. But how could the entire family share in their union when Iorlando and Frank were imprisoned? Somebody came up with the inspired idea of holding the wedding celebration in the prison yard. All they needed was Sheriff Marrero's approval.

Venal and corrupt though he was, Sheriff Marrero was not heartless. He had children of his own and had recently lost a son. Frank pointed out that if they hanged him, this was the last family celebration he'd see. The sheriff saw no harm and agreed.

On Sunday afternoon, January 4, Lena Jordano and Anthony Spera were married at Saint Joseph's Church in Gretna, and after the ceremony the entire wedding party made their way from the church to the parish prison. There they found a table set up in the prison yard covered with "tempting dishes of chicken, ham, potted meats, cakes, pies and soft drinks." Sixty or so relatives and friends ate and drank, offering the bride their best wishes and congratulating the groom. Laughing and delighting in the presence of so many friends, Iorlando and Frank moved easily among the guests. Except for the presence of a couple of deputy sheriffs, no one would have guessed that the shadow of the scaffold loomed over the festivities. No one was saying what everyone was thinking: this was probably the last time they would celebrate as a family.

But then Saint Joseph answered their prayers and gave them a miracle.

Rosie couldn't sleep.

Things had not gone well for the Cortimiglias in the months since the trial. Losing a child produces unfathomable stress; surviving the murder of one's child so strains a marriage that, in the early twenty-first century at least, most marriages don't survive it. Divorce might not have been such an easy option a hundred years ago, but for Charlie and Rosie Cortimiglia, Mary's murder was no less damaging. The pressure on their lives and their marriage exacted such a toll that Charlie wasn't able to manage his business. The grocery—earlier so successful—began to founder.

Most of the specifics of the Cortimiglias' business failure and marriage breakdown are lost, and only a few details of their lives in the months immediately after the trial are known. In mid-June, about three weeks after the verdict, Rosie was somehow accosted by Lillie and Lena Jordano, who accused her of lying on the witness stand about Iorlando and Frank. A few days later, Charlie carelessly shot himself in the hand while cleaning his pistol. The injury wasn't life-threatening, but he ended up in Charity again a few weeks later when the wound became infected. At the end of August, he was sued by a wholesale company to which he owed money. The police didn't return the $134 that had been in the bedroom the night of the attack. Exactly how these particular events contributed to the decline of the Cortimiglia grocery business isn't known, but by the autumn of 1919, things had become so bad that the Cortimiglias became desperate. So desperate that Rosie found her way to Storyville.

Officially, of course, the federal government had shuttered Storyville two years before. The sixteen-block district outside of the French Quarter where vice and sin had been officially tolerated had been a cornucopia of carnality, a galleria of luxurious whorehouses, saloons, and cabarets that flaunted their immorality. Suppressing Storyville meant closing the more ostentatious establishments but leaving many prostitutes in business, mostly the down-market whores, many of whom operated out of cheap one-room "cribs," standing in their doorway, provocatively advertising their wares.

It was there, on November 1, in one of their periodic vice raids on the "ancient restricted district," that two detectives arrested Rosie Cortimiglia in a squalid Bienville Street rooming house with a traveling salesman named Ralph Rogers. Rosie tried to pretend that she was his wife, but the detectives recognized her.

Rogers was released, as the prostitutes' customers unfailingly were. Only later, when the police realized that he'd given them a false name, that he was really a former New Orleans Police Department patrolman named Edward Hickey, was Rosie's paramour tracked down and locked up on a "dangerous and suspicious" charge. Rosie was taken to the Third Precinct, where she was charged with prostitution. Her arrest report also records that she had a venereal disease. She admitted that she met Hickey for money—several times since he had first picked her up at the corner of Canal and Dauphine Streets a month before. She didn't have a choice, she sobbed. The store was failing; she and Charlie were broke.

When Chief Mooney found out about her arrest, he was inclined to be suspicious. Was this a ploy to besmirch Rosie's character and aid the Jordanos' appeal? Had someone been hired to entice Rosie into immorality in order to stain her moral character? When he questioned Hickey he uncovered no connection to the Jordanos, but he still felt sorry for Rosie and wanted to send her home.

Charlie Cortimiglia was soon summoned to police headquarters, where he was informed of the charges against his wife. If he'd had any idea of what Rosie had been doing, he didn't admit it to Superintendent Mooney. Charlie raged with the predictable fury of a wronged husband and swore that he'd turn his wife out immediately: "Nothing in the world will ever make me consent to forgive her and take her back!" he declared to the police superintendent. Mooney tried to calm Charlie down and talk him around, without much success, even when he explained his hunch that some Jordano supporter had been behind this. Charlie was adamant that Rosie had to go.

Rosie was mortified and contrite. She told the police department social worker that Charlie was right: "I sinned . . . my husband is right by refusing to forgive me." There was nothing for her to do, she said tearfully, but to kill herself.

Afraid that she meant it, Mooney had Rosie committed to the Isolation Hospital, a relatively new public institution on Rampart Street for contagious diseases, especially prostitutes with venereal disease. There she stayed for almost a week, until Charlie softened and took her home to Gretna.

Their reconciliation didn't last. Neighbors, taking pity on the couple that had endured so much misfortune, arranged a benefit to help with their money problems. But the Cortimiglias had been through too much. After only a few months, which they spent quarreling constantly, they separated. Rosie left Gretna and went to New Orleans, where she got a job at the American Can Company's tin can factory.

Since that awful night in March, Rosie had been plagued with chronic headaches as a result of the head wounds she'd sustained. But now the torment from her uneasy conscience was greater. Maybe, as one newspaper later suggested, she remembered Frank Jordano's statement when he'd been sentenced to death. "I would rather go to the gallows than tell a lie in order to have an innocent man executed," the boy had said, with more sadness than anger. "If Mrs. Cortimiglia is possessed of her faculties, she knows that she is lying and I would not swap places with her today."

Rosie Cortimiglia, who accused two innocent men of one of the Axeman's worst crimes.

Maybe it was his words that gnawed at her day after day. Or maybe it was simply the knowledge that she'd been responsible for sending an old man to prison for life and a boy to the gallows. But something unsettled her, causing her to doubt her own sworn testimony. She should come forward, Rosie thought to herself, and make things right. But she was afraid. What would they do to her if she admitted she'd sworn falsely in court? Would they understand why she had done it? Would they put her in jail? Increasingly anxious and agitated, the distressed and indecisive Rosie was restless at night, fighting off pricks of conscience, the specter of the old man and teenaged boy haunting her sleep.

Rosie's indecision reached an end on Monday night, February 2, 1920, when she dreamed that she lay dying, and Saint Joseph, the patron saint of Sicilians, came to her. "He raised his hand and pointed a finger at me," she recalled with awe later. "Oh, it was terrible, and yet it was beautiful." The saint spoke: "Rosie, you cannot die with that boy's life and that old man's liberty on your conscience." She woke up, tears running down her face, and determined to see the Jordanos free as soon as possible.

It's not clear exactly how *Times-Picayune* police reporter Jim Coulton was involved in all this, but it seems likely that he followed up on his promise to Frank by staying in touch with Rosie, perhaps playing some role in awakening her conscience. The *New Orleans States* reported that after her dream, Rosie "sought out friends, and to them she unbosomed the truth." These friends immediately encouraged her to go public with her story. That, presumably, is what led to Rosie going to the *Times-Picayune*. She had met Jim Coulton during the trial, and after the verdict he had determined to get at the truth of her story, and if he was one of her encouraging friends, it is easy to see why she went to the *Times-Picayune* office and why one of the paper's attorneys was so conveniently there to witness her statement. Coulton had promised Frank Jordano that he would do what he could to help him, and convincing Rosie to retract her accusation—which Coulton certainly believed was false—would help him the most.

On Tuesday, February 3, Rosie Cortimiglia officially recanted her identification of the Jordanos as her assailants. In the office of the newspaper, she signed a statement in which she said her family had been attacked by two tall, black-haired men whose faces were hidden by red bandanas and that she didn't recognize the Jordanos "either by their faces, figures or voices as the men who killed my baby." The statement was officially witnessed by Jim Coulton and James E. Edmonds, managing editor of the *Times-Picayune*.

"Oh, God," sighed Rosie after signing her statement, "I hope I can sleep now!"

The next morning, word of Rosie's confession flashed through Gretna with the speed of a brushfire. Reaction was swift and intense. Those many community members who had for almost a year been firmly, incontrovertibly convinced of the Jordanos' guilt now loudly declared that Iorlando and Frank were the victims and that it was Rosie who should be jailed. Indeed, in less than twenty-four hours, popular opinion reversed itself completely.

William Byrnes was ecstatic when he got the news. He had been convinced of his clients' innocence, repeatedly telling reporters that he knew the truth would eventually come out, "as surely as there is a heaven above us." He had only feared that the truth might not be known until it was too late for Frank. He told reporters that he hoped that with the cooperation of District Attorney Rivarde and the state attorney general, in light of Rosie's confession, he could ask the state supreme court for the case to be sent back down to the district court for a new trial. There, he assumed, the charges would be dropped.

At first light on Wednesday morning, February 4, Frank heard John Bruno, Josie's stepbrother, yelling for him. He looked through his cell window to see John sprinting toward the prison gate, all the while shouting up at him and waving a newspaper. Frank couldn't make out what he was saying, but his throat tightened in dread. Had something happened to his mother? Or to Lena? Why else would John be making such a fuss? How will Papa stand it? he thought. With mounting anxiety, he could barely force himself to go downstairs to greet his friend in the prison yard.

The words were fairly bursting out of John. *Miss Rosie has told the truth! Miss Rosie said she lied!* He shoved the *Times-Picayune* into Frank's hand. Bewildered, Frank opened the paper to see Rosie's face and his own face staring back at him. He gaped at the headline for a few seconds as the meaning began to sink in: ROSIE CORTIMIGLIA RETRACTS HER IDENTIFICATION. CONFESSION THAT PUT NOOSE AROUND TWO MEN DENIED.

Frank was soon joined by his father, and with growing elation, he read the story to Iorlando. Shortly afterward, a call came from Mr. Byrnes, confirming the paper's good news. It wasn't long before Jordanos were fairly streaming into the Gretna jail—mother, brother, sisters, nieces, nephews, cousins, brothers-in-law, and fiancée—the entire clan returned for another party in the jail's courtyard, spontaneously rejoicing that their family would soon be made whole again.

There was much talk of forgiveness; now that the shadow of death seemed lifted, no one seemed to bear Rosie a grudge. "Both of us are happy that she has told the truth," Frank told reporters. "She need not be afraid to come to see us. We will both welcome her and forgive her. She must have been out of her head, like she said."

Frank's mother, Lillie, too, was magnanimous: "Of course, I forgive Rosie Cortimiglia. But she's not the one who needs forgiveness most. I even forgive those who forced her to tell that lie . . . I forgive them all. I'm going to get my boy and my husband back."

There also was talk of gratitude. "It must have been the blessed Saint Joseph made this happen," Frank told Jim Coulton as he held one of his little cousins on his lap. "We must all pray to thank him for making Miss Rosie tell the truth by coming to her in a dream like he did. I was praying hard last night. It must have been right when Miss Rosie was taking it all back."

The defense's contention that a vulnerable Rosie had been bullied into implicating the Jordanos is probably accurate. Rosie herself said that after her release from the hospital, she was bombarded by voices insisting that the Jordanos must be guilty. Remembering the falling out over the grocery store, she admitted, "I made up my mind to say it was the Jordanos who had committed the crime," despite her uncertainty that it was true. In all probability, young, uneducated Rosie, still recovering from a serious injury, felt scared and alone in the Jefferson Parish jail. Sheriff Marrero, District Attorney Rivarde, and her jailer, Deputy Sheriff Burgbacher, must have made it clear what they wanted her to say. She eventually complied, probably even convincing herself for a time that Frank and Iorlando were actually guilty. Everybody said so. Questioned over and over again in the hospital while drugged with painkillers, then again in the intimidating surroundings of the Gretna jail, asked the same questions—"Did the Jordanos do it? Was it Frank Jordano [who] hit you?"—Rosie wouldn't have found it hard to persuade herself that everybody was right; they must have done it.

After the trial, she no longer had the constant reinforcement of the sheriff or the DA checking that she hadn't changed her story. When she moved to New Orleans, she also escaped the citizens of Gretna who were so set against the Jordanos. There, she let her doubts overtake her. Rosie knew she hadn't seen the assailants, and perhaps she realized how improbable it was that Iorlando, a kindly, crippled old man, and Frank, an ambitious, likable boy, would kill a child over an old quarrel. Perhaps fully realizing that young Frank, who had played so often and so lovingly with Mary, was going to be hanged, she recovered her doubts about his guilt, and she wanted no part in his death. In New Orleans, supporting herself, away from her husband, she found an inner strength that perhaps no sheriff or lawyer had suspected.

Rosie's amended account of the attack was very similar to the story she told at trial, save that she didn't see the assailants' faces. But it remained an implausible tale: two men entered her bedroom; one handed the other an axe, and the man with the axe told her "he would have to kill the baby because the baby was crying." Rosie pleaded, but the intruder hit the baby three times, then knocked Rosie unconscious. Charlie slept through all of this but was then assaulted.

Memory isn't a literal recording of the past that people play back in their heads. Memories are highly subjective. They're malleable constructs that can be created through suggestion or manipulation. When Rosie was subjected to suggestive questioning and told over and over that the Jordanos *must* have done it, it's easy to see that in trying to remember, she could have imagined—and eventually came to believe as real—a scene in which she saw two men enter her room, even if, as she eventually acknowledged, she never convinced herself that she saw the Jordanos or heard Frank's voice. Repeated efforts on Rosie's part to remember the attack in all probability led to a false, created memory. The prosecutors' insistence on the Jordanos' guilt made the Axeman into two men in Rosie's mind, even when she had decided that Frank and Iorlando were innocent.

Not everyone was rejoicing in the Jordanos' apparent salvation. Robert Rivarde was having none of it. The district attorney was convinced of their guilt and wasn't to be deterred by the defection of his star witness. He refused to cooperate with the defense attorneys and had no intention of asking the state supreme court to send the case back to the trial court. Rivarde knew full well that Rosie's admission would have no bearing on the high court's decision if he opposed the appeal because the court decided on matters of law, not matters of fact.

He let it be known that if the Jordanos won their appeal and the case was remanded to the district court for retrial, he would charge Rosie with perjury for changing her original testimony. Rosie's fears of getting into serious trouble were likely to be realized. And not everybody was convinced that she was willing to go to prison to free the convicted men.

In the face of the DA's resolve, Byrnes prepared to present his appeal. No doubt he knew that the state supreme court was legally required to ignore Rosie's statement. But Byrnes could hope that the justices would agree that "where human life was at stake . . . her retraction of that damaging testimony could not, in justice to the accused, be utterly ignored." He could hope that the justices' knowledge that the men were almost certainly innocent would have an effect, even if an unconscious, extralegal one.

On March 6, in the marble and granite neoclassical court building on Royal Street in the Vieux Carré, the Louisiana Supreme Court heard oral arguments on the defense's motion to send the Jordano case back to the Twenty-Eighth District Court. The appellants went first. Andrew Thalheim and Archie Higgins were present, but chief counsel William Byrnes did most of the talking.

The defense had amassed thirty-two bills of exception, or objections to the trial court's ruling. Not all of them could be addressed during oral arguments, but any one of them might be grounds for overturning the jury's verdict. For the defense, the most significant issues were multifold. It had been the district attorney's tactic to ask the defendants if they made certain threatening statements, warning that he would introduce witnesses who would contradict their statements, but never doing so, and so unfairly introducing unsubstantiated, prejudicial accusations to the jury. The judge refused to permit evidence that the Cortimiglia attack was an Axeman attack. The state's attorneys made prejudicial statements against the defendants during the trial. And the state had refused to turn over to the defense the statement Rosie Cortimiglia made in the Gretna jail.

Oral arguments before the five justices took two days. When arguments ended on the second day, Byrnes was entitled to a rush of optimism. The state's performance hadn't been particularly strong. At one point, Rivarde declared, "It is a significant thing that since the Jordanos have been in jail there have been no axe murders." Not only had no one ever accused either of the Jordanos of being the Axeman, the accusation contradicted the prosecution's stated motive for the crime—jealousy. It made the state look a little desperate.

Several of the justices had voiced concern about the issue Byrnes felt most strongly about: the prosecution's questioning of the defendants about threats they were alleged to have made, without putting on the stand witnesses who could support the allegations. One of the justices said he didn't understand why the prosecutor didn't call these witnesses, if he had them. Yes, Byrnes had reason to be cheerful.

It was a long three weeks for Iorlando and Frank Jordano, but the decision when it came vindicated their lawyer's optimism. On April 5, the Louisiana Supreme Court ruled that the jury's guilty verdict was set aside and Iorlando and Frank's convictions overturned. The State of Louisiana would have to try them again.

The court found that the trial judge made two reversible errors. Rosie Cortimiglia's statement to Clay Gaudet, which he had written down, should have been turned over to the defense. "As a matter of fact and law," the court wrote, "it was a piece of substantive evidence concerning questions of vital importance in the defense of two men who were on trial for their lives, and we know of nothing in the law or in reason which authorized the refusal to produce it."

The court also rejected the strategy of asking the Jordanos if they had made specific threats but never producing the witnesses who—Rivarde claimed—could discredit the defendant's denials. The justices found that a jury might easily have concluded that the district attorney could have produced witnesses to contradict the accused, if he'd chosen to do so. But the high court determined that "the only reasonable presumption" is that Rivarde couldn't have done so. It was unacceptable, the court ruled, "to import into a case material facts which have not been established or attempted to be established by evidence; and . . . such action is . . . good ground for the reversal of a conviction." The court had, quite properly, ignored Rosie's recent confession. But the Jordanos were granted a retrial without it.

Now the state had to retry the Jordanos. Which would be hard to do without Rosie Cortimiglia's testimony.

When can we get out of jail? the Jordanos quizzed their lawyers. Iorlando and Frank had been locked up for a year. Mr. Byrnes counseled patience. The state had a right to request a rehearing before the high court. But the deadline for making application to do so came and went, so the state supreme court's ruling became final, and the case was officially sent to the Twenty-Eighth District Court for retrial. Byrnes could tell his clients that their new court date might be as early as the next month.

In the meantime, Byrnes had other things to do. Thomas Semmes Walmsley, Louisiana's assistant attorney general arguing on behalf of the state, had disparaged Rosie's retraction before the Louisiana Supreme Court, arguing that it couldn't be considered an affidavit because she hadn't been legally sworn in. The statement didn't even reflect Rosie's own words, he maintained. It was too well written for someone with her lack of education. Clearly the document had been composed by someone else. And she hadn't just walked into the newspaper office by herself. Someone had talked her into making these allegations, which he doubted she'd actually swear to. In order to assure that Rosie's confession was taken seriously, he needed to address these criticisms.

But where was Rosie? Shortly after her startling admission in February, she'd been admitted to the Isolation Hospital with smallpox. That year, New Orleans experienced an unusually virulent outbreak of the disease, which overwhelmed the resources of the Isolation Hospital. Despite the dismaying mortality rate in the hospital's smallpox ward, Rosie recovered, her youthful prettiness permanently marred by the disease. The smallpox patients suffered from a desperate shortage of nursing staff, so she stayed on for several weeks to help. Rosie discovered that the Jordanos' convictions had been thrown out only when she finally left the hospital on April 23.

She must have gotten in touch with Byrnes or Jim Coulton immediately, because the next day she repeated her statement under oath in front of a notary and a handful of witnesses. She swore that the statement she'd given the *Times-Picayune* was absolutely true and again retracted her trial testimony identifying Frank and Iorlando as the killers. She affirmed that the statement she made to the *Times-Picayune* had been "of her own free will" and that she hadn't been coerced or compensated in any way. The statement was in the third person, although in the *Times-Picayune* story reporting it, Rosie was quoted as saying, "On the last night of my confinement in jail I was told by Charles F.

Burgbacher, jailer, that I would be kept in prison unless I testified that the Jordanos had killed my baby. I wanted to get out and so I said the Jordanos murdered my baby."

When the Jordanos were retried, Rosie would need to go back to Gretna to testify. But now she was afraid. She'd heard that Jefferson Parish was offering a fifty-dollar reward for her arrest. Sheriff Marrero denied the rumor. Still, she refused to cross the river until May when a new sheriff, one of a wave of reform candidates who'd swept Ring politicians out of office in the 1920 elections, would replace him.

Byrnes, meanwhile, needed to get his clients out on bail. They'd been sitting in jail for over a year, and now that virtual proof of their innocence had emerged, it seemed outrageous that they should stay there. On May 12, in the Gretna courthouse, Byrnes asked Judge Fleury to allow them to post bond. Rosie had overcome her misgivings about entering Jefferson Parish, and Byrnes called her to the stand.

Was the testimony you gave in the defendants' trial a year ago true? Byrnes asked.

Rosie's new attorney, Sam Montgomery, intervened. He objected to his client answering the question, pointing out that if she incriminated herself, she could be prosecuted. He pointed to the district attorney: *Mr. Rivarde is waiting for Mrs. Cortimiglia to admit that she gave false testimony under oath*, he said. *Then he will charge her with perjury.*

Byrnes was exasperated. "If Rosie Cortimiglia is convicted of perjury by telling the truth which will save this boy from the gallows and his father from life imprisonment, I am willing to serve her jail sentence," he retorted.

Despite Byrnes's gallant offer, Montgomery still refused to allow Rosie to testify.

Under the circumstances, Judge Fleury had no choice but to turn down the request for bail. Although their conviction had been thrown out, the Jordanos were still under indictment for murder, and murder suspects were usually not accorded bail. Weary with disappointment, Frank and Iorlando returned to their cells.

The same day, in the same courthouse, a grand jury began investigating both Rosie's charge that she had been coerced into identifying the Jordanos and the possibility that Rosie had committed perjury. When Judge Fleury issued his instructions, he "laid special stress on the crime of perjury," reported the *New Orleans States*. Again, Sam Montgomery would not let Rosie say anything. And, unsurprisingly, since the key witness would not testify, the grand jury's investigation came to nothing. Rosie's continued silence led some observers to wonder if she actually would testify at the Jordanos' retrial. Frank and Iorlando could be forgiven for wondering too.

The new trial was scheduled to begin on Monday, May 17. Coincidently, that was also the day that John Parker was inaugurated as Louisiana's new governor. William Byrnes and Archie Higgins (as former and current state representatives) were up in Baton Rouge for the inauguration and didn't appear at the trial. One wonders why the trial still took place under such circumstances. In fact, the week before, the *Times-Picayune* had speculated that the trial would have to be postponed for this very reason. At any rate, the trial was delayed for two days. When the defense attorneys failed to appear on Wednesday, however, both the judge and the DA were visibly irritated. When Judge Fleury learned that Andrew Thalheim, one of the Jordanos' lawyers, was in the courthouse, he immediately summoned him to account for the attorneys' absence. The flustered associate counsel stammered that there was some miscommunication; Byrnes and Higgins were still in Baton Rouge and hadn't been notified that the trial was due to start that day.

Whatever the causes of the misunderstanding, less than a week of the criminal term remained, not enough time to postpone the trial yet again and still have the case heard before the summer break. The murder trial would have to be postponed until the next criminal term—in November. Instead of an immediate trial, likely acquittal, and imminent freedom, Frank and Iorlando faced another six months in jail. Father and son dejectedly "returned to the sweltering heat of the Gretna jail . . . for the summer."

One would like to know what Frank had to say to his attorneys when they arrived home from the inauguration festivities. But as was his nature, he made the best of his situation. Life wasn't too unbearable for the Jordanos in the parish jail now anyway. Once it became clear that in all likelihood the Jordanos would eventually be released, Deputy Sheriff Burgbacher (the man Rosie blamed for coercing her into accusing Frank) handed Frank the keys to the jail and a revolver and informed him that he was now a turnkey. Frank also put his business experience to good use, keeping the jail's books for Burgbacher. He proved as good and conscientious a jailer as he had been a real estate agent, and the only time Frank and Iorlando had to spend in their cells was when they slept. Having something to occupy his time was good for Frank; still the summer dragged by as they waited for the fall and the acquittal they were convinced would send them home.

Sometime during the summer and fall Frank's personal life suffered a blow when his fiancée Josie dropped him; this was the girl he'd tried to protect by fibbing to the coroner's jury. Perhaps the stress of having a jailed boyfriend proved too much for her. But another young woman (whose name we don't know), who perhaps was attracted by Frank's notoriety, quickly took Josie's place in his affections, and Frank was still determined to get married as soon as he could get out and earn some money.

Finally, the November criminal court term arrived. This time, public opinion was firmly in the defendants' favor. Many in Jefferson Parish wondered why the district attorney persevered with his prosecution; without Rosie Cortimiglia's testimony, he didn't have a case. Rivarde must not have been convinced that Rosie would change her story. And he was determined that as long as Rosie would not admit to perjury under oath, he had a case. Once she resolved to take the risk, he knew, it was over. Why he couldn't concede the Jordanos' probable innocence is a mystery.

The fall criminal term of the Twenty-Eighth District Court opened on November 3. Almost immediately, the trial schedule was set back because the presiding judge, Fred Middleton, dismissed the first jury pool over improprieties in the way its members had been selected. The process of summoning people for jury duty and selecting jurors had to start all over again. At best, the Jordano trial would start two weeks late.

The criminal term finally began on Monday, November 15, and William Byrnes entered the courtroom with his clients, eager to go to trial. Rivarde, however, asked for a continuance. Over William Byrnes's opposition, and the visible disappointment of the defendants, Judge Middleton delayed the case for another week. He assured the defense that the trial would begin the next Monday. The Jordanos' case was now set for the second week of the term, Monday, November 22.

But Judge Middleton wasn't able to keep his promise. When the next week came, Rivarde stood up before the judge and sheepishly explained that he'd need another continuance. The state had mislaid its records of the case and consequently hadn't been able to summon any witnesses. Byrnes was furious. "This is the second time [since] this case came back from the supreme court that we have been ready for trial and the state has asked continuance," he sputtered. "I believe Iorlando and Frank Jordano are innocent men. Why should they have to stay in jail waiting for the state to prepare its case when the records are lost?"

Judge Middleton tried to soothe him. "If the state is not ready for trial next Friday," he promised, "I will entertain a motion for bail."

Byrnes wasn't happy with it, but there was little he could do but agree. *Just a few more days*, he must have assured his clients. Frank left the courtroom to spend another birthday—his nineteenth, on November 23—in jail.

When Friday came, the attorneys were ready, but now Rosie Cortimiglia was missing. She'd not responded to the subpoena, and no one seemed to know where she was. Once again, the judge granted a continuance, this time until December 6.

Frank and Iorlando couldn't even take comfort in the promised bail. Judge Middleton was no longer hearing the case. He was no longer even on the bench. District judges were not well-paid, at least compared to lawyers in private practice, and Fred Middleton had not run for reelection. His term expired on December 2, but he resigned a week early to take a potentially lucrative case defending a bootlegger who'd gotten into a shootout that had killed a deputy sheriff. The governor appointed H. N. Gautier, who'd been elected to succeed him, to fill the week remaining in Middleton's term. On Friday, November 26, Judge Middleton opened court just long enough to turn the proceedings over to Judge Gautier.

Judge Gautier, who had made no assurances to the Jordanos, promptly denied bail.

By now the two men must have been in despair, wondering if the State of Louisiana would ever get around to trying them again. Perhaps they were beginning to worry that their retrial would be delayed again and they'd spend another five or six months in jail until the next criminal term in May. They had even more reason now to long for release. Lena was having her first child. Iorlando and Frank wanted to be home to cradle their newest family member when he or she arrived.

The morning of December 6 dawned bleak and rainy in Gretna, sheets of rain alternating with a dull drizzle that reduced the unpaved streets to a boggy mess. The temperatures were only in the fifties, but the wet and wind made it colder and more depressing. Crowds streaming toward the courthouse trudged on, many soaked to the skin, heads down into the wind, braving rain and mud. Sinister dark clouds filling the sky seemed to portend nothing good for this day.

Rosie Cortimiglia quietly entered the district attorney's office down the hall from the packed courtroom where Iorlando and Frank Jordano waited for their trial to begin. She and Robert Rivarde sat in serious conversation, speaking in low tones. She spoke to him quietly and earnestly. He asked her a question; she answered with a determined shake of her head. He pressed her: *Are you certain?* She nodded: *Yes, I am certain.*

Frank and Iorlando sat at the defense table with their attorneys. Frank, conspicuous by his great size and flashy green suit, was turned around chatting with friends, confident about the outcome and anxious to be out of jail and back at work. Iorlando appeared a slight figure next to the bulk of his son. He sat quietly, his wife occasionally reaching up from where she sat behind him to touch his shoulder reassuringly. The atmosphere was different from that of the previous trial, with the hum of the crowd now sympathetic to the two men sitting at the defense table.

At noon, the court crier solemnly intoned the traditional opening of court: "Oyez, oyez, oyez. The Honorable Twenty-Eighth District Court of Jefferson Parish is now in session, the Honorable H. N. Gautier presiding. All those having business before this honorable court draw nigh and ye shall be heard. God save the United States and this Honorable Court."

Silence descended on the courtroom as Judge Gautier entered and took his seat. When the court crier solemnly announced "the Jordano case," Robert Rivarde stood up. Rivarde addressed the judge: "Your honor, just before court opened the material witness in this case came to my office. She informed me that if the case comes to trial again, she will reverse the testimony she gave in the original case, the testimony on which the accused were convicted. In order to save this court and many of our good citizens the discomfort of serving on a jury, I make a motion that the case be dropped."

Without hesitation, Judge Gautier nol-prossed the case, dismissing the two defendants. "You can go, Frank," he said to the younger man.

Relief flooded through Frank. Even though he'd fully expected to be freed, it still came as a shock. It took the old man a moment or two longer to understand what had just happened. After a shocked silence, the courtroom erupted, and friends and relatives and supporters thronged around the two men, slapping them on the back, shaking their hands, congratulating them, and wishing them well.

As fast as the arthritic Iorlando could move, father and son hurried out of the courtroom and outside into the drizzle, savoring the drops of rain on their faces, enjoying the sweet thrill of freedom for the first time in almost two years. They were both in a hurry, headed for different places. Iorlando wanted to go home with his wife while Frank headed to New Orleans. He had someone he needed to thank. He left without noticing the woman who'd nearly destroyed him. Rosie Cortimiglia left the courthouse alone, headed back to New Orleans to take up her lonely life.

Frank caught the ferry to New Orleans with his brother-in-law Tony Spera and a couple more of his pals. On the way, he experienced a tense confrontation that was at once dramatic yet utterly pedestrian. The meeting was no great coincidence. He should have expected it. They were both on their way to New Orleans straight from the courthouse, and the Jackson Avenue ferry was the only convenient means across the river. Nevertheless, Frank was taken by surprise when in the middle of the Mississippi River, he came face to face with the woman who'd almost cost him his life.

He recovered from the shock before Rosie did and, betraying no bitterness, walked up to her and shook her hand. Rosie told him she was happy he was free. She couldn't stop the tears as she added that she did sometimes think of her dead baby. Then, overcome with grief and regret, she sank to the floor in a silent fit of weeping.

Embarrassed by the tears and her unmistakable wretchedness, "That's all right. God bless you," was all Frank could manage before he escaped outside onto the deck.

Later that afternoon, Frank gazed introspectively out the window of the *Times-Picayune* office at the corner of Camp and North Streets, watching the rain fall on the leafy Lafayette Square. He knew he and his parents were worse than penniless; they were in debt. The money, grocery store, and land they had slowly and thriftily accumulated over the past thirty years had all been liquidated toward their defense. But Frank, as was his nature, was cheerful and confident. He could take care of his parents and his younger brother Louis. He'd been offered a job in New Orleans selling real estate. He was young. He was hardworking. Like the biblical figure Job, he could get it all back.

He turned to look at Jim Coulton and he smiled. "Ain't it fine?"

14

The Final Chapter?

I ORLANDO'S JOY AT BEING released was crushed two months later when his daughter, Lena, died in childbirth. His heart was broken. He died four years later. But he died at home surrounded by his family, not on a prison farm.

Meanwhile, Frank went back to work for Paul Dupas and soon had his own real estate company, becoming what the *Times-Picayune* called "probably the youngest realtor in the state." After working, like so many Italians before him, fourteen hours a day, seven days a week (with an hour off on Sundays to go to church), he made his fortune in real estate development as the wetlands surrounding New Orleans were drained and the population spread inexorably over former swampland. And Frank didn't just sell real estate. He branched out into lumber, construction, mortgages, and cattle ranching.

While it isn't clear whether Frank married the girl he met while in jail, we know that in 1926 he married twenty-one-year-old Linzy Hamilton, and that it was a mistake. Just a year later, he filed for divorce. All we know about Hamilton is that she ran up debts she then didn't, or couldn't, pay. Maybe an attraction driven by the notoriety of a murder accusation wasn't enough to make a good marriage. But in 1936, he married a woman a couple of years older than him named Mary Shambra, this time for life. They never had children. In 1961,

Frank's huge size and years of overwork finally caught up to him; at the age of fifty-nine, he died of congestive heart failure.

There is no record of what happened to Charlie and Rosie Cortimiglia after Rosie's December 1920 appearance in the Gretna courtroom.

In 1924, Robert Rivarde, the DA who had been so thoroughly convinced of the Jordanos' guilt, defeated both his Jordano case opponent Andrew Thalheim and the incumbent judge Prentice Edrington in a primary election and went on to be elected judge of the Twenty-Fourth District Court at Gretna, where he served until his retirement in 1958. He and John Fleury remained friends until Rivarde's death in 1967, and the Jefferson Parish juvenile detention center is named for him.

John Fleury was elected district attorney for the Twenty-Fourth Judicial District in 1924 and was reelected for three more terms. After his retirement from the DA's office in 1948, he practiced law in Gretna and was a fixture in Jefferson Parish politics until he was in his nineties. He died in Gretna in 1984 at the age of ninety-eight.

William Byrnes, too, had a long career in Louisiana law and politics. He was a civil district court judge for twenty years, as well as a lecturer at Loyola University Law School and, briefly, its dean. In the 1930s, he turned down a spot on the state supreme court because of philosophical differences with Louisiana law.

Police Superintendent Frank Mooney was out of office by the time the Jordanos walked free, and he left widely regarded as a failure. He'd never quite fit in with the police department, too much a disciplinarian to have been a favorite of the rank and file, his tenure marred by scandals involving corrupt and incompetent policemen and the flourishing trades of prostitution, gambling, and illegal sale of alcohol, as well as his failure to find the Axeman.

He stepped down from office in December 1920, stating emphatically, and with great relief, "There'll be no more political jobs or detective work ever again for me."

Mooney went back to the railroad world that he knew and understood. Ironically, the man who failed to track down the killer of Italian grocers took a position with the Standard Fruit Company, founded and run by the Sicilian immigrant Vaccaro brothers. He ran the company's railroad lines in Honduras with great success, and it was there, in La Ceiba, that he died suddenly of a heart attack on August 22, 1923. His body was returned via steamship to New Orleans where it was met by a police honor guard in full uniform. The next day, the white-gloved honor guard escorted him to his final resting place in the family vault in Metairie.

What became of the Axeman, the "fiend" Mooney so fruitlessly sought? Previous accounts of the Axeman story note that he vanished after 1919, dropping out of sight as mysteriously as he had materialized, never to be heard from again. But while it's true that he disappeared from New Orleans, there is good reason to believe that he left the city only to terrorize victims elsewhere.

On a mild December morning in 1920, in Alexandria, Louisiana, two hundred miles northwest of New Orleans, Rosa Spero woke abruptly at 1 AM, sensing a presence in her bedroom. Later, all she could remember was that someone hit her husband with an axe and then turned to her, raising the weapon and bringing it crashing down on her head. Then nothing. She woke at 4 AM, covered in blood, a dull throbbing pain in her head and jaw and shoulder. On the bed lay her husband Joseph, dead, drenched in blood. Her baby, twenty-month-old Josephine, was unconscious and bleeding. Her five boys were still asleep in the next room. Cradling the infant in her arms, she fled the house, calling for help.

Frank Mooney would have instantly recognized the crime scene. Forty-eight-year-old Joseph and thirty-one-year-old Rosa Spero were the Italian proprietors of a grocery store at the corner of Wise and Turner Streets. Their assailant had broken in through a kitchen window. Entering the bedroom with an axe taken from the backyard and a butcher knife from the grocery, he struck Joseph Spero with the axe, breaking his jaw, then slashed the grocer's throat, slicing through his carotid artery. Spero bled out in minutes. After striking the woman and infant, the murderer abandoned the bloody axe and a railroad coupling pin (similar to the shoe pin left by the "Cleaver" when he'd broken into the Crutti home in 1910) in the bedroom. Police found the bloody butcher knife on the grocery counter. There was no evidence of robbery; hundreds of dollars in cash in the residence and store had not been touched.

Mrs. Spero's cuts were not severe enough to kill her, and by Monday afternoon she could speak to the police but could tell them nothing about the assailant. That evening her little girl died without regaining consciousness.

The police had no real leads. They briefly took into custody Louis Hughes, a sixty-year-old black carpenter. He'd recently done some work for Spero and had bloodstains on his trousers. But he satisfactorily explained the blood as the result of a cut on his hand, and with no other evidence against him, the investigation quickly came to a dead end.

A month later in DeRidder, Louisiana, seventy miles southwest of Alexandria, early on the morning of January 14, 1921, neighbors discovered thirty-eight-year-old Sicilian grocer Giovanni "John" Orlando, hacked and bloody, along with his wife and two small children. His skull had been cracked with an axe. Rushed to the hospital, he died on the operating table. The doctor estimated that his injury occurred about 2 AM.

Again, the assailant had broken in through a window and apparently hadn't taken anything. He'd left the axe, hair still sticking to the blade, in the blood-splattered bedroom. Mary Orlando, and the children who'd been sleeping in their parents' bed—Paul, age eight, and Josephine, age six—had all been badly cut but survived.

Once again, no real suspects were ever identified. Once again, the police collared a black man—this time, a "half-witted Negro," known as "Fittified Sol" on account of the seizures he suffered—who was jailed while the police investigated. And, again, the investigation turned up nothing. The murder remained unsolved.

Three months later, at around three o'clock in the morning on April 12, 1921, another incident occurred, this time in Lake Charles, Louisiana, fifty miles south of DeRidder. Neighbors of Marlena Scalisi were startled out of their beds by her screams for help. They hurried to the house at Opelousas and Blake Streets to find Mrs. Scalisi covered with blood, her husband Frank lying in their bed with a broken neck.

Frank Scalisi, a thirty-five-year-old immigrant from Palermo, worked at the Powell Lumber Company, while his wife Marlena ran the grocery store at the front of their house. In addition to eleven-month-old Johnnie, who slept in his parents' bed, the Scalisis had four other children in the next room.

The murderer had opened a dining room window and crawled into the house with an axe stolen from a backyard several blocks away. Entering the bedroom, he'd struck Frank one blow, killing him instantly. Then he'd raised his weapon against the sleeping Marlena and Johnnie. Fortunately for them, as he swung down, the blunt old axe head flew harmlessly off against the wall, and only the old wooden handle cracked against their heads.

Startled out of sleep by the blow, Marlena screamed. The intruder bolted. Marlena stumbled out of bed to turn on the bedroom light. Seeing her husband dead, she snatched up the baby and darted into the adjoining room where her ten-year-old daughter Mary had woken. Marlena handed Johnnie to Mary and ran off to call for help.

The Lake Charles sheriff arrived to find a scene that was very similar to the ones in Alexandria and DeRidder: a mysterious break-in, a shadowy assailant, and a dead body. This time, however, there was a witness.

Marlena had woken to see only a silhouette of a man at the foot of her bed, but she was able to describe him only as "short [and] chunky." But as the intruder had run through the children's room, ten-year-old Mary had gotten a look at him. She described him as a "short and stout" black man.

Was the murderer of Joseph Spero, Giovanni Orlando, and Frank Scalisi the Axeman of New Orleans? Was another killer at work? Was the same person even responsible for all three of these deaths?

The modus operandi was clearly that of the New Orleans killer: a break-in into the home of an Italian grocer in the middle of the night, the use of an axe found at or near the scene to murder the grocer in his bed, little or nothing stolen, and no apparent motive. Joseph Spero's throat had been cut, as had the throats of Joe and Catherine Maggio in May 1918. Also, the killer had taken care to tread softly by wearing rubber soles, as had Joe Romano's killer.

The New Orleans Axeman, however, was a white man. He'd been clearly seen by Harriet Crutti and her neighbors, and by Mary Davi; Pauline Bruno, too, told police she had the impression that her uncle's killer was white, although she could not be certain. And, based on descriptions, his height ranged from five feet six inches to perhaps six feet. Only one witness, one of the Crutti neighbors, had described him as "a short, heavy-set man."

The newspaper reported that robbery was the motive for the Scalisi crime. Drawers had been pulled open and a box on top of the dresser had been opened. However, the intruder had not found the significant amount of cash tucked away in a trunk, and while he had grabbed Frank's trousers containing two dollars, he abandoned them two blocks away. Eleven dollars in the grocery's cash register had not been disturbed.

The New Orleans Axeman was also known to have opened and rummaged through wardrobes. When he killed Joe Romano, he had also grabbed his trousers and wallet. But was robbery the primary motive for the attack on the Scalisis? Or was it, as some New Orleans detectives believed of the Axeman attacks, only an attempt to disguise his murders as robberies? Maybe the killer would have discovered the savings and cash register money if given enough time. But then, why try to kill the Scalisis? Did the grocer wake up, prompting the robber to strike? He had only been hit once, unusual for the Axeman. If that's what happened, why did he turn on the wife who was only woken when hit on the head? On balance, it seems more likely that the intruder chose to abandon his search for valuables, if that's what it was, in order to attack.

As for Mary's identification of the intruder as a black man, could she have been mistaken? A light had been shining in her room, but the girl had only just been woken up; she only got a fleeting look at the fleeing man. Moreover, her identification appears to have become more certain overnight. On the day of the attack, the newspaper reported that Mary "said she did not see the man plainly but he seemed short and stout and to her he seemed a negro." She was much more confident the next day when she testified in front of the coroner's jury: "The man was short and stout. He was dark, a colored man."

Not only are children less reliable as witnesses than adults, but studies demonstrate that memories can be unconsciously influenced by others, who can make witnesses more positive in their identification of a suspect, regardless of whether the identification is correct. Mary, no doubt, discussed her experience with her family before she gave testimony, and perhaps they gave her reason to (subconsciously) want to pin the blame on a black man.

The sheriff's first suspect was Mary's uncle and Marlena's brother, Joe Mansueto. But Marlena and her mother firmly rejected that possibility, and Mary insisted that the person she saw was not her uncle. As she ruminated over the incident or discussed it with her mother or grandmother before she gave evidence to the coroner's jury (and it's hardly likely that she did not), the idea that the assailant couldn't have been Uncle Joe solidified in her mind. Certainly, it would have been convenient for the culprit to have been black; that way, he couldn't have been Uncle Joe.

Moreover, Mary might have been subtly conditioned in other ways to identify her father's killer as a black man if she didn't get a good look at him. Witnesses often see—and remember—what they expect to see. People fit what they observe into preexisting paradigms, or schemas, of how they understand the world. The black axe murderer was a common racist stereotype at the time. That's why, in many of the Axeman cases, a black man was among the first to be detained for the crime. Given assumptions about black criminality, it wouldn't be surprising for the girl to subconsciously assume a black man was responsible for breaking into the grocery and killing her father.

If the Scalisi killer was, indeed, the Axeman of New Orleans, it is problematic that both mother and daughter described him as short; almost all the New Orleans witnesses had stated otherwise. But witnesses make mistakes. And Mary's characterization of the man could have been influenced by her mother's description. Waking up in pain and fright, Mrs. Scalisi got a fleeting glimpse of a silhouette in the room and decided she'd seen a short, pudgy man. Mary's memory of the intruder was conceivably influenced by her mother's.

Or perhaps the girl was right and the killer was a stocky black man. It could have been nothing more than a botched or brutal robbery. Such crimes weren't unknown. Around the same time, a series of robberies and axe or hammer murders of shopkeepers—some Italian—took place in Birmingham, Alabama, which would end only with the arrest and conviction of five black suspects.

However, the axe murder of an Italian grocer amid little evidence of robbery in much the same way as the grocers in New Orleans seems too remarkable a coincidence to ignore. Of course, it's possible that the Scalisi murder was the work of a would-be African American burglar, and the Spero and Orlando killings were Axeman murders. Or, perhaps, Mary Scalisi was mistaken and the Axeman was responsible for all three of these crimes. The possibility that the Axeman continued killing after leaving New Orleans must be balanced against the possible but improbable scenario of someone *else* with no apparent motive preying on Italian grocers with an axe.

Did anyone in New Orleans see a connection between these killings and the Axeman murders? The only evidence of an effort to connect the murders is a single line in the *New Orleans States* that referred to the Spero killing as "an ax murder identical in detail with those which stirred the state more than a year ago."

The Scalisi murder, too, remained unsolved.

So who, then, was the Axeman? He has never been identified and is unlikely to be given a name now. Had the murders occurred today, sophisticated investigative techniques—better fingerprinting, DNA analysis, forensic psychology—would have given Dantonio and Mooney tools to make it easier to identify and track him down. Criminal profilers would provide more sophisticated insights into a killer who struck with no apparent motive and would suggest tactics for flushing him out. The police could release information about how the murderer would act and his likely personality. Profilers also could advise them on how to turn up the killer's stress level to make him nervous enough to exhibit unusual behavior such as becoming obsessed with the investigation, trying to change his appearance, drinking too much, having trouble sleeping, or planning to leave town. This behavior might, in turn, alert his family and/or coworkers that something was wrong. Of course, there's still no guarantee that modern methods would have yielded success; too many serial killers still go uncaught.

Even if the Axeman cannot be identified, however, the modern study of serial killers provides insight into what kind of person he probably was. Without benefit of real forensic evidence and detailed crime scene evidence, conclusions can only be provisional and sketchy, but it's possible to construct a likely profile of the Axeman.

From witness descriptions (and with all the caveats that go with these), he appears to have been a white working-class male in his mid-to-late thirties when he began his attacks in 1910–1911. That he was familiar with burglary tools and had the confidence to break in armed with only an axe or cleaver when grocers routinely kept handguns next to their beds suggests that he was an old hand at breaking and entering. As with many sociopaths, he may well have had a history of other petty crimes.

Likely uneducated, the Axeman was probably a laborer of some sort, who could move freely all over the city without attracting attention and easily enter a shop to scout the premises. He'd choose a familiar weapon. Perhaps he started with a butcher's cleaver because he worked in the meat-packing industry. But leaving a murder scene with a bloody cleaver was risky, and having to steal a new instrument every time posed its own risks. Maybe he switched to axes because he knew he could reasonably expect to find one at any grocer's residence. And an axe was not only a more convenient weapon, it was a more lethal one.

Superficially, the killer would have seemed normal, except perhaps that he'd have a history of run-ins with the law. Anyone who got to know him well, however, would realize there was something slightly "off" about him. Chief Reynolds and Superintendent Mooney both thought he was a drug fiend of some sort; they were probably right. His early thefts might have been to support a morphine or cocaine habit. And he likely carried out his crimes under the influence of some drug, which would explain his odd behavior at the Crutti crime.

Serial killers crave power and control. They need it to give them a sense of superiority, especially over the people they're convinced have wronged them. It isn't unusual for psychopathic killers to target a specific group of people who represent an injustice to be redressed, a humiliation to be avenged. An inadequate personality, the Axeman would have blamed the failures in his own life on his victims. The man was his primary target; sometimes a wife or child just happened to be there; they were collateral damage. The Axeman was a coward who could only face his victims as they slept. He was a predator who could only prey on the helpless.

Why Italian grocers? Perhaps because these not-quite-white foreigners and small businessmen had the temerity to be more successful than he was. Maybe he resented their growing success as Italian corner groceries spread over the city. Could he have come from a family whose own business venture had failed? Alternatively, maybe he'd been caught and jailed for breaking into an Italian-owned grocery. Perhaps an Italian grocer had been instrumental in sending him to jail for an earlier crime. Or perhaps an Italian grocer had thrown him out of his store, publicly humiliating him.

Whatever the reason, he hated them as a group, not as individuals; he was unlikely to have known any of his victims personally. But by standing over his sleeping prey in the night, holding an axe, he could feel God-like, with the power of life or death. Bringing down the axe, crushing the skull, seeing blood spray the walls, made the pitiless psychopath feel like he'd conquered his enemy and avenged his humiliation, real or imagined. Even when his victim was a blameless toddler, killing gave his life a purpose and a sense of success. The extensive press coverage of his crimes would have added to the Axeman's sense of accomplishment; it would have been the only thing of note he would ever do.

The mystery of the Axeman's identity probably will never be solved, but in some ways it's appropriate that he remains a faceless phantom. He was certainly a nobody, a loser, a nonentity with no sense of self who felt that he had no control over anything, not even his own life.

He may not always remain unknown, however. His path led from New Orleans to Alexandria and then to western Louisiana. Perhaps he continued moving west on to Texas or beyond. Or turned north toward Shreveport, Louisiana. The killing wouldn't have stopped. Perhaps in some obscure small-town newspaper there's a story of an intruder caught fleeing an Italian grocery in the middle of the night after attacking the proprietor and his wife, or a tale of an Italian grocer who shot a man trying to crawl through his window with an axe. That would be the Axeman.

The Axeman of New Orleans may yet be discovered.

Acknowledgments

This book could not have been written without the aid of many people to whom I am hugely indebted and immensely grateful.

First, I must thank all of the archivists and librarians who made this project possible. At the top of this list is the staff of the Louisiana Division/City Archives at the New Orleans Public Library—Nancy Aloisio, Charlie Brown, Christina Bryant, Stephen Kuehling, Yvonne Loiselle, Maya Lopez, Greg Osborn, and Cheryl Picou. Special thanks are owed to Irene Wainwright, former head of the Louisiana Division, who patiently and courteously endured years of what must have seemed like endless requests for information.

I also want to thank the staff of the Louisiana State Archives, particularly reference librarian John Fowler, who tracked down a thesis on the Axeman for me. Daniel Hammer of the Williams Research Center at the Historic New Orleans Collection provided me with a copy of "The Mysterious Axman's Jazz." Gratitude is due, too, to Tara Laver and the staff at Louisiana State University's Special Collections; Florence Jumonville at the University of New Orleans' Special Collections; Connie L. Phelps at the University of New Orleans' Services Department; Ann Case at the Louisiana Research Collection at Tulane University; Michelle Riggs at the University Archives at LSU at Alexandria; and the staffs of McNeese State University's Frazar Memorial Library, Auburn University's Ralph Brown Draughon Library, and the library at Notre Dame Seminary in New Orleans.

The Church of Jesus Christ of Latter Day Saints' Family History Center greatly assisted my research, and I'm especially grateful to the local staff of the Family History Library who graciously helped me on Tuesday and Thursday mornings at the LDS Church on Carter Hill Road, Montgomery, Alabama.

I also made use of records in parish and county courthouses. Thanks are due to Sha Carter and Kay Gilliland at the Criminal Records division of the Calcasieu Parish Clerk of Court's office; Maria Hall at the Los Angeles Superior Court Archives and Records Center; and the staffs of the Ouachita Parish Clerk of Court's office, the Marriage License and Passport Department, Jefferson Parish General Government Center, and the Old Records and Evidence Department, Jefferson Parish, Gretna.

I wouldn't have been able to complete this book without the interlibrary loan staff at Delta State University, Mississippi University for Women, and Auburn University at Montgomery. Diane Coleman was a cheerful colleague for many years. Gail Gunter continued to answer questions long after I left Mississippi. I appreciate DSU's history program and former DSU provost Ann Lotven for allowing me to retain my ties to DSU for several years after I left.

Harry Laver, John C. Rodrigue, Chuck Westmoreland, and Edith Ambrose answered questions about Southern history. Roger Lane offered guidance on homicide and homicide investigation in the early twentieth century. Kenneth Gravois from the Sugar Research Station at the LSU AgCenter was an indispensable resource on the sugarcane industry in Louisiana.

Many other scholars, writers, and researchers answered questions and shared their findings with me, including Patricia Cohen, David Critchley, Mike Dash, Marianne Fisher-Giorlando, Anita Guerinni, Tom Hunt, Elizabeth Loftus, Michael Newton, Katherine Ramsland, Harold Schechter, and Richard Warner. Keven McQueen of Eastern Kentucky University, too, shared with me the fruits of his own research on the Axeman; I'm particularly indebted to him for his exceptional generosity. I also benefited from Doug Casey's willingness to give me access to his years of research on early New Orleans criminal gangs.

I'm grateful to Professor Elliot Leyton for taking the time to speak with me by phone.

In the New Orleans Police Department, thanks are due to Lieutenant Gwendolyn M. Nolan, Captain H. M. Kouts, and NOPD historian Ruth Ashur.

Dr. Carol Terry, chief medical examiner for Gwinnet County, Georgia, shared her expertise on death in all its forms. I'll never forget (much as I will try) what she told me about "biscuit brain." I greatly profited from the expertise of profiler Ralph Stone, retired Georgia Bureau of Investigation special agent; Rick Chambers, former City of Atlanta homicide detective and now chief investigator at Chambers Consulting & Security; and Lieutenant Tina Miller, retired, Atlanta Police Department.

Working on the Axeman brought home to me how many lawyers I know. While I'm not sure if that's good or bad, it's been very helpful in writing this book. For their assistance in answering numerous legal questions, I want to acknowledge and thank Polly Price, Robin Hutchinson, Jean Powers, and Ben Farrow.

Several people read part or all of the manuscript. Thomas Easterling and Donnie Nobles read chapters. Michael Burger read numerous drafts of the manuscript. Adam Lynde read and gave perceptive comments under the most uncomfortable conditions. Kara Bryant brought an English teacher's eye to my grammar. Corey-Jan Albert has twice now gone above and beyond the call of friendship by reading and editing a manuscript. My editor at Chicago Review Press, Yuval Taylor, improved the manuscript. Developmental editor Devon Freeny and copyeditor Mark Bast saved me from many embarrassing mistakes. All remaining errors, omissions, oversights, inaccuracies, misunderstandings, misinterpretations, and typos are solely my responsibility.

A few miscellaneous thank-yous are in order: to Christal Varholdt for carrying out some freelance research, Blythe Camenson for reading my original proposal, Maureen Ogle for advice on agents and arcs, and my agent Eric Myers for taking me on.

I'm especially obliged to Francine Loveless Cloud for talking to me about her grandmother, Josephine Orlando, her great-grandmother, Maria Conchetta Liggio Orlando, and her great-grandfather, Giovanni Orlando, three of the Axeman's likely victims.

I owe all the people listed here for helping bring this work to fruition. It's entirely possible that I've overlooked or forgotten someone who helped in some way. If so, please forgive me. My memory is less reliable than my gratitude, which is always profound.

And, finally, I want to note three very important individuals: my mother, Maxine Reynolds Davis, who rather belatedly I need to thank for her commitment to my education; Michael for supporting me (in more ways than one) while I wrote this book; and Cocktail, for his support and love, despite insisting on sitting on my lap when I was trying to write.

Notes

Preface

I got hold of Robert Tallant's Ready to Hang: An earlier version of Tallant's story, apparently unknown to many who wrote about the Axeman, appeared in *Gumbo Ya-Ya: A Collection of Louisiana Folk Tales*, published in 1945. Tallant appears not to have known about another version of the Axeman in an article published by Kendall, "Blood on the Banquette."

may well have gotten much of his information: Tallant does seem to have consulted the *Times-Picayune*.

Most of the available sources basically repeated: E.g., Everitt, *Human Monsters*, 76–78; Jeffers, *With an Axe*, 14–15; Lane and Greg, eds., *Encyclopedia of Serial Killers*, 35–38; Lester, "Axeman of New Orleans," 67–75; Newton, *Encyclopedia of Unsolved Crimes*, 274–276; Ramsland, "All About the Axeman"; Reid, *Mafia*, 184–187; Schechter, *Serial Killer Files*, 145–146; and Wilson and Wilson, *Killers Among Us*, 167–171.

In a list of male serial killers: Hickey, *Serial Murderers*, 131.

crime writer Jay Robert Nash argued: Nash, *Bloodletters and Badmen*, 358.

city records showed that no Italian grocers: Newton, *Hunting Humans*, 18. Newton revised this account in subsequent books, e.g., *Encyclopedia of Unsolved Crimes* (2004) and *Encyclopedia of Unsolved Crimes*, 2nd ed. (2009), but *Hunting Humans* is what I had when I first began reading about the Axeman.

a sleeping Italian grocer named Joseph Davi: NOPD, *Reports of Homicide*, vol. 14 (1911), in New Orleans Public Library; Coroner's Office, *Record Book Journals*, vol. 7 (1911), in New Orleans Public Library.

1. Evil Descends

It was a moonless night: According to the Naval Observatory (http://aa.usno.navy.mil/data/docs/RS_OneYear.php, accessed August 31, 2015), the moon set just after midnight.

"There will be no gorgeous pageants": *NOTP*, March 4, 1919.

"modest, even . . . somber Carnival": *NOTP*, March 5, 1919.

They also shared the streets: I don't have any direct evidence that either Frank Jordano and his girlfriend or the murderer known as the Axeman of New Orleans were at Mardi Gras in 1919. But it doesn't stretch the imagination to envisage the high-spirited young couple joining in the celebrations. And the killer? Well, he had to be somewhere; he was almost certainly in the city at the time.

"Oh, Jesus! Oh, Jesus! Oh, Jesus!": Direct quotations of dialogue in the immediate aftermath of the attack on the Cortimiglias are taken from the Jordano trial transcript.

in the direction of Amesville: By 1914, the growing settlement of Amesville was officially renamed Marrero, although most people still called it by its older name.

At thirty-nine: 1920 US Census, Ancestry.com.

Only last year, a man: NOPD, *Reports of Homicide*, February 19, 1918, in New Orleans Public Library.

"sent her back to the ward": State v. Guagliardo and Guagliardo, 186, in Supreme Court of Louisiana Historical Archives.

"I must see her!": NOI, March 11, 1919.

"one of the saddest funerals": NODS, March 10, 1919.

2. The Cleaver

Details of the attack on August Crutti come from *Daily News*, August 13, 1910; *NODP*, August 14, 1910; *NODS*, August 13 and 14, 1910; *NOTD*, August 14 and 15, 1910; and *NOI*, August 13 and 14, 1910.

For a description of the attack on the Rissettos and the subsequent police investigation, see *Daily News*, September 20–22, 1910; *NOI*, September 20, 21, and 23, 1910; *NODP*, September 20–24 and 27, 1910; *NOB*, September 21, 1910; and *NOTD*, September 21–22, 1920.

For information on Conchetta and Joseph Rissetto's family background and deaths, see New Orleans Marriage Records, Ancestry.com; 1920 US Census, Ancestry.com; *NODP*, November 25, 1910; *NODS*, November 25, 1912; and *NOTP*, May 29, 1940.

Information on John T. Flannery comes from *State v. Flannery*, in New Orleans Public Library; *NOI*, August 29 and October 25, 1910; *NOTD*, August 29–30 and October 26, 1910; and *NODP*, August 29–30 and October 26, 1910.

August and Harriet shared the small house: 1910 US Census, Ancestry.com.

"drunk or crazy": NODP, August 14, 1910.

"some half-witted fellow": Ibid.

"well-known police character": Daily News, August 13, 1910; *NOTD*, August 14, 1910.

"insane and irresponsible": Drs. Hummel and O'Hara to Hon. P. D. Chretien, *State v. Flannery*, in New Orleans Public Library. See also *NODP*, October 26, 1910; and *NOTD*, October 26, 1910.

A man crept up: Like many Italian names, the Rissettos' name is spelled a variety of ways in the newspapers, and I have standardized the spelling.

With no children: The 1910 US Census (Ancestry.com) lists no one else living with the Rissettos.

"slaughtering pen": Daily News, September 20, 1910.

"domestic strife": Daily News, September 22, 1910.

"of Italian descent": NOI, September 20, 1910; *NODP*, September 21, 1910.

"I am certain that burglars": NOI, September 23, 1910.

"a fiendish thirst for blood": *Daily News*, September 21, 1910.
"dime store novel flavor": *Daily News*, September 21, 1910.
"the trail is very warm": *NOI*, September 23, 1910.
"murder stamped on his countenance:" *NODP*, August 14, 1910.

3. *Dagoes, Sugarcane, and Muffulettas*

Iorlando Guagliardo left the barest record of his existence in official documents. I know his date of birth, where he came from, the year he emigrated, whom he married, and where he owned businesses. The account in this chapter is built around those known facts, but it also attempts to flesh out his life based on the typical experiences of Sicilian immigrants into Louisiana.

For Italians in Louisiana, I have relied on Adams, "Mafia Riots"; Baiamonte, "New Immigrants in the South" (MA thesis) and *Immigrants in Rural America*; Boneno, "Migrant to Millionaire" (PhD diss.); Edwards-Simpson, "Sicilian Immigration" (PhD diss.); Macaluso, *Italian Immigrant Families*; Magnaghi, "Louisiana's Italian Immigrants"; Margavio, "Reaction of the Press"; Margavio and Molyneaux, "Residential Segregation of Italians"; Margavio and Salomone, *Bread and Respect*, "Passage, Settlement, and Occupational Characteristics," and "Economic Advantages of Familism"; Maselli and Candeloro, *Italians in New Orleans*; Jean Ann Scarpaci, "Immigrants in the New South" and "Italian Immigrants" (PhD diss.); Clive Webb, "Lynching of Sicilian Immigrants"; "Our Italian Fellow-Citizens," *NODP*, October 17, 1890; "Italian Colony," *NODP*, October 18, 1890; "Italian Immigration," *NODP*, August 12, 1904; and "Thirteen Hundred Italian Immigrants," *NODP*, October 17, 1907.

Details of nineteenth-century New Orleans from Cable, *Lost New Orleans*; Jewell, *Jewell's Crescent City Illustrated*; and Thomas Ruys Smith, *Southern Queen*.

For population in New Orleans, I have relied on Sublette, *World That Made New Orleans*; City of New Orleans, *Population, Total and by Race*, http://nutrias.org/facts/aq150_1981p.pdf; and University of Virginia Library, Historical Census Browser.

For information on the sugarcane industry and the importation of foreign workers, see Berthoff, "Southern Attitudes"; Carter, *Southern Legacy*; Conrad and Lucas, *White Gold*; J. Vincenza Scarpaci, "Labor for Louisiana's Sugar Cane"; Jean Ann Scarpaci, "Immigrants in the New South" and"Italian Immigrants" (PhD diss.); Schmitz, "Transformation of the Southern Cane Sugar Sector"; Shrugg, "Survival of the Plantation System"; Sitterson, *Sugar Country*; and Smalley, "Sugar Making in Louisiana."

Background for the cult of Saint Joseph is found in Margavio and Salomone, *Bread and Respect*; McColloster, "New Light"; Plemer, "Feast of St. Joseph"; "History of the Saint Joseph Altar," CatholicCulture.org; and Warren, "Sicilian St. Joseph Altar." Because they are preserved through oral tradition, there are many variations of the Saint Joseph's Day tradition.

Personal information on Iorlando Guagliardo (aka Jordano) comes from *State v. Guagliardo and Guagliardo*, in Supreme Court of Louisiana Historical Archives; *NODS*, March 18, 1919; and "Giolando Guagliardo aka Jordano" and "Frank Guagliardo" in Ancestry.com, One World Tree Project.

For ethnic clusters in New Orleans, see Campanella, *Bienville's Dilemma* and *Geographies of New Orleans*; Hintz, *Ethnic New Orleans*; Lewis, *New Orleans*; Margavio, "Reaction of the Press"; Margavio and Molyneaux, "Residential Segregation of Italians"; Maselli and Candeloro, *Italians in New Orleans*; and Richey and Kean, *New Orleans Book.*

For descriptions of "Little Palermo," I drew on Adams, "Mafia Riots"; Gambino, *Vendetta*; McMain, "Behind the Yellow Fever"; and Tallant, *Romantic New Orleanians.*

For the history of the muffuletta, see Tusa, *Marie's Melting Pot.*

"hard-working, money-saving race": Quoted in Sitterson, *Sugar Country*, 315.

"like school girls": "Immigrants from Italy," *NODP*, December 17, 1880.

"foggy cities of the North": Adamoli, "Letters from America," 271.

"Americans, Brazilians, West Indians": Quoted in Campanella, *Bienville's Dilemma*, 169.

"are ready to start a fruit shop": Quoted in Jean Ann Scarpaci, "Italian Immigrants" (PhD diss.), 211.

"black dagoes": Gambino, *Vendetta*, 56.

"Negroes made unabashed distinction": Carter, *Southern Legacy*, 106.

"filthy paupers": Adams, "Mafia Riots," 15.

seat of Saint James Parish: According to Saint James Parish, State of Louisiana, Conveyance Record vol. 52, 1889–1893, in April 1892 "Benedict Jurdano" bought an "oyster saloon . . . consisting of assorted fruits and general merchandise" for $200. Iorlando Guagliardo used the name Benedict or Benedetto Jordano for business purposes. He is referred to as "Benedict" or "Benedetto" Jordanno in several New Orleans newspapers, and a newspaper article mentions he was in business in Saint James Parish. The 1900 Census (Ancestry.com) lists "Benedict Jordano", a fruit dealer, living in Saint James Parish with his wife Lillie and his daughters "Marywarard" and "Annie." It's likely that the names were garbled in the census, as they often were; almost certainly this refers to Jordano's daughters Mary and Anna (also known as Lena). See also *NODS*, March 18, 1919.

"filth and . . . intolerable stench": Adams, "Mafia Riots," 16.

"humble, loud-voiced vendor": Richey and Kean, *New Orleans Book*, 129.

4. The Davi Murder

Details of Joe Davi's murder and the police investigation come from *NOI*, June 27–29, 1911; *NODS*, June 27–28 and July 2, 1911; *NODP*, June 28–30, July 1, and August 3, 1911; *NOB*, June 28–29, 1911; *NOTD*, June 28–29 and July 2 and 4, 1911; Coroner's Office, *Record Book Journals*, June 28, 1911, in New Orleans Public Library; and NOPD, *Reports of Homicide*, June 28, 1911, in New Orleans Public Library.

For murder in New Orleans, see Adler, "Murder, North and South"; Asbury, *French Quarter*; Metcalf, "Race Relations"; Wheeler, "Homicides and Suicides"; NOPD, *Reports of Homicide*, in New Orleans Public Library; and NOPD, Annual Report, 1910, in New Orleans Public Library.

For the development of the police force in New Orleans, see Jackson, *New Orleans in the Gilded Age*; Metcalf, "Race Relations"; Rousey, "Cops and Guns" and *Policing the Southern City*; Vyhnanek, *Unorganized Crime*; NOPD, Annual Reports, in New Orleans Public Library; *Rules and Regulations Governing the Police Department*, in New Orleans Public Library; NOPD, *Fifty Years of Progress*; and *NODP*, February 19, 1912.

Information on Martin Berhman's administration and the Ring comes from Berhman, *Martin Behrman*; Deacon and Coleman, *Martin Behrman Administration*; Kendall, "Sixteen Years"; Reynolds, *Machine Politics*; Schott, "New Orleans Machine"; and Williams, "Martin Behrman."

For James Reynolds as chief of police, see *NOTD*, February 10, 1911; *NOI*, February 10–11, 1911; and *NODP*, February 19 and April 19, 1912.

For the development of scientific police investigation, see James Morton, *Catching the Killers*; Ramsland, *Beating the Devil's Game*; Thorwald, *Century of the Detective*; and Wilson and Wilson, *Written in Blood.*

For the tools the NOPD had to solve crimes with, see *Rules and Regulations Governing the Police Department*, in New Orleans Public Library; *NOTD*, February 28, 1908; *NODP*, July 18–19, 1908; and *NOI*, August 3, 1917.

To understand why suspects confess, see Tousignant, "Why Suspects Confess."

For use of the third degree, see Keedy, "The Third Degree"; Skolnick and Fyfe, *Above the Law*; *NOTD*, December 9, 1907; *NOI*, February 10, 1911; *NOTP*, March 17, 1915; *NODS*, August 19, 1917; and *NOTP*, April 10, 1920. In 1919, a grand jury found that New Orleans policemen frequently relied on the third degree to "extort a confession," per *NOI*, February 27, 1919. See also *NODS*, February 28, 1919; and *NOTP*, February 28, 1919.

For accusations that George Long used the third degree to attempt to coerce a confession from a suspect, Andrew Whitfield, for the murder of Leopold Cordova, see *NOTP*, April 16–18, 1920.

Details of John Dantonio's career are found in *NODP*, October 21, 1900, and September 13, 1910; *NODS*, July 13, 1911; *NOTP*, March 28 and April 2, 1920; and NOPD, Annual Reports, especially for 1896 and 1902, in New Orleans Public Library.

For the relationship between police and newspapermen, see Ramelli, "Scenes in the 'Underworld'"; Kendall, "Old-Time New Orleans"; and *NODS*, August, 3, 1917. For Andy Ojeda, see *NOTP*, April 12, 1950.

For a description of police headquarters, see Kendall, "Notes on the Criminal History"; NOPD, *Fifty Years of Progress*; and sketch in *NODS*, August, 3, 1917.

For John Flannery's plea to DA Adams and his ultimate fate, see *NODS*, July 3, 1911, and August 14, 1916; and *NOTP*, August 15, 1916.

a city of 339,000: University of Virginia Library, Historical Census Browser.

Robberies and burglaries were common: In the period 1900–1910, the homicide rate for New Orleans was 22.2 per 100,000 residents, which made it among the most violent of southern cities and gave it a murder rate three times that of Chicago. Adler, "Murder, North and South," 301.

a hundred years later: "Historical Crime Data 1990–2004," City of New Orleans official website, accessed October 13, 2016, www.nola.gov/getattachment/NOPD/Crime-Data/Crime-Stats/Historic-crime-data-1990-2014.pdf.

"keep the police force entirely out": *NOI*, February 11, 1911.

"steady, sober and good young man": *NODP*, June 28, 1911.

a man near the wardrobe: The *New Orleans Item* says she didn't see him rummaging in the wardrobe, that people took stuff out of it to wipe her face. *NOI*, June 28, 1911.

"Where is your money?": *NOI*, June 29, 1911.

"Call your husband": *NOI*, June 27, 1911.

"a blow with a sharp-edged though heavy blade": *NOTD*, June 29, 1911.

"Are you sure about the man": *NODP*, June 29, 1911.

"delicate state": *NODP*, June 29 and July 6, 1911.

two Bertillon operators: NOPD, Annual Reports, 1897, 1898, and 1911, in New Orleans Public Library.

"All he needs is to use his eyes": NOI, August 3, 1917.
"motive is the clew [sic]": NOTD, July 4, 1911.
"I've forced confessions": Quoted in Skolnick and Fyfe, *Above the Law*, 44.
"knew the effect of moral suasion": NODP, February 11, 1911.
"through persuasion and without": NOTD, October 17, 1910.
"There is no apparent motive:" NOTD, June 29, 1911.
Sam Pitzo: Sometimes spelled Pizzo.
Philip Daguanno: Sometimes given as Diavani.
"beat his brains in": NOTD, July 2, 1911.
"The man who attacked my husband": NOTD, July 2, 1911.
"closely allied to the [police] department": Ramelli, "Scenes in the 'Underworld.'"
"I came back early": NODP, July 3, 1911; *NOI*, July 3, 1911.
"I do not believe any of these jobs": NOTD, July 4, 1911.
named Joseph P. Davi for his father: The 1920 US Census (Ancestry.com) shows Joseph P. Davi living with his maternal grandparents in New Orleans.
"in very much the same manner": NODP, July 8, 1911.
the victims of "vengeance": NOI, September 20, 1910.
"fact that all the victims": NODP, June 29, 1911.

5. *The Black Hand*

For the Mafia generally, see Critchley, *Origin of Organized Crime*; Dash, *First Family*; Dickie, *Cosa Nostra*; Fentress, *Rebels and Mafiosi*; Hess, *Mafia and Mafioso*; and Nelli, *Business of Crime.*

For the New Orleans "Mafia," see Asbury, *French Quarter*; Ralph Carroll, "Mafia in New Orleans" (MA thesis); Chandler, *Brothers in Blood*; Dulitz, "Myth of the Mafia" (BS thesis); Kendall, "Who Killa de Chief?"; Kurtz, "Organized Crime"; and Nelli, *Business of Crime.*

For the true story of the ill-fated Francisco Domingo, see *DTD*, January 6, 1855; and Orleans Parish Coroner's Office. For Sicilian criminals in New Orleans in the 1860s, see *DTD*, June 22 and August 15, 1861; and *New Orleans Times*, March 19, 1869. For Esposito as merely a bandit, see Baiamonte, "'Who Killa de Chief' Revisited"; Kurtz, "Organized Crime"; Nelli, *Business of Crime*; and *NODP*, July 9 and July 22, 1881, and November 9, 1881.

For crime in Sicily in the nineteenth century, see table 1 in Eisner, "Long-Term Historical Trends."

Details of David Hennessy's involvement with the Matrangas and Provenzanos, his murder, and the subsequent lynching of suspected Italians are from the substantial literature on the case: Baiamonte, "'Who Killa de Chief' Revisited"; Botein, "Hennessy Case"; Richard Carroll, "Impact of David Hennessey"; Coxe, "New Orleans Mafia"; Dash, *First Family*; Gambino, *Vendetta*; Hunt and Sheldon, *Deep Water*; Katz, "Hennessy Affair"; Kendall, "Who Killa de Chief?"; Marr, "New Orleans Mafia"; Nelli, *Business of Crime*; Tom Smith, *Crescent City Lynchings*; and Wilds, *Afternoon Story.* See also numerous newspaper articles, especially *NOTD*, May 7, 1890; *NODP*, May 6–7, July 17–20, and October 16–19, 1890; *NODS*, October 16–17, 1890; *NODP*, October 17–21, 1890, and March 13–23, 1891; *NOTD*, March 14 and 18, 1891; *Daily City Item*, March 17, 1891; *NODS*, March 18, 1891; *New York Tribune*, March 18, 1891; *Mascot*, March 21, 1891.

For Black Hand crime, see Lombardo, *Black Hand*; Nelli, *Business of Crime*; and Pitkin and Cordasco, *Black Hand*. In New Orleans, see, for example, *NOTD*, April 12, 1908; *NODP*, September 10, 1910; and *NOTD*, May 31, 1912. For examples of the Black Hand as an organization, see *NOI*, May 20, 1908; and *NODP*, July 14, 1910.

For the career of Joseph Mumfre, see Convict Record of the Louisiana State Penitentiary, in Louisiana State Archives; *State v. Monfre* [*sic*], in New Orleans Public Library; *State v. Pamelia*, Westlaw, 122 La. 207, 47 So. 508 (1908); *State v. Monfre* [*sic*], Westlaw, 122 La. 251, 47 So. 543 (1908); and *State v. Monfre* [*sic*], Westlaw, 122 La. 513, 47 So. 846 (1908). Also *NOTD*, December 6–9, 1907; *NOI*, December 7–8, 1907, and July 23–25, 1908; *NODS*, July 24–25, 1908; *NOTD*, July 24–25, 1908; and *NODP*, July 24–25, 1908.

"It's not necessary for you": *NODP*, October 16, 1890; and *NODS*, October 16, 1890.

"They've given it to me": *NODP*, October 16, 1890; and *NODS*, October 16, 1890.

"was in essence the Mafia": Kendall, "Who Killa de Chief?" 506.

suspected by some later writers: In *Deep Water*, Hunt and Sheldon argue that Joseph Macheca established the New Orleans Mafia.

"the law and the evidence": *NODP*, August 10, 1890.

"Scour the whole neighborhood": *NODP*, October 16, 1890.

"We must teach these people": *NODP*, October 19, 1890.

"Who killa de chief?": Quoted in Wilds, *Afternoon Story*, 99; and Coxe, "New Orleans Mafia," 1085.

"Hang the Dago murderers!": *NOTD*, March 15, 1891.

"a form of behavior": Lombardo, *Black Hand*, 122.

"part armed criminal gang": Dickie, *Cosa Nostra*, 52.

"fact that all the victims were Italians": *NODP*, June 29, 1911.

"Dear Friend": *NODP*, August 3, 1911.

Joseph Mumfre was just: Like many immigrants' names, Mumfre's name appears in a variety of spellings: Monfre, Munfre, Monfee, Manfre. I have chosen one of the most common variations to use consistently.

6. The Cleaver Returns

For understanding serial killers, I've relied on Brown, *Killing for Sport*; Carlisle, "Divided Self"; Douglas and Dodd, *Inside the Mind of BTK*; Douglas and Olshaker, *Cases That Haunt Us*; Hale, "Application of Learning Theory"; Holmes, "Psychological Profiling"; Holmes and Holmes, *Serial Murder*; Jenkins, "Serial Murder"; Leyton, *Hunting Humans*; Robert Morton, "Serial Murder"; Newton, *Century of Slaughter*; and Ramsland, *Inside the Minds*. I've also benefited from discussions with profiler Ralph Stone, retired Georgia Bureau of Investigation special agent and instructor in criminal justice at Columbus State University, Rick Chambers, former city of Atlanta homicide detective and now chief investigator at Chambers Consulting & Security, and Dr. Elliot Leyton, professor emeritus of anthropology at Memorial University of Newfoundland.

For the aftermath of Joe Davi's murder, see *NOI*, July 10, 1911; and *NODP*, December 30, 1912.

Details of the attack on the Andollinas are found in *NODS*, December 22–23, 1917; *NOI*, December 22–23, 1917; and *NOTP*, December 23, 1917. Additional information about the Andollina family comes from 1920 US Census, Ancestry.com; WWI Draft

Registration Cards, Ancestry.com; New Orleans Death Records, Ancestry.com; Louisiana State Board of Health, death certificate for Epifanio Andollina, Parish of Orleans, October 23, 1918; New Orleans Marriage Records, Ancestry.com.

The story of Chief Reynolds's murder comes from *NODS*, August 2–6, 13, 1917; *NOTP*, August 3–8 and 13–15, 1917; *NOI*, August 2–10 and 12–14, 1917; and "Testimony, Murder of Superintendent Reynolds" in New Orleans Public Library.

Background on the development of the New Orleans railroads is found in Downey, *Illinois Central Railroad*; Jessup, "Golden Age"; Murray, *Illinois Central Railroad*; Solomon, *North American Railroads*; and Stover, *History of Illinois Central Railroad.*

For Frank Mooney's background and selection as police superintendent, see *NODP*, May 21, 1905; *NOI*, February 7, 12, 1911, and August 8–9, 1917; *NODS*, August 8, 1917; *NOTP*, August 8–9, 1917; *NODS*, August 23, 1923; *NOI*, August 23, 1923; and *NOTP*, August 24, 1923.

For Mooney as head of the ICR, see *NOTP*, June 20 and July 22, 1914, and January 22, 1916; *NODS*, February 24, 1916; and *NOTP*, July 16, 1916.

Details on John Dantonio's departure come from *NOI*, August 3, 1917; *NOTP*, March 28, 1920; *NODS*, April 1, 1920; *NOI*, April 1, 1920; and *NOTP*, April 2 and 20, 1920.

Details of Arthur Marullo's career are from *NOI*, October 14 and December 25, 1917, and March 11, 1918; *NOTP*, March 11, 1918; *New Orleans States-Item*, July 7, 1965; and *NOTP*, July 8, 1965.

Information about Vincent Miramon's murder found in *NODS*, May 19, 23, and 25, 1917; *NOI*, May 19–20, 22, and 25, 1917; *NOTP*, May 20, 1917; and Coroner's Office, autopsy report, May 24, 1919, in New Orleans Public Library.

Particulars on the attack on the Girard family and subsequent Sumner trial taken from *NODS*, May 28–29, 1917; *NOI*, May 28–29, 1917; *NOTP*, May 29–30, 1917; *NODS*, August 14–15, 1917; *NOTP*, August 15 and September 2, 1917; and *State v. Sumner*, in New Orleans Public Library.

Information on the murder of Joseph and Catherine Maggio and the subsequent investigation taken from *NOI*, May 23–26, 1918; *NODS*, May 23–26, 28, 1918; *NOTP*, May 24–26, 1918; NOPD, *Reports of Homicide*, May 23, 1918, in New Orleans Public Library; and Coroner's Office, autopsy report, May 23, 1918, in New Orleans Public Library.

For the homicide investigations Mooney had been involved in before the Maggio killings, see *NOI*, January 15 and February 15, 1918; and *NOTP*, March 20, 1918.

Details of Franz Reidel's murder are from *NOI*, October 11–12, 15–17, and 19, 1910; *NOTD*, October 12, 16–18, 1910; *NODP*, October 12–14 and 16–19, 1910; *NODS*, October 12–15, 17, 1910; *State v. Rodin and Bescanon*, in New Orleans Public Library; NOPD, *Reports of Homicide*, October 11, 1910, in New Orleans Public Library; and Coroner's Office, autopsy report, October 11, 1910, in New Orleans Public Library.

For details of the Sciambra murders, see *NODS*, May 16, 18, 26–27, 1912; *NOI*, May 16–18, 25, and 27, 1912; *NOTD*, May 17–19 and 27, 1912; *NODP*, May 17–19 and 27, 1912; Coroner's Office, autopsy report, May 16, 1912, and May 26, 1912, in New Orleans Public Library; and NOPD, *Reports of Homicide*, May 16, 1912, and May 26, 1912, in New Orleans Public Library.

For Joseph Mumfre's involvement with Vito Di Giorgio, see *NODP*, June 12, 1908; and *NOTD*, June 12, 1908. Also, for Di Giorgio, see Warner, "First Mafia Boss?"

For Detective Obitz's murder, see *NOI*, May 27, 1918; *NOTP*, May 27, 1918; and *NODS*, May 28, 1918.

"Shut up!": *NOTP*, December 23, 1917.
"It was too dark": *NOI*, December 23, 1917.
"I have no enemies": *NOI*, December 23, 1917.
"how a man could be shot": *NOI*, August 12, 1917.
"Murder! Murder!": *State v. Sumner*, in New Orleans Public Library.
"Come at once!": *NOI*, May 23, 1918.
"Do you have a father, mother": WWI Draft Registration Cards, Ancestry.com.
"Robbery was the motive": *NODS*, May 23, 1918.
"just like Mrs. Toney": *NOTP*, May 25, 1918.
"Just write Mrs. Toney": *NODS*, May 23, 1918.
"just write. Mrs. Tony": *NOI*, May 23, 1918.
"unusually mysterious": Ibid.
"the unsettled state": *NODS*, May 25, 1918.
"How could you think I could kill": *NOI*, May 26, 1918.
"Up to the time we conducted": *NODS*, May 26, 1918.
"We don't know where to start": *NOTD*, October 12, 1910.
"one of the criminal mysteries": *NODS*, October 12, 1910.
"award[ing him] the first honors": *NOI*, October 19, 1910.
"the better class of Italians": *NOI*, May 25, 1912.
"lust for blood": *NOTD*, May 17, 1912.
unclear how long: On May 15, 1916, the *NOTP* noted that Henry Sciambra sold his store "a few days after [his brother's] murder," but since it gets the date of the murder wrong (saying it happened in 1914), the information may not be entirely reliable. The New Orleans City Directory records that in 1913–1914 Henry Sciambra was still at 2302 Dauphine St. and Di Giorgi on N. Rocheblave St.; Di Giorgio is not listed as owner of the grocery at 2302 Dauphine until 1915–1916.
"considerably worried because of an Italian": *NODP*, May 17, 1912.
George Musacchia: Sometimes appearing as Masuchia or Musachia.
"bore all the earmarks": *NOI*, May 27, 1912.

7. A German Spy?

Particulars of the attack on Louis Besumer and Harriet Lowe, and the police investigation, found in *NODS*, June 27–29, 1918; *NOI*, June 27–30, 1918; *NOTP*, June 28–30, 1918; *NODS*, July 3, 5, 7–8, 12, 15, and 30, 1918; *NOTP*, July 1, 3–7, 9–10, 12, and 15, 1918; and *NOI*, July 1, 3–4, 7–8, 1918.

For German spies in WWI and US counterespionage measures, see Witcover, *Sabotage at Black Tom*. For treatment of Germans in the United States during the First World War, see Peterson and Fite, *Opponents of War*; and Schaffer, *America in the Great War*, chapter 2, "Controlling Dissent."

For James G. Coulton's career, see *NODS*, February 7, 1949; *NOI*, February 7, 1949; and *NOTP*, February 7–8, 1949.

For Mooney's demotion of detectives, see *NOI*, July 3, 1918; *NODS*, July 7, 1918; and *NOTP*, July 7, 1918.

Details of the attack on Mary Schneider from *NODS*, August 5–7, 1918; *NOI*, August 5–7, 1918; and *NOTP*, August 6–7, 1918. Additional details on the Schneider family from 1920 US Census, Ancestry.com.

named Louis Besumer: His name is also sometimes spelled Besemer or Bessemer.

Come around to the front: The New Orleans papers contained two or three different versions of Zanca knocking on the door and entering the grocery. My version is based on the report in the *NOI*, June 30, 1918; and NOPD, *Reports of Homicide*, September 14, 1918, in New Orleans Public Library. See also *NODS*, June 27, 1918; *NOI*, June 27, 1918; *NOTP*, June 28, 1918; and *NOTP*, May 1, 1919.

"My God, what's happened?": Zanca's conversation with Besumer has been reconstructed based on NOPD, *Reports of Homicide*, in New Orleans Public Library; *NODS*, June 27, 1918; *NOI*, June 27, 1918; *NOTP*, June 28, 1918; and *NOI*, June 30, 1918.

"one of the queerest [mysteries]": *NOTP*, July 4, 1918.

Harriet Anna Lowe: Her name sometimes appears as Annie Harriet Lowe or Harriet Annette Lowe. Besumer referred to her as "Annie." *NOI*, September 16, 1918.

"My husband is a German": *NOI*, June 28, 1918.

HATCHET MYSTERY: *NOTP*, June 29, 1918.

schools abolished German language instruction: My husband's Swedish grandfather was bullied during the war for speaking Swedish, which some, apparently, could not distinguish from German.

"proceeded to tell about the people": *NOTP*, July 4, 1918.

"a born investigator": *NOI*, July 3, 1918.

"I am a man who leaves nothing undone": *NOTP*, July 4, 1918.

"The other articles in my store": *NOTP*, July 7, 1918.

his former wife lived in Cincinnati: Eventually, Besumer admitted to two ex-wives. *NOTP*, August 20, 1918.

"twitche[d] uncontrollably": *NODS*, August 25, 1918.

"I feel sure he and I are married": *NOTP*, July 7, 1918.

their memory of the details was a little foggy: The *Item* reported that these attacks had occurred during the last two years. *NOI*, June 27, 1918.

usually on moonless nights: According to the Naval Observatory (http://aa.usno.navy.mil/data/docs/RS_OneYear.php, accessed August 31, 2015).

a greater risk of being spotted: In addition to the evidence of fresh blood, Lowe said that she was attacked in daylight. *NODS*, June 27, 1918.

Caring for three small children: The 1920 US Census (Ancestry.com) shows Edward and Mary Schneider and their four children living next to Emile and Kate Gonzales.

"Struck? Oh, no": *NODS*, August 7, 1918.

POLICE BELIEVE AX-MAN: *NOTP*, August 6, 1918.

connecting the Schneider attack: Jim Coulton was the *Times-Picayune*'s crime reporter and so presumably was responsible for the paper's coverage of the crimes.

"it probable that Mrs. Schneider": *NOTP*, August 6, 1918.

VICTIM OF AX-MAN NOW HAPPY: *NOTP*, August 7, 1918.

Andy Ojeda took a different tack: Ojeda was probably covering police headquarters at this time. *NODS*, April 1, 1950.

"It is nothing more or less": *NODS*, August 7, 1918.

AXE-MAN'S VICTIM CAN'T RECALL: *NOI*, August 7, 1918.

ARMED MEN GUARD SLEEPING FAMILIES: *NOI*, August 8, 1918.

AX-VICTIM TO BE TAKEN: *NOI*, August 15, 1918.

8. Axeman Hysteria

For details of Joe Romano's murder, see *NODS*, August 10, 1918; *NOI*, August 10, 1918; *NOTP*, August 11, 1918; NOPD, *Reports of Homicide*, August 10, 1918, in New Orleans Public Library; and Coroner's Office, autopsy report, August 10, 1918, in New Orleans Public Library. Additional information about the Romano/Bruno family from the 1920 US Census, Ancestry.com.

For Axeman panic, see *NOI*, August 10–12, 1918; *NOTP*, August 11–12, 1918; and *NODS*, August 11 and 13, 1918. For examples of Axeman spotting, see *NOI*, August 12 and 16, 1918; *NODS*, August 12, 16–17, 1918; and *NOTP*, August 12 and 17 and October 31, 1918.

Accounts of Axeman-like break-ins that came to light after Joe Romano's murder come from *NOI*, August 10 and 15, 1918; *NODS*, August 11, 1918; and *NOTP*, August 12 and 16, 1918.

For evidence of thefts at Italian stores after the Romano murder, see *NODS*, August 19–21, 1918; *NOI*, August 20, 1918; and *NOTP*, August 21–22, 1918.

For examples of Axeman-like burglaries/panel robberies, see *NOI*, September 15, 25, and 27, 1918; *NOTP*, September 15 and 25, 1918; *NODS*, September 15 and 23, 1918; *NODS*, March 10, 1919; and *NOTP*, March 16, 1919.

For Piggly Wiggly and the rise of supermarket chains, see Levinson, *The Great A&P*.

Harriet Lowe's account of her assault is based on details in *NOI*, August 19, 1918; *NODS*, August 19, 1918; and *NOTP*, August 20, 1918.

For the bloodstains found in Besumer's trunk, see *NODS*, August 5, 1918; *NOI*, August 21, 1918; *NODS*, May 1, 1919; and *NOTP*, May 1, 1919.

My account of Besumer's response to Lowe's charges is based on information in *NODS*, August 20, 1918; *NOI*, August 20, 1918; and *NOTP*, August 20–21, 1918.

Information on Besumer's arrest and murder charge found in *NODS*, August 19–20, 23, and 25, 1918; *NOI*, August 19–21 and 23, 1918; *NOTP*, August 20–21 and 24, 1918; *NODS*, September 16, 24, and 27, 1918; *NOTP*, September 17, 1918; *NOI*, September 17 and 25, 1918; *NOI*, November 24 and December 6, 1918.

For details of Harriet Lowe's operation and death, see *NOI*, August 21, 1918; *NOTP*, August 21, 1918; *NODS*, September 6–7, 14, and 16, 1918; *NOI*, September 6, 16–17, 1918; *NOTP*, September 6–8, 14, and 17–18, 1918; NOPD, *Reports of Homicide*, September 16, 1918, in New Orleans Public Library; and Coroner's Office, autopsy report, May 24, 1919, in New Orleans Public Library.

To understand the dynamics of domestic abuse, see Bancroft, *Why Does He Do That?*; and Barnett, "Why Battered Women Do Not Leave," parts 1 and 2.

For evidence of Mooney's views on the Axeman, see *NOI*, August 10, 1918; *NODS*, August 11, 1918; *NOTP*, August 12, 1918; *NODS*, March 11, 1919; and *NOTP*, March 11 and 16, 1919.

My understanding of the workings of memory is based on Loftus, "Make-Believe Memories" and "Malleability of Human Memory"; and Schacter, *Seven Sins of Memory*.

Information about the Spanish flu in New Orleans comes from *NODS*, September 16 and 19, 1918; *NOI*, September 18, 1918; *NOTP*, September 18, 1918; *NODS*, October 8–9, 20, and 29, 1918; and *NOTP*, October 10, 16, 31, 1918.

"Something has happened": *NOTP*, August 11, 1918.

"He was awfully light on his feet": *NOI*, August 10, 1918.

"The skull was not shattered": NOPD, *Reports of Homicide*, August 10, 1918, in New Orleans Public Library.
"I believe it is criminal": *NODS*, August 16, 1918.
"this blood-mad creature": *NOI*, August 15, 1918.
"badly frightened negro woman": *NOTP*, August 17, 1918.
"scathing criticism": *NOI*, August 12, 1918.
"exhaustive investigation": *NODS*, August 11, 1918.
"thinly settled sections": *NOTP*, August 17, 1918.
Jim Coulton sought out: Jim Coulton was the *Times-Picayune*'s crime reporter, so presumably he conducted the interview.
"This is very probably the man": *NOTP*, August 13, 1918.
"The homes of all the victims": Ibid.
"Take this for the gospel": *NOI*, August 10, 1918.
"Attention Mr. Mooney and All Citizens": *NOTP*, August 23, 1918.
"I met Mr. Besumer in Jacksonville": *NOTP*, August 20, 1918.
"You'll get your money and more": *NODS*, August 20, 1918.
"Annie, you are going to make a fire": *NOI*, August 19, 1918.
"As I lay in bed": *NOTP*, August 20, 1918.
"gave me some trouble": Ibid.
"peculiar disposition": *NODS*, August 20, 1918.
"I feel that I am going to die": *NOTP*, September 6, 1918. A slightly different version is found in *NOI*, September 6, 1918.
Writing over thirty years later: Robert Tallant mentions the story of Besumer's and Lowe's violent bickering in *Ready to Hang*.
when she said she couldn't remember: The black-haired man she recalled bending over her was probably John Zanca.

9. The Mysterious Axeman's Jazz

Information about Iorlando Guagliardo (aka Jordano) and his family comes from *State v. Guagliardo and Guagliardo*, in Supreme Court of Louisiana Historical Archives; "Orlando Guagliardo Jordano" and "Frank Guagliardo" in Ancestry.com, One World Tree Project; 1920 US Census, Ancestry.com; New Orleans Death Records, Ancestry.com; *NODS*, March 18, 1919; and *NOI*, March 18, 1919.

For Charlie Cortimiglia's background, see *State v. Guagliardo and Guagliardo*, in Supreme Court of Louisiana Historical Archives; *NOI*, March 10 and 12, 1919; *NOTP*, March 10, 1919; *NODS*, March 10, 1919, and February 4, 1920.

Description of Rosie Cortimiglia based on information in *State v. Guagliardo and Guagliardo*, in Supreme Court of Louisiana Historical Archives; and *NOTP*, February 4, 1920.

For a description of Frank Jordano, see *NODS*, March 15, 1919; *NOTP*, March 15, 1919; *NOI*, March 18, 1919; *NOTP*, February 5, 1920; *NOTP*, June 17, 1923, and March 14, 1926; and *State v. Guagliardo and Guagliardo*, in Supreme Court of Louisiana Historical Archives.

Details of the conflict between the Cortimiglias and Jordanos over the grocery business come from *NOTP*, March 10, 1919; *NOI*, March 10 and 15, 1919; *NODS*, March 15, 1919; and *State v. Guagliardo and Guagliardo*, in Supreme Court of Louisiana Historical Archives.

Details of the events of the night of Saturday, March 8, 1919, and the following Sunday morning come from *State v. Guagliardo and Guagliardo*, in Supreme Court of Louisiana Historical Archives.

Manny Fink's account of hearing the Axeman taken from his testimony in *State v. Guagliardo and Guagliardo*, in Supreme Court of Louisiana Historical Archives.

For Sheriff Louis Marrero Sr.'s history, see Chambers, *History of Louisiana*; Curry, *Gretna*; Fortier, *Louisiana*; Goodspeed, *Biographical and Historical Memoirs*; *NOI*, May 2, 1912; *NODS*, October 25, 1917; *NOI*, January 15, 1920; *NOI*, February 26–27, 1921; and *NOTP*, February 27, 1921.

For details of the initial investigation of the Cortimiglia crime scene, see *NOI*, March 10–11, 1919; *NOTP*, March 10–11, 1919; and *State v. Guagliardo and Guagliardo*, in Supreme Court of Louisiana Historical Archives.

For details of the Vicari break-in, see *NOI*, March 11, 1919; *NODS*, March 11, 1919; and *NOTP*, March 11, 1919. Also *State v. Guagliardo and Guagliardo*, 587–589, in Supreme Court of Louisiana Historical Archives.

Information about Dr. Fernandez's coroner's jury comes from *State v. Guagliardo and Guagliardo*, in Supreme Court of Louisiana Historical Archives; *NOTP*, March 10–11, 1919; *NODS*, March 15, 1919; *NOI*, March 17, 1919; *NODS*, April 16, 1919; and *NOTP*, April 17, 1919.

For Frank's testimony before the coroner's jury, see *State v. Guagliardo and Guagliardo*, in Supreme Court of Louisiana Historical Archives; *NOI*, March 10, 1919; *NOTP*, March 10, 1919; and *NODS*, March 15, 1919.

For details of the Cortimiglias' recovery in Charity Hospital, see *NOI*, March 10–11, 1919; *NOTP*, March 10–12, 1919; *NODS*, March 11–13, and 15–16, 1919; and *State v. Guagliardo and Guagliardo*, in Supreme Court of Louisiana Historical Archives.

Details on interrogation of suspect Charles Anderson found in *NODS*, March 12, 1919; *NOTP*, March 12, 1919; *NOI*, March 12–14, 1919; and *State v. Guagliardo and Guagliardo*, in Supreme Court of Louisiana Historical Archives.

For accusation against Frank and Iorlando, see *NODS*, March 15–19, 1919; *NOTP*, March 15–16 and 18, 1919; *NOI*, March 15–19, 1918; and *State v. Guagliardo and Guagliardo*, in Supreme Court of Louisiana Historical Archives.

Details of J. J. Davilla's career from *NOTP*, July 30, 1916, March 10, 1918, and March 18 and 20, 1919; *NODS*, March 20, 1919; *NOTP*, March 23, 1919; *NODS*, May 10, 1919; *NOTP*, May 11, 1919; *NOTP*, July 20, 1947; and *NOTP*, May 26, 1957.

For Saint Joseph's Day in New Orleans, see Chupa, "St. Joseph's Day Altars"; McColloster, "New Light"; Orso and Kaveski, "Undisclosed Aspects"; Plemer, "Feast of St. Joseph"; and Tallant, Dreyer, and Saxon, *Gumbo Ya-Ya*, 6.

For Saint Joseph's Day 1919, see *NODS*, March 16 and 18–19, 1919; *NOTP*, March 18–19, 1919; *Herald*, March 20, 1919; and *NOTP*, July 20, 1947.

For Robert Rivarde's background, see Louisiana District Judges, *Biographies*; *NODP*, February 19, 1912; *NOI*, December 4 and 7, 1916; *NODS*, December 7–8 and 17, 1916; *NOI*, January 30, 1967; *NOTP*, January 31, 1967; *States-Item*, January 30 and 31, 1967.

For Rosie's arrest as a material witness, see *NOI*, March 28, 1919; *NOTP*, March 28, 1919; *NODS*, March 28–29, 1919; *NODS*, February 4, 1920; *NOI*, February 4, 1920; *NOTP*, April 26, 1920; and *State v. Guagliardo and Guagliardo*, in Supreme Court of Louisiana Historical Archives.

"all crippled up": State v. Guagliardo and Guagliardo, in Supreme Court of Louisiana Historical Archives.

"it would just kill her": State v. Guagliardo and Guagliardo, in Supreme Court of Louisiana Historical Archives.

"a pronounced Italian type": NOTP, February 4, 1920.

"of a manly bearing": NOTP, March 15, 1919.

They set March 19, Saint Joseph's Day: State v. Guagliardo and Guagliardo, in Supreme Court of Louisiana Historical Archives.

"Mama, have you got anything": State v. Guagliardo and Guagliardo, in Supreme Court of Louisiana Historical Archives.

"nonfeasance, malfeasance, extortion": NODP, May 25, 1912.

Santo Vicari: Sometimes spelled Vaccarri or Viccari.

"the murder was the deed": NOTP, March 10, 1919.

"Do you know who attacked you": NOTP, March 12, 1919.

"Who hit you?": State v. Guagliardo and Guagliardo, in Supreme Court of Louisiana Historical Archives.

"That son-of-a-bitch Cortimiglia": Ibid.

"Frank Jordano and the old man": Ibid.

"They've arrested Frank Jordano": NODS, March 15, 1919.

"How are you feeling?": Ibid.; *State v. Guagliardo and Guagliardo*, in Supreme Court of Louisiana Historical Archives.

"Editor of the Times-Picayune": NOTP, March 16, 1919.

The real killer didn't send: Newspapers refer to two letters to Mooney from an anonymous "student of criminology" about the series of axe murders (*NOI*, August 8, 1918; *NOTP*, August 9, 1918). Seven months later the *Times-Picayune* reported that the superintendent received two letters he believed to be from the Axeman (*NOTP*, March 11, 1919), and when the paper printed the letter purporting to be from the Axeman, it noted that it was "similar in some respects" to the letters received by Mooney (*NOTP*, March 16, 1919). In *Empire of Sin*, Krist (p. 275) suggests that the letters may have come from the killer himself. He may be right, but so little is known of these letters that it is difficult to speculate.

"I keep on hearing the police": Rumbelow, *Jack the Ripper*, 118.

WAIT—WATCH THE AXMAN'S JAZZ: NOTP, March 23, 1919.

"think[ing] of the great amount of harm": Herald, March 20, 1919.

"Did Frank Jordano attack you": NODS, March 16, 1919.

Q: "Did Frank Jordano hit you": NOI, March 18, 1919.

Q: "Was Iorlando Jordano with Frank Jordano": NOI, March 17, 1919.

"was unable to give details": NOTP, March 18, 1919.

"I am confident we have the right men": Ibid.

"You must make up your mind:" NOTP, February 4, 1920.

"useless and unnecessary": NOTP, May 8, 1919.

10. "Hung by the Neck Until Dead, Dead, Dead"

All direct quotations during the trial are taken from the trial transcript in *State v. Guagliardo and Guagliardo*, in Supreme Court of Louisiana Historical Archives. I have edited and rearranged testimony for narrative purposes.

Details of Louis Besumer's trial are from *NODS*, April 30 and May 1–2, 1919; *NOI*, April 30 and May 1–2, 1919; *NOTP*, April 30 and May 1–2, 1919.

Description of the Gretna courthouse based on evidence in *NOI*, February 6–7, 1907; *NODP*, February 7, 1907; and "Parish of Jefferson" in Inventory of the Parish Archives, Louisiana State University Archives.

For Judge Fleury's background, see *NOI*, June 2, August 28, and November 3, 1914; and *NOTP*, November 6, 1914.

For Robert Rivarde's background, see sources listed in chapter 9.

For the difficulties empaneling a jury, see *NOI*, May 19–20, 1919; *NODS*, May 20, 1919; *NOTP*, May 20, 1919; and *State v. Guagliardo and Guagliardo*, in Supreme Court of Louisiana Historical Archives.

Details of the Jordano trial are from *NODS*, May 21–24 and 27, 1919; *NOTP*, May 22–27, 1919; *NOI*, May 23–24 and 26–27, 1919; and *State v. Guagliardo and Guagliardo*, in Supreme Court of Louisiana Historical Archives.

cases of Spanish influenza were declining: NODS, October 21 and 25, 1918; *NOTP*, October 22, 1918; and *NODS*, February 7, 1919.

"largely circumstantial": NOTP, March 18 and May 1, 1919.

He'd been locked up in the parish prison: NODS, October 4, 1918; *NOI*, March 17, 1919; *NOTP*, March 17–18, 1919; *NOI*, April 12 and April 27, 1919; and *NOTP*, April 27, 1919.

"victims of the murderous Axeman": NOTP, May 2, 1919.

"temple of justice": NOI, February 7, 1907.

"obliterated their awe of death": NOI, May 20, 1919.

11. Verdict

All direct quotations during the trial are taken from the trial transcript in *State v. Guagliardo and Guagliardo*, in Supreme Court of Louisiana Historical Archives. I have edited and rearranged testimony for narrative purposes.

the way a coroner or, today, a medical examiner: My thanks to Dr. Carol Terry, chief medical examiner, Gwinnett County, Georgia, for pointing out that surgeons often don't know as much about forensics as they think they do.

"It is true, judge, that I may hang": Composite speech based on accounts in *NODS*, October 11, 1919; *NOI*, October 11, 1919; and *NOTP*, October 11, 1919.

12. False Lead

For discussions of Joseph Mumfre as an Axeman suspect, see Krist, *Empire of Sin*; McQueen, *Axman Came from Hell*; and sources listed in the preface.

Information about Angola from Vodicka, "Prison Plantation"; *Daily States* (Baton Rouge), June 6, 1908; and *NODP*, October 29, 1908. Convict Record of the Louisiana State Penitentiary, in Louisiana State Archives, states that Mumfre was discharged on June 2, 1915.

For Vincent Moreci's murder and Mumfre's arrest as a suspect, see *NODP*, March 13 and December 22, 1910; *NODS*, November 19, 1915; *NOTP*, November 20–21, 1915; and *NOI*, November 21, 1915.

Story of Mumfre held by Sheriff Marrero and finally sent back to the penitentiary comes from *NODS*, February 3–5, 12, 14, and 16–18, 1916; *NOTP*, February 4–6, 12, 15, and 17, 1916; *NODS*, March 10, 1916; *NOTP*, March 11, 1916; *NODS*, July 10, 1916; and *NOTP*, July 11, 1916. See also *Monfre* [*sic*] *v. Marrero*, Westlaw, 138 La. 737, 70 So. 786 (1916); and *Monfre* [*sic*] *v. Marrero*, Westlaw, 138 La. 739, 70 So. 787 (1916)

For Mumfre's trial, see *NOTP*, February 17, 1916; *NODS*, February 17–18, 1916; *NODS*, March 10, 1916; and *NOTP*, March 11, 1916.

For Mumfre being released from prison and quickly rearrested, see Convict Record of the Louisiana State Penitentiary, in Louisiana State Archives; *NOTP*, May 18, 1918, and January 20, 1919.

For Mumfre being run out of New Orleans, see *NOTP*, May 18, 1918; *NODS*, January 20, 1919; *NOTP*, January 20, 1919; *NODS*, January 24, 1919; and *NODS*, December 15, 1921.

Details of the attack on Sarah Laumann from *NODS*, August 4–5, 1919; *NOI*, August 4–5, 1919; and *NOTP*, August 4–5, 1919. Additional details about Sarah Laumann family from 1910 and 1920 US Census, Ancestry.com.

For the robbery on the night after the Laumann attack, see *NODS*, August 5, 1919; and *NOI*, August 5, 1919.

The story of Steve Boca and William Carlson is told in Tallant, "Axman Wore Wings" in *Ready to Hang*.

Details of the murder of Mike Pepitone in *NOI*, October 27, 1919; *NODS*, October 27–28, 1919; *NOTP*, October 27–29, 1919; *NODS*, May 15, 1921; NOPD, *Reports of Homicide*, October 27, 1919, in New Orleans Public Library; and Coroner's Office, autopsy report, October 27, 1919, in New Orleans Public Library.

For the murder of Paul Di Christina and Peter Pepitone's fear of retaliation, see *NODP*, April 14, 1910; *NOI*, April 14–15, 1910; *NOTP*, November 10, 1915; *NOI*, November 10 and 19, 1915; and *NODS*, May 15, 1921.

Details of Esther Pepitone's move to California and marriage to Angelo Albano come from the 1920 US Census, Ancestry.com; Louisiana State Board of Health, death certificate for Jenny Albano, Parish of Orleans, October 14, 1918; *NODS*, October 27, 1919; and *LAT*, December 6, 17, and 25, 1921.

For Albano and Mumfre's history, see *NODP*, April 16, 1908; *NODS*, February 5 and 24, 1916; *NOTP*, February 17, 1916; *NODS*, March 10, 1916; and *LAT*, December 6, 10, and 17, 1921.

Details of Albano's disappearance in *LAT*, November 6 and December 10, 11, 17, and 25, 1921; *Los Angeles Examiner*, December 10 and 16, 1921; and *NOTP*, December 16, 1921.

Details of Mumfre's death in *LAT*, December 6, 7, 17, 25, and 29, 1921; *Los Angeles Examiner*, December 8, 10, and 16, 1921; *NODS*, December 16, 1921; and *Los Angeles Evening Herald*, April 10, 1922.

For L.A. detectives learning about Mumfre's identity and history from New Orleans, see *LAT*, December 10, 1921; *NOTP*, December 15, 1921; and *Los Angeles Examiner*, December 16, 1921. In addition, Esther Pepitone's defense subpoenaed an identification officer with police records of "Joseph P. Monfre," Superior Court, case no. CR17593, subpoena of A. R. Kallmeyer.

Details of Esther Pepitone's trial taken from *Los Angeles Evening Herald*, April 8 and 10, 1922; and *Los Angeles Examiner*, April 11, 1922. See also *NODS*, December 16, 1921; *LAT*, December 17 and 25, 1921; and list of witnesses subpoenaed by the state, Superior Court, case no. CR17593.

Esther's testimony at her trial is based on newspaper accounts of her trial but also on earlier newspaper accounts. The Los Angeles papers didn't cover Esther Albano's April 1922 trial in great detail. Some details of her testimony are taken from earlier newspaper coverage of the investigation and criminal proceedings against her on the assumption that she told substantially the same story on the witness stand in April 1922.

For biographical information on Robert Tallant, see Robert Tallant Papers, in New Orleans Public Library; and *NOTP*, April 2, 1957.

For biographical information on Andy Ojeda and Jim Coulton, see *NODS*, February 7, 1949; *NOI*, February 7, 1949; *NOTP*, February 7, 1949; *NOTP*, February 8, 1949; *NODS*, April 1, 1950; and *NOTP*, April 2, 1950.

a continuation of the vendetta: And, indeed, police suspected that subsequent shootings of Italians were part of the same vendetta. See *NODS*, January 30 and May 14–15, 1916; and Kendall, "Blood on the Banquette."

"no bondsman [was] forthcoming": NODS, February 14, 1916.

paid intervention: Convict Record of the Louisiana State Penitentiary, in Louisiana State Archives, notes: "Parole approved by Gov. L. E. Hall."

"For years Monfre": NODS, January 24, 1919.

"It would do the city no good": Ibid.

Doc Mumfre left: That Mumfre left New Orleans for California about January 1919 is confirmed by his death certificate (in the name of "Leone J. Manfre"), California Department of Public Health, dated December 1921, which said that he had been living in Los Angeles for three years.

"I felt a stinging": NODS, August 4, 1919.

"About 26 years old": NOTP, August 4, 1919.

"a thick, blunt instrument": NOTP, August 5, 1919.

"if he had hit her": NOI, August 4, 1919.

MYSTERIOUS "AXMAN": NOTP, August 4, 1919.

"probably six feet": NODS, August 10, 1918.

Esther Pepitone: Sometimes spelled Pipitone.

"Oh, Lord!": NODS, October 27, 1919.

"it looks like the Axeman": NOPD, *Reports of Homicide*, October 27, 1919, in New Orleans Public Library.

Detectives theorized that he'd heard: Another theory was that Pepitone was attacked outside his bedroom and his murderers dragged him back to his bed or he managed to stagger back to bed. The homicide report records the finding of blood in the room next to Pepitone's bedroom. But no subsequent New Orleans news story mentions this, so it may have been an early misapprehension by the reporting officer. Yet this version of events is also attributed to Mrs. Pepitone in *LAT*, December 25, 1921.

believed he was involved: Mike Pepitone was actually a nasty piece of work. He'd recently been arrested for physically abusing his six-year-old son. *NODS*, September 13, 1919; and *NOTP*, September 13, 1919.

"another vendetta mystery": NODS, October 28, 1919.

fed the Axeman narrative: I'm presuming that Coulton wrote these articles because he was the police and crime reporter at the time.

"Mooney does not connect": NODS, October 28, 1919.

"bore some of the characteristics": NOTP, October 27, 1919.

"the Pepitone case is not unlike": NOTP, October 29, 1919.

Leone J. Manfre: Without a doubt, Joe Mumfre and Leone J. Manfre were the same man. Mumfre's 1917–1918 draft registration form records that he had a daughter Lena, who lived in Los Angeles. In 1915, the *NODS* noted that Mumfre had a twelve-year-old daughter in California. In 1921, "Leone J. Manfre" had a nineteen-year-old daughter in L.A. named Lena Manfre, which would give her the right name and right age to be Joseph Mumfre's daughter (see *Los Angeles Examiner*, December 8, 1921). Also, L.A. court records show that for the trial of Esther Pepitone for killing Leone J. Manfre, the L.A. Police Department requested the police records of "Joseph Monfre" [*sic*] from New Orleans, suggesting that L.A. officials believed Manfre and Monfre/Mumfre to be the same man. See Superior Court, case no. CR17593, subpoena of Lena Vera Manfre, and subpoena of A. R. Kallmeyer for police records of Joseph P. Monfre.

Esther tried to carry on: Esther filed for divorce in early November and had a receiver named for Albano's property so she could get into his safety deposit box. *LAT*, November 6, 1921; *States*, December 16, 1921.

testified that the dead man was her father: LAT, December 29, 1921. I'm assuming Lena testified for the same reason in April as she had in December.

"Albano has a big house": The accounts of the trial in the newspapers covered only Esther Albano's testimony. But the case records include copies of those subpoenaed by the defense for a pretrial hearing in March, and it only makes sense that the defense would call these witnesses during the actual trial. Mrs. Griffith's testimony is taken from *LAT*, December 25, 1921.

not guilty: Esther Pepitone returned to New Orleans, where she died in 1940. She never remarried. *NOTP*, August 25, 1940.

"motive and probable solution": NOTP, December 15, 1921. New Orleans police also told Los Angeles investigators that Mumfre killed Pepitone. *Los Angeles Examiner*, December 16, 1921.

"Perhaps it was just a coincidence": NODS, December 15, 1921.

pointing out that Joseph Mumfre: NOI, December 16, 1921.

Tallant thought he was the first: Tallant, Dreyer, and Saxon, *Gumbo Ya-Ya*, vii. Tallant didn't know about Kendall's "Blood on the Banquette," published in 1939.

"He was the Axeman": Tallant, *Ready to Hang*, 215. In an earlier telling of the story published in 1945, Tallant didn't quote Mrs. Pepitone as alleging that Mumfre was the Axeman. In fact, although he claimed that the Axeman crimes could be matched to the times Mumfre was out of prison, he added that "there was no evidence of his connection with the ghastly [Axeman] crimes." Tallant, Dreyer, and Saxon, *Gumbo Ya Ya*, 89.

13. Rosie and Saint Joseph

For Frank's reaction to the verdict, see *NOTP*, May 28, 1919.

For Jim Coulton's firm belief in the Jordanos' innocence, see *NOTP*, December 7, 1920. For Coulton's personal experience with corrupt cops, see *NOI*, February 5, 1919.

For the appeals and delays in the Jordano case, see *NOTP*, June 30 and July 6 and 11, 1919; *NODS*, July 10, 1919; and *NOTP*, October 4, 1919.

Description of hanging based on accounts in *NODP*, April 29, 1905, and March 6, 1909; *NOI*, January 13, 1910; *NOTP*, July 24, 1918; *NODS*, November 28, 1919, and August 13, 1920.

Details of Lena's wedding from *NOI*, January 4, 1920; *NODS*, January 4–5, 1920; and *NOTP*, January 4–5, 1920.

Evidence for the Cortimiglias' difficulties after the trial found in *NOTP*, June 18, 1919; *NODS*, June 20, 1919; *NOI*, June 21, 1919; *NOTP*, July 11, 1919; *NOTP*, August 30, 1919; *NOI*, August 31, 1919; and *NODS*, May 22, 1920.

For Storyville and prostitution, I have relied on Krist, *Empire of Sin*; Rose, *Storyville*; and Vyhnanek, "Seamier Side of Life" (PhD diss.).

For the details of Rosie Cortimiglia's arrest for prostitution, see *NOI*, November 1–2, 1919; *NODS*, November 2, 1919; and arrest record for Rosie Cortimiglia, November 1, 1919, in NOPD, Arrest Cards.

Details of Rosie and Charlie's failed reconciliation in *NOTP*, November 7, 1919; *NODS*, February 4, 1920; *NOI*, February 4, 1920; and *NOTP*, February 4, 1920.

For the story of Rosie's confession, see *NODS*, February 4, 1920; *NOI*, February 4, 1920; *NOTP*, February 4–5, 1920; and statement of Rosie Salama Cortimiglia to *Times-Picayune*, in Supreme Court of Louisiana Historical Archives.

For reaction to news of Rosie's retraction, see *NOI*, February 4, 1920; and *NODS*, February 4, 5, and 7, 1920.

For memory, see Loftus and Hoffman, "Misinformation and Memory"; Loftus and Ketcham, *Myth of Repressed Memory*; Loftus and Thomas, "Creating Bizarre False Memories"; and Loftus works cited in chapter 8.

For details of the Jordanos' state supreme court appeal, see *NOI*, February 4, 1920; *NODS*, February 7–8, 1920; *NOTP*, February 8, 1920; *NOI*, March 6, 7, and 14, 1920; *NOTP*, March 7 and 14, 1920; *NODS*, March 13–14 and April 5, 1920; *NOI*, April 5, 1920; and *NOTP*, April 6 and 22, 1920. See also the state supreme court decision, *State v. Guagliardo et al.*, in Westlaw; and Supplemental Brief on Behalf of Defendants and Appellants, in Supreme Court of Louisiana Historical Archives.

For Rosie ill with smallpox, see *NOTP*, January 30, 1920; *NOI*, January 31 and February 11, 1920; and *NOTP*, December 7, 1920.

For Rosie swearing to affidavit, see *NODS*, April 26, 1920; and *NOTP*, April 26, 1920.

For grand jury investigation into Rosie's charges, see *NODS*, May 12, 1920; and *NOTP*, December 7, 1920.

For fears that Rosie would not recant her testimony under oath, see *NODS*, May 16, 1920; and *NOTP*, May 19, 1920.

For details of attempts to get bail for Jordanos, see *NOTP*, April 26–27 and May 9, 13, and 20, 1920; *NOI*, May 28 and November 22 and 26, 1920; and *NODS*, November 26, 1920.

For failed attempts to retry Jordanos, see *NOTP*, May 9, 17, 19, and 20, 1920; *NOI*, May 28, 1920; *NODS*, November 14, 15, 21, 22, and 26, 1920; and *NOTP*, November 15, 16, and 27, 1920.

For details of the Jordanos' life in the parish jail, see *NOTP*, February 5, 1920; *NOI*, November 15, 1920; and *NODS*, November 15, 1920.

For the Jordanos finally freed, see *NODS*, December 6, 1920; *NOI*, December 6, 1920; and *NOTP*, December 7, 1920.

"nonchalance": *NODS*, February 4, 1919.
"I believe you": *NOTP*, December 7, 1920.
"tempting dishes of chicken": *NODS*, January 5, 1920.
"ancient restricted district": *NOI*, January 29, 1919.
"Nothing in the world will ever": *NODS*, November 2, 1919.
"I sinned": Ibid.
"I would rather go to the gallows": Composite statement based on *NODS*, October 11, 1919; and *NOTP*, October 11, 1919.
"He raised his hand": *NODS*, February 4, 1920.
"Rosie, you cannot die": Statement of Rosie Salama Cortimiglia to *Times-Picayune*, in Supreme Court of Louisiana Historical Archives.
"sought out friends": *NODS*, February 4, 1920.
"either by their faces, figures or voices": Statement of Rosie Salama Cortimiglia to *Times-Picayune*, in Supreme Court of Louisiana Historical Archives.
"I hope I can sleep": *NOTP*, February 4, 1920.
"as surely as there is": *NODS*, February 4, 1919.
How will Papa stand it?: *NOTP*, February 5, 1920.
"Both of us are happy": Composite quote from *NODS*, February 4, 1920; and *NOTP*, February 5, 1920.
"Of course, I forgive Rosie Cortimiglia": *NOI*, February 4, 1920.
"It must have been the blessed Saint Joseph": *NOTP*, February 5, 1920.
"I made up my mind to say": Statement of Rosie Salama Cortimiglia to *Times-Picayune*, in Supreme Court of Louisiana Historical Archives.
"Did the Jordanos do it?": *NOI*, February 4, 1920.
she no longer had the constant reinforcement: In the courthouse, Chief Leson was locked up with Rosie in the witness room. *State v. Guagliardo and Guagliardo*, 179, in Supreme Court of Louisiana Historical Archives.
"he would have to kill the baby": Statement of Rosie Salama Cortimiglia to *Times-Picayune*, in Supreme Court of Louisiana Historical Archives.
"where human life was at stake": *NOTP*, March 7, 1920.
"It is a significant thing": *NOI*, March 14, 1920; Supplemental Brief on Behalf of Defendants and Appellants, in Supreme Court of Louisiana Historical Archives.
"As a matter of fact and law": *State v. Guagliardo et al.*, in Westlaw.
"the only reasonable presumption": Ibid.
"to import into a case material facts": Ibid.
"of her own free will": *NOTP*, April 26, 1920.
"On the last night of my confinement": Ibid.
"If Rosie Cortimiglia is convicted": *NOTP*, May 13, 1920.
"laid special stress on the crime": *NODS*, May 12, 1920.
"returned to the sweltering heat": *NOI*, May 19, 1920.
"This is the second time": *NOI*, November 22, 1920.
"If the state is not ready": Ibid.
"Your honor, just before court opened": *NODS*, December 6, 1920.
"You can go": Ibid.
"That's all right": Ibid.
"Ain't it fine?": *NOTP*, December 7, 1920.

14. The Final Chapter?

Details of Lena's and Iorlando's deaths from *NODS*, February 10, 1921; *NOI*, February 10, 1921; *NOTP*, February 10, 1921, and October 18, 1925; "Giolando Guagliardo aka Jordano" and "Orlando Guagliardo Jordano" in Ancestry.com, One World Tree Project.

For the remainder of Frank Jordano's life, see *NOTP*, June 17, 1923, December 20, 1925, May 3, 1927, and February 21, 1961; Jefferson Parish, marriage license (no. 1609) for Frank Jordano and Linzy Hamilton, February 7, 1926; Jefferson Parish, marriage license (no. 1812) for Frank Jordano and Mary Shambra, April 6, 1936; Louisiana State Board of Health, death certificate for Frank Jordano; "Frank Guagliardo" in Ancestry.com, One World Tree Project.

For Robert Rivarde's career, see *NOTP*, September 11, 1924, and July 2, 1965; *States-Item*, January 30–31, 1967; *NOTP*, January 31 and October 3, 1967.

For John Fleury's career, see *NOTP*, September 30, 1984.

For William Byrnes's career, see *NOTP*, February 26–28, 1942; "Judge William H. Byrnes, Jr." in *Louisiana Today*, by James M. Thomson, 337, 396; and "Judge William H. Byrnes, Jr.," in *Book of the South*, ed. by John Temple Graves, 276.

For Frank Mooney's failings as police chief, see *NOTP*, December 30, 1917, and January 17, 1919; *NODS*, February 27, 1919; *NOTP*, February 28 and April 6, 1919; *NOI*, March 17 and 20, 1920; and *NOTP*, November 27, 1920, and August 23, 1923. The Axeman crimes weren't the only murders he was criticized for not solving; see *NOI*, April 25, 1919.

For Mooney's resignation and the remainder of his life, see *NOTP*, August 24 and 26 and November 28, 1920; *NODS*, November 28, 1920; *NOI*, August 23, 1923; *NODS*, August 23 and 26, 1923; and *NOTP*, August 28, 1923.

Details of the Spero murder are from *ADTT*, December 13, 14, and 17, 1920; *NODS*, December 13–14, 1920; and *NOTP*, December 15 and 18, 1920.

Description of the Orlando murder from *NODS*, January 12, 1921; *NOI*, January 12, 1921; *NOTP*, January 13, 1921; *LCWAP*, January 14 and 21, 1921; and *DeRidder Enterprise*, January 15, 1921.

Additional information for John Orlando and family from Louisiana State Board of Health, death certificate for John Orlando; 1920 US Census, Ancestry.com; WWI Draft Registration Cards, Ancestry.com; Texas, Naturalization Records, 1881–1992, Ancestry .com, accessed June 26, 2015, http://search.ancestry.com/search/db.aspx?dbid=2509; Francine Cloud, interview with the author, February 6, 2015.

Details of the Scalisi murder are from *LCWAP*, April 12, 14, and 19, 1921; Criminal Records Archives, Calcasieu Parish, coroner's certificate for Frank Scalisi, April 13, 1921.

On the reliability of eyewitness testimony, see Cutler and Penrod, *Mistaken Identification*; Douglass and Pavletic, "Eyewitness Confidence"; Engelhardt, "Problem with Eyewitness Testimony"; Poole et al., "Children as Witnesses"; Putwain and Sammons, *Psychology and Crime*; and Steblay, "Eyewitness Memory." For racist stereotypes, see Jenkins, "Serial Murder."

For robbery and murder spree in Birmingham, Alabama, see McQueen, *Axman Came from Hell*; and Kazek, *Forgotten Tales*.

For serial killers, see sources cited in chapter 6.

"probably the youngest realtor": *NOTP*, December 20, 1925.

"There'll be no more political jobs": *NOI*, November 28, 1920.

The murder remained unsolved: Josephine Orlando told her granddaughter, Francine Cloud, that several men broke in, poured chloroform on the floor, and attacked the family. Revenge was ostensibly the motive. But none of the contemporary newspaper accounts mention such a possibility. The idea that assailants would chloroform their victims was a common convention of the time, and many people (including Italians) assumed that any attack on Italians was motivated by revenge. Josephine was only six years old at the time of the attack, and her memory probably reflects the speculation she subsequently heard from the adults around her. For created memories, see Loftus, "Make-Believe Memories" and "Malleability of Human Memory." Moreover, Mrs. Cloud also heard growing up that her great-grandfather was killed by "the Axeman." This term was used by both her grandmother and her great-grandmother (who spoke little English).

"short [and] chunky": Criminal Records Archives, Calcasieu Parish, coroner's certificate for Frank Scalisi, April 13, 1921.

"short and stout": Ibid.

"a short, heavy-set man": NODP, August 14, 1910.

"said she did not see": LCAP, April 12, 1921.

"The man was short": Criminal Records Archives, Calcasieu Parish, coroner's certificate for Frank Scalisi, April 13, 1921.

"an ax murder identical": NODS, December 13, 1920.

a morphine or cocaine habit: At the time both drugs could be had from any drugstore with a prescription.

Bibliography

Archival Sources

Criminal Records Archives, Calcasieu Parish, Clerk of Court, Lake Charles, Louisiana.

- Coroner's certificates.

Jefferson Parish General Government Center (Gretna Courthouse), Marriage License and Passport Department.

- Marriage licenses.

Louisiana State Archives, Baton Rouge.

- Convict Record of the Louisiana State Penitentiary.

Louisiana State Board of Health, Bureau of Vital Statistics.

- Death certificates.

Louisiana State University Archives.

- Inventory of the Parish Archives of Louisiana. Prepared by the Historical Records Survey, Division of the Professional and Service Projects Work Projects Administration. No. 26. Jefferson Parish (Gretna). The Department of Archives, Louisiana State University, January 1940.

New Orleans Public Library, Louisiana Division/City Archives.

- City Directories of the United States, vol. 4 (1902–1935).
- Coroner's Office, Autopsy Reports, vol. 1 (1904–1913).
- Coroner's Office, Autopsy Reports, vol. 2 (1913–1924).
- Coroner's Office, *Record Book Journals*.
- New Orleans Police Department, Annual Reports.
- New Orleans Police Department, Arrest Cards, 1914–1947.
- New Orleans Police Department, *Reports of Homicide*.
- Orleans Parish Criminal District Court Records.
    - *State of Louisiana v. John T. Flannery*. Docket no. 38,264 (1910).
    - *State of Louisiana v. Joseph Monfre* [*sic*]. Docket no. 35,993 (1908).
    - *State of Louisiana v. Francis Rodin and Eugene Bescanon*. Docket no. 38,403 (1911).
    - *State of Louisiana v. John Wesley Sumner*. Docket no. 46,575 (1917).

- Orleans Parish, Louisiana, Coroner's Office, vol. 9, January 1, 1855–September 12, 1855.
- Robert Tallant Papers, Manuscript Collection.
- *Rules and Regulations Governing the Police Department of the City of New Orleans* (1921).
- "Testimony, Murder of Superintendent of Police James W. Reynolds," 1917.

State of California Department of Public Health Center for Health Statistics and Informatics, Vital Records.

- Death certificates.

Superior Court of the County of Los Angeles, Archives and Records Center.

- *The People of the State of California v. Esther Albano*. Case no. CR17593 (1922).

Supreme Court of Louisiana Historical Archives, Louisiana and Special Collections Department, Earl K. Long Library, University of New Orleans.

- *State of Louisiana v. Frank Guagliardo, alias Frank Jordano, and Iorlando Guagliardo, alias Jordano*. Docket no. 23,815 (1919–1920).
    - Statement of Rosie Salama Cortimiglia to *Times-Picayune*.
    - Original Brief on Behalf of the Defendants.
    - Original Brief on Behalf of the State.
    - Supplemental Brief on Behalf of the Defendants and Appellants.
    - Trial transcript. 3 vols. No. 4458.
    - Opinion and Judgement.

Newspapers

New Orleans

- *Daily City Item*
- *Daily News*
- *Daily True Delta* (*DTD*)
- *Herald*
- *Mascot*
- *New Orleans Bee* (*NOB*)
- *New Orleans Daily States* (*NODS*); after 1918 becomes the *States*
- *New Orleans Item* (*NOI*)
- *New Orleans States-Item*
- *New Orleans Times*
- *New Orleans Times-Democrat* (*NOTD*)
- *New Orleans Times-Picayune* (*NOTP*); before 1913 the *New Orleans Daily Picayune* (*NODP*)

Others

- *Alexandria Daily Town Talk* (*ADTT*)
- *DeRidder Enterprise*
- *Lake Charles Weekly American Press* (*LCWAP*)
- *Los Angeles Evening Herald*
- *Los Angeles Examiner*

- *Los Angeles Times* (*LAT*)
- *New York Tribune*

Online Sources

Ancestry.com

- New Orleans, Louisiana, Death Records Index, 1804–1949. http://search.ancestry.com/search/db.aspx?dbid=6606.
- New Orleans, Louisiana, Marriage Records Index, 1831–1964. http://search.ancestry.com/search/db.aspx?dbid=6500.
- One World Tree Project. http://awtc.ancestry.com/cgi-bin/igm.cgi.
- US, World War I Draft Registration Cards, 1917–1918. http://search.ancestry.com/search/db.aspx?dbid=6482.
- US Federal Census Collection. http://search.ancestry.com/search/group/usfedcen.

City of New Orleans. *Population, Total and by Race, of Orleans, Jefferson, St. Bernard, and St. Tammany Parishes, the State of Louisiana, and Five Southern Cities Comparable to New Orleans, 1810–1980*. Prepared by City Planning Commission, with the assistance of New Orleans Public Library, 1981. http://nutrias.org/facts/aq150_1981p.pdf.

Family Search. Conveyance Records, Saint James Parish Clerk of Court, Saint James Parish Courthouse. Vol. 52 (1889–1893). Family History Library, microfilm no. 04026371. https://familysearch.org.

Supreme Court of Louisiana. *State v. Guagliardo et al.* Docket no. 23815. Westlaw. 146 La. 949, 84 So. 216 (1920).

University of Virginia Library. Historical Census Browser. Geospatial and Statistical Data Center, accessed January 9, 2012. http://fisher.lib.virginia.edu/collections/stats/histcensus/index.html (site discontinued).

Unpublished Theses and Dissertations

Adams, Margaret. "Outline of Mafia Riots in New Orleans." MA thesis, Tulane University, 1924.

Baiamonte, John V., Jr. "New Immigrants in the South: A Study of the Italians of Tangipahoa Parish, Louisiana." MA thesis, Southeastern Louisiana College, 1969.

Boneno, Roselyn Bologna. "From Migrant to Millionaire: The Story of the Italian-American in New Orleans, 1880–1910." PhD diss., Louisiana State University, 1986.

Botein, Barbara. "The Hennessy Case: An Episode in American Nativism, 1890." PhD diss., New York University, 1975.

Carroll, Ralph Edward. "The Mafia in New Orleans, 1900–1907." MA thesis, Notre Dame Seminary, New Orleans, 1956.

Carroll, Richard Louis. "The Impact of David Hennessey on New Orleans Society and the Consequences of the Assassination of Hennessey." MA thesis, Notre Dame Seminary, New Orleans, 1957.

Dulitz, Harris Myron. "The Myth of the Mafia in New Orleans." BS thesis, Tulane University, 1956.

Edwards-Simpson, Louise Reynes. "Sicilian Immigration to New Orleans, 1870–1910: Ethnicity, Race, and Social Position in the New South." PhD diss., University of Minnesota, 1996.

Metcalf, Christina. "Race Relations and the New Orleans Police Department: 1900–1971." BA thesis, Tulane University, 1985.

Scarpaci, Jean Ann. "Italian Immigrants in Louisiana's Sugar Parishes: Recruitment, Labor Conditions and Community Relations, 1880–1910." PhD diss., Rutgers University, 1972.

Vyhnanek, Louis Andrew. "The Seamier Side of Life: Criminal Activity in New Orleans During the 1920s." PhD diss., Louisiana State University, 1979.

Warren, Karen Wright. "The Sicilian St. Joseph Altar Celebration in Southeastern Louisiana." MA thesis, Southeastern Louisiana University, 1983.

Webb, Michael E. "Horror in a Time of Social Upheaval: The New Orleans 'Axman' Murders, 1910–1920." MA thesis, University of New Orleans, 2002.

Books and Articles

Adamoli, Giulio. "Letters from America, 1867." *Louisiana Historical Quarterly* 6 (April 1923): 271–279.

Adler, Jeffrey S. "Murder, North and South: Violence in Early-Twentieth Century Chicago and New Orleans." *Journal of Southern History* 74, no. 2 (May 2008): 297–324.

American Historical Society. *Louisiana*. Chicago: American Historical Society, 1925.

Asbury, Herbert. *The French Quarter: An Informal History of the New Orleans Underworld.* New York: Knopf, 1936; Thunder's Mouth, 2003.

Baiamonte, John V. *Immigrants in Rural America: A Study of the Italians of Tangipahoa Parish, Louisiana.* New York: Garland, 1990.

———. "'Who Killa de Chief' Revisited: The Hennessy Assassination and Its Aftermath, 1890–1991." *Louisiana History* 33 (1992): 117–146.

Bancroft, Lundy. *Why Does He Do That? Inside the Minds of Angry and Controlling Men.* New York: Berkley Books, 2002.

Barnett, Ola W. "Why Battered Women Do Not Leave, Part 1." *Trauma, Violence, & Abuse* 1, no. 4 (2000): 343–372.

———. "Why Battered Women Do Not Leave, Part 2." *Trauma, Violence, & Abuse* 2, no. 1 (2001): 3–35.

Begnaud, Allen. "The Louisiana Sugar Cane Industry: An Overview." In *Green Fields: Two Hundred Years of Louisiana Sugar. A Catalogue Complementing the Pictorial Exhibit.* Lafayette, LA: Center for Louisiana Studies, University of Southwestern Louisiana, 1980.

Behrman, Martin. *Martin Behrman of New Orleans: Memoirs of a City Boss.* Edited by John R. Kemp. Baton Rouge: Louisiana State University Press, 1977.

Berthoff, Rowland T. "Southern Attitudes Toward Immigration, 1865–1914." *Journal of Southern History* 17, no. 2 (August 1951): 328–360.

Brock, Eric J. *New Orleans.* Charleston, SC: Arcadia, 1999.

Brown, Pat. *Killing for Sport: Inside the Minds of Serial Killers.* Beverly Hills, CA: New Millennium Press, 2003.

Cable, Mary. *Lost New Orleans*. Boston: Houghton Mifflin, 1980.

Campanella, Richard. *Bienville's Dilemma: A Historical Geography of New Orleans*. Lafayette, LA: Center for Louisiana Studies, University of Southwestern Louisiana, 2008.

———. *Geographies of New Orleans: Urban Fabrics Before the Storm*. Lafayette, LA: Center for Louisiana Studies, University of Southwestern Louisiana, 2006.

Carlisle, Al C. "The Divided Self: Toward an Understanding of the Dark Side of the Serial Killer." In *Contemporary Perspectives on Serial Murder*, edited by Ronald M. Holmes and Stephen T. Holmes. Thousand Oaks, CA: Sage, 1998.

Carter, Hodding. *Southern Legacy*. Baton Rouge: Louisiana State University Press, 1950.

CatholicCulture.org. "History of the Saint Joseph Altar." Accessed August 31, 2016. www.catholicculture.org/culture/liturgicalyear/activities/view.cfm?id=1029.

Chambers, Henry E. *A History of Louisiana: Wilderness, Colony, Province, Territory, State, People*. Chicago: American Historical Society, 1925.

Chandler, David. *Brothers in Blood: The Rise of the Criminal Brotherhoods*. New York: E. P. Dutton, 1975.

Chupa, Anna Maria. "St. Joseph's Day Altars." Houston Institute for Culture, Louisiana Project. www.houstonculture.org/laproject/stjo.html.

Conrad, Glenn R., and Ray F. Lucas. *White Gold: A Brief History of the Louisiana Sugar Industry, 1795–1995*. Lafayette, LA: Center for Louisiana Studies, University of Southwestern Louisiana, 1995.

Coxe, John E. "The New Orleans Mafia Incident." *Louisiana Historical Quarterly* 20, no. 4 (October 1937): 1067–1110.

Critchley, David. *The Origin of Organized Crime in America: The New York City Mafia, 1891–1931*. New York: Routledge, 2008.

Curry, Mary Grace. *Gretna: A Sesquicentennial Salute*. Metairie, LA: Jefferson Parish Historical Commission, 1986.

Cutler, Brian L., and Steven D. Penrod. *Mistaken Identification: The Eyewitness, Psychology, and the Law*. Cambridge: Cambridge University Press, 1995.

Dash, Mike. *The First Family: Terror, Extortion, Revenge, Murder and the Birth of the American Mafia*. New York: Random House, 2009.

Deacon, William A., and John P. Coleman. *Martin Behrman Administration Biography, 1904–1916*. New Orleans: John J. Weihing Printing, 1917.

Dickie, John. *Cosa Nostra: A History of the Sicilian Mafia*. London: Hodder & Stoughton, 2004.

Douglas, John, and Johnny Dodd. *Inside the Mind of BTK: The True Story Behind Thirty Years of Hunting for the Wichita Serial Killer*. San Francisco: Wiley, 2007.

Douglas, John, and Mark Olshaker. *The Cases That Haunt Us: From Jack the Ripper to JonBenet Ramsey, the FBI's Legendary Mindhunter Sheds Light on the Mysteries That Won't Go Away*. New York: Scribner, 2000.

Douglass, Amy Bradfield, and Afton Pavletic. "Eyewitness Confidence Malleability." In *Conviction of the Innocent: Lessons from Psychological Research*. Washington, DC: American Psychological Association, 2012.

Downey, Clifford J. *Chicago and the Illinois Central Railroad*. Charleston, SC: Arcadia, 2007.

Edward, Wallace. *The Axeman: The Brutal History of the Axeman of New Orleans*. Anaheim, CA: Absolute Crime Books, 2013.

Eisner, Manuel. "Long-Term Historical Trends in Violent Crime." *Crime and Justice* 30 (2003): 83–142.

Engelhardt, Laura. "The Problem with Eyewitness Testimony." *Stanford Journal of Legal Studies* 1, no. 1 (1999): 25–29.

Everitt, David. *Human Monsters: An Illustrated Encyclopedia of the World's Most Vicious Murderers*. Chicago: Contemporary Books, 1993.

Fentress, James. *Rebels and Mafiosi: Death in a Sicilian Landscape*. Ithaca, NY: Cornell University Press, 2000.

Fortier, Alcée. *Louisiana: Comprising Sketches of Parishes, Towns, Events, Institutions, and Persons, Arranged in Cyclopedic Form*. Madison, WI: Century Historical Association, 1914.

Gambino, Richard. *Vendetta: A True Story of the Largest Lynching in U.S. History*. Toronto: Guernica, 1998.

Garvey, Joan B., and Mary Lou Widmer. *Beautiful Crescent: A History of New Orleans*. New Orleans: Garmer Press, 2006.

Goodspeed Publishing. *Biographical and Historical Memoirs of Louisiana*. Vol. 3. Chicago: Goodspeed Publishing, 1892; Louisiana Classic Series Reprint, Baton Rouge: Claitor's, 1975.

Graves, John Temple, ed. *A Book of the South*. New Orleans: Southern Editors Association, 1940.

Hale, Robert. "The Application of Learning Theory to Serial Murder, or 'You Too Can Learn to Be a Serial Killer.'" In *Contemporary Perspectives on Serial Murder*, edited by Ronald M. Holmes and Stephen T. Holmes. Thousand Oaks, CA: Sage 1998.

Hess, Henner. *Mafia and Mafiosi: Origin, Power and Myth*. Translated by Ewald Osers. New York: New York University Press, 1996.

Hickey, Eric W. *Serial Murderers and Their Victims*. 3rd ed. Belmont, CA: Wadsworth/Thomason Learning, 2002.

Hintz, Martin. *Ethnic New Orleans. A Complete Guide to the Many Faces & Cultures of New Orleans*. Lincolnwood, IL: Passport Books, 1995.

Holmes, Ronald M. "Psychological Profiling: Uses in Serial Murder Cases." In *Contemporary Perspectives on Serial Murder*, edited by Ronald M. Holmes and Stephen T. Holmes. Thousand Oaks, CA: Sage, 1998.

Holmes, Ronald M., and James E. DeBurger. "Profiles in Terror: The Serial Murderer." In *Contemporary Perspectives on Serial Murder*, edited by Ronald M. Holmes and Stephen T. Holmes. Thousand Oaks, CA: Sage, 1998.

Holmes, Ronald M., and Stephen T. Holmes. *Serial Murder*. 2nd ed. London: Sage, 1998.

Hunt, Thomas, and Martha Macheca Sheldon. *Deep Water: Joseph P. Macheca and the Birth of the American Mafia*. Lincoln, NE: iUniverse, 2007.

Industrialist Publishing. *New Orleans Police Souvenir Book, 1906*. New Orleans: Industrialist Publishing, 1906.

Italian-American Digest. "Who Really Killed the Chief?" Vol. 7 (Spring 1981): 3.

Jackson, Joy J. "Crime and the Conscience of a City." *Louisiana History* 9, no. 3 (Summer 1968): 229–244.

———. *New Orleans in the Gilded Age: Politics and Urban Progress, 1880–1896*. Baton Rouge: Louisiana State University, 1969.

Jeffers, H. Paul. *With an Axe: 16 Horrific Accounts of Real-Life Axe Murders*. New York: Kensington Publishing, 2000.

Jenkins, Philip. "Serial Murder in the United States: 1900–1940: A Historical Perspective." *Journal of Criminal Justice* 17 (1989): 377–392.

Jessup, Steve. "The Golden Age, 1900–1950." In *The Complete Book of North American Railroading*, by Kevin EuDaly et al. Minneapolis, MN: Voyager Press, 2009.

Jewell, Edwin L. *Jewell's Crescent City Illustrated: The Commercial, Social, Political and General History of New Orleans, Including Biographical Sketches of Its Distinguished Citizens*. New Orleans: E. L. Jewell, 1873.

Katz, Allan. "The Hennessy Affair: A Centennial," *New Orleans*, October 1990, 58–62, 81.

Kazek, Kelly. *Forgotten Tales of Alabama*. Charleston, SC: History Press, 2010.

Keedy, Edwin R. "The Third Degree and Legal Interrogation of Suspects." *University of Pennsylvania Law Review and American Law Register* 85, no. 8 (June 1937): 761–777.

Kendall, John S. "Blood on the Banquette." *Louisiana Historical Quarterly* 22, no. 3 (1939): 819–856.

———. "Notes on the Criminal History of New Orleans." *Louisiana Historical Quarterly* 34 (1951): 147–173.

———. "Old-Time New Orleans Police Reporters and Reporting." *Louisiana Historical Quarterly* 29, no.1 (January 1946): 43–58.

———. "Sixteen Years of Martin Behrman." In *History of New Orleans*, 547–564. Chicago: Lewis Publishing, 1922.

———. "Who Killa de Chief?" *Louisiana Historical Quarterly* 22, no. 2 (1939): 492–530.

Krist, Gary. *Empire of Sin: A Story of Sex, Jazz, Murder and the Battle for Modern New Orleans*. New York: Crown, 2014.

Kurtz, Michael L. "Organized Crime in Louisiana History: Myth and Reality," *Louisiana History* 24 (1983): 355–376.

Lane, Brian, and Wilfred Greg, eds. *The Encyclopedia of Serial Killers*. New York: Berkley Books, 1995.

Lester, Henry. "The Axeman of New Orleans." In *Unsolved Murders and Mysteries*, edited by John Canning. London: Time Warner, 1992.

Levinson, Marc. *The Great A&P and the Struggle for Small Business in America*. New York: Hill & Wang, 2011.

Lewis, Peirce F. *New Orleans: The Making of an Urban Landscape*. 2nd ed. Chicago: Center for American Places, 2003.

Leyton, Elliot. *Hunting Humans: The Rise of the Modern Multiple Murderer*. 2nd ed. New York: Carroll & Graf, 2001.

Loftus, Elizabeth. "Make-Believe Memories." *American Psychologist* (November 2003): 867–873.

———. "The Malleability of Human Memory." *American Scientist* 67, no.3 (May–June 1979): 312–320.

Loftus, Elizabeth, and A. K. Thomas. "Creating Bizarre False Memories Through Imagination." *Memory & Cognition* 30 (2002): 423–431.

Loftus, Elizabeth, and H. G. Hoffman. "Misinformation and Memory: The Creation of New Memories." *Journal of Experimental Psychology* 118, no. 1 (1989): 100–104.

Loftus, Elizabeth, and Katherine Ketcham. *The Myth of Repressed Memory: False Memories and Allegations of Sexual Abuse.* New York: Saint Martin's Press, 1994.

Lombardo, Robert M. *The Black Hand: Terror by Letter in Chicago.* Urbana and Chicago: University of Illinois Press, 2010.

Louisiana District Judges Association. *Biographies of Louisiana Judges.* New Orleans: New Orleans Public Library, Louisiana Division, 1961.

Macaluso, Joseph N., Sr. *Italian Immigrant Families: Grocers, Proprietors, and Entrepreneurs.* Pittsburgh: RoseDog Books, 2004.

Magnaghi, Russell. "Louisiana's Italian Immigrants Prior to 1870." *Louisiana History* 27 (Winter 1996): 43–68.

Margavio, A. V. "The Reaction of the Press to the Italian American in New Orleans, 1880 to 1920." *Italian Americana* 4, no. 1 (1978): 72–83.

Margavio, A. V., and J. L. Molyneaux. "Residential Segregation of Italians in New Orleans and Selected American Cities." *Louisiana Studies* 12 (1973): 639–645.

Margavio, A. V., and Jerome Salomone. *Bread and Respect: The Italians of Louisiana.* Gretna, LA: Pelican, 2002.

———. "Economic Advantages of Familism." *Sociological Spectrum* 7 (1987): 101–119.

———. "The Passage, Settlement, and Occupational Characteristics of Louisiana's Italian Immigrants." *Sociological Spectrum* 1 (1981): 345–359.

Marr, Robert H., Jr. "The New Orleans Mafia Case." *American Law Review* 25 (1891): 414–431.

Maselli, Joseph, and Dominic Candeloro. *Italians in New Orleans.* Charleston, SC: Arcadia, 2004.

McColloster, Mary Ann Tusa. "New Light on the New Orleans St. Joseph Day Altar. *Louisiana Folklore Miscellany* 3, no. 1 (April 1970): 38–45.

McMain, Eleanor. "Behind the Yellow Fever in Little Palermo." *Charities and the Commons* 15 (October 1905–March 1906): 150–159.

McQueen, Keven. *The Axman Came from Hell and Other Southern True Crime Stories.* Gretna, LA: Pelican, 2011.

Morton, James. *Catching the Killers: The Definitive History of Criminal Detection.* London: Ebury Press, 2001.

Morton, Robert J. "Serial Murder: Multi-Disciplinary Perspectives for Investigators." Behavioral Analysis Unit-2, National Center for the Analysis of Violent Crime, Critical Incident Response Group, Federal Bureau of Investigation. www.fbi.gov/stats-services/publications/serial-murder.

Murray, Tom. *Illinois Central Railroad.* Saint Paul, MN: Voyageur Press, 2006.

Nash, Jay Robert. *Bloodletters and Badmen: A Narrative Encyclopedia of American Criminals from the Pilgrims to the Present.* New York: M. Evans, 1973.

Nelli, Humbert S. *The Business of Crime. Italians and Syndicate Crime in the United States.* Chicago: University of Chicago Press, 1981.

New Orleans Police Department. *Fifty Years of Progress, 1900–1950.* New Orleans: Franklin Print, 1951.

Newton, Michael. *Century of Slaughter.* Lincoln, NE: toExcel, 2000.

———. *The Encyclopedia of Unsolved Crimes.* 2nd ed. New York: Checkmark Books, 2009.

———. *Hunting Humans: The Encyclopedia of Serial Killers.* Vol. 1. New York: Avon Books, 1990.

Orso, Ethelyn, and Peggy Kaveski. "Undisclosed Aspects of Saint Joseph Altars." *Louisiana Folklore Miscellany* 3, no. 5 (1975): 14–18.

Persico, Joseph. "Vendetta in New Orleans." *American Heritage* 24, no. 4 (June 1973): 65–72.

Peterson, H. C., and Gilbert C. Fite. *Opponents of War, 1917–1918.* Madison: University of Wisconsin Press, 1957.

Pitkin, Thomas Monroe, and Francesco Cordasco. *The Black Hand: A Chapter in Ethnic Crime.* Totowa, NJ: Litchfield, Adams, 1977.

Plemer, Roslynn. "The Feast of St. Joseph." *Louisiana Folklore Miscellany* 2, no. 4 (August 1968): 85–90.

Poole, Debra Ann, Sonja P. Brubacher, and Jason J. Dickinson. "Children as Witnesses." In *APA Handbook of Forensic Psychology*, vol. 2, *Criminal Investigation, Adjudication, and Sentencing Outcomes.* Washington, DC: American Psychological Association, 2015.

Putwain, David, and Aidan Sammons. *Psychology and Crime.* New York: Routledge, 2002.

Ramelli, Rudolph. "Scenes in the 'Underworld.'" In *New Orleans Police Souvenir Book, 1906.* New Orleans: Industrialist Publishing, 1906.

Ramsland, Katherine. "All About the Axeman of New Orleans." Crime Library, truTV, accessed March 28, 2006. www.trutv.com/library/crime/serial_killers/weird/axeman/index.html (site discontinued).

———. *Beating the Devil's Game: A History of Forensic Science and Criminal Investigation.* New York: Berkley Books, 2007.

———. *Inside the Minds of Serial Killers: Why They Kill.* Westport, CT: Praeger, 2006.

Reid, Ed. *Mafia.* New York: Random House, 1952.

Reynolds, George M. *Machine Politics in New Orleans, 1897–1926.* New York: Columbia University Press, 1936.

Richey, Emma Cecilia, and Evelina Prescott Kean. *The New Orleans Book.* New Orleans: L. Graham, 1915.

Rose, Al. *Storyville, New Orleans: Being an Authentic, Illustrated Account of the Notorious Red-Light District.* Tuscaloosa: University of Alabama Press, 1979.

Rousey, Dennis C. "Cops and Guns: Police Use of Deadly Force in Nineteenth Century New Orleans." *American Journal of Legal History* 28, no. 1 (January 1984): 41–66.

———. *Policing the Southern City: New Orleans, 1805–1889.* Baton Rouge: Louisiana State University Press, 1996.

Rumbelow, Donald. *Jack the Ripper: The Complete Casebook*. New York: Berkley Books, 1988.

Scarpaci, J. Vincenza. "Labor for Louisiana's Sugar Cane Fields: An Experiment in Immigrant Recruitment." *Italian Americana* (Spring–Summer 1981): 19–41.

Scarpaci, Jean Ann. "Immigrants in the New South: Italians in Louisiana's Sugar Parishes, 1880–1910." *Labor History* 16, no. 2 (Summer 1974): 165–183.

Schacter, Daniel L. *The Seven Sins of Memory: How the Mind Forgets and Remembers*. Boston: Houghton Mifflin, 2001.

Schaffer, Ronald. *America in the Great War: The Rise of the War Welfare State*. New York: Oxford University Press, 1991.

Schechter, Harold. *The Serial Killer Files*. New York: Ballantine, 2004.

Schmitz, Mark. "The Transformation of the Southern Cane Sugar Sector: 1860–1930." *Agricultural History* 53, no. 1 (January 1979): 270–285.

Schott, Matthew J. "The New Orleans Machine and Progressivism." *Louisiana History* 24, no. 2 (Spring 1983): 141–153.

Shrugg, Roger Wallace. "Survival of the Plantation System in Louisiana." *Journal of Southern History* 3, no. 3 (August 1937): 311–325.

Sitterson, J. Carlyle. *Sugar Country: The Cane Sugar Industry in the South, 1753–1950*. Lexington: University of Kentucky Press, 1953.

Skolnick, Jerome H., and James J. Fyfe. *Above the Law: Police and the Excessive Use of Force*. New York: Free Press, 1993.

Smalley, Eugene V. "Sugar Making in Louisiana."*Century Magazine* 35 (November 1887): 100–120.

Smith, Thomas Ruys. *Southern Queen: New Orleans in the Nineteenth Century*. New York: Continuum, 2011.

Smith, Tom. *The Crescent City Lynchings: The Murder of Chief Hennessy, the New Orleans "Mafia" Trials, and the Parish Prison Mob*. Guilford, CT: Lyons Press, 2007.

Solomon, Brian. *North American Railroads: The Illustrated Encyclopedia*. Minneapolis, MN: MBI and Voyageur Press, 2012.

Stahls, Paul J. *Jefferson Parish: Rich Heritage, Promising Future*. San Antonio, TX: Historical Publishing Network, 2009.

Steblay, Nancy K. "Eyewitness Memory." In *APA Handbook of Forensic Psychology*, vol. 2, *Criminal Investigation, Adjudication, and Sentencing Outcomes*. Washington, DC: American Psychological Association, 2015.

Stover, John F. *History of the Illinois Central Railroad*. New York: Macmillan, 1975.

Sublette, Ned. *The World That Made New Orleans*. Chicago: Lawrence Hill, 2008.

Swanson, Betsy. *Historic Jefferson Parish: From Shore to Shore*. Gretna, LA: Pelican, 1975.

Tallant, Robert. *Mardi Gras . . . As It Was*. Garden City, NY: Doubleday, 1948.

———. *Ready to Hang: Seven Famous New Orleans Murders*. New York: Harper, 1952.

———. *The Romantic New Orleanians*. New York: E. P. Dutton & Co., 1950.

Tallant, Robert, Edward Dreyer, and Lyle Saxon. *Gumbo Ya-Ya: A Collection of Louisiana Folk Tales*. Boston: Houghton Mifflin, 1945.

Thomson, James M. *Louisiana Today*. Louisiana Society, 1939.

Thorwald, Jürgen. *The Century of the Detective*. Translated by Richard and Clara Winston. New York: Harcourt, Brace & World, 1965.

Tousignant, David D. "Why Suspects Confess." *FBI Law Enforcement Bulletin* (March 1991): 14–18.

Tusa, Marie Lupo. *Marie's Melting Pot*. New Orleans: Distributed by the Spielman Co., 1980.

Vodicka, John. "Prison Plantation: The Story of Angola." *Southern Exposure* 6, no. 4 (1978): 32–38.

Vyhnanek, Louis Andrew. *Unorganized Crime: New Orleans in the 1920s*. Lafayette, LA: Center for Louisiana Studies, University of Southwestern Louisiana, 1998.

Warner, Richard. "The First Mafia Boss of Los Angeles? The Mystery of Vito Di Giorgio, 1880–1922." *On the Spot Journal* (Summer 2008): 46–54.

Webb, Clive. "The Lynching of Sicilian Immigrants in the American South, 1886–1910." *American Nineteenth-Century History* 3, no. 1 (March 2000): 45–76.

Wheeler, Thomas B. "Homicides and Suicides in New Orleans." *Daily Picayune*, January 8, 1911.

Widmer, Mary Lou. *New Orleans 1900 to 1920*. Gretna, LA: Pelican, 2007.

Wilds, John. *Afternoon Story: The History of the New Orleans States-Item*. Baton Rouge: Louisiana State University Press, 1976.

Williams, Robert W. "Martin Behrman and New Orleans Civic Development, 1904–1920." *Louisiana History* 2, no. 4 (Autumn 1961): 373–400.

Wilson, Colin, and Damon Wilson. *The Killers Among Us, Book II: Sex, Madness & Mass Murder*. New York: Warner, 1995.

———. *Written in Blood: A History of Forensic Detection*. New York: Carroll & Graf, 2003.

Witcover, Jules. *Sabotage at Black Tom: Imperial Germany's Secret War in America, 1914–1917*. Chapel Hill, NC: Algonquin Books of Chapel Hill, 1989.

Index

Italicized page references denote illustrations